Student Manual

for

Theories of Psychotherapy and Counseling
Concepts and Cases

Third Edition

Richard S. Sharf
University of Delaware

THOMSON

BROOKS/COLE

Australia • Canada • Mexico • Singapore • Spain • United Kingdom • United States

Printer: Phoenix Color Corp

ISBN: 0-534-53105-9

For more information about our products, contact us at:
Thomson Learning Academic Resource Center
1-800-423-0563

For permission to use material from this text, contact us by:
Phone: 1-800-730-2214
Fax: 1-800-731-2215
Web: http://www.thomsonrights.com

Brooks/Cole—Thomson Learning
10 Davis Drive
Belmont, CA 94002-3098
USA

Asia
Thomson Learning
5 Shenton Way #01-01
UIC Building
Singapore 068808

Australia/New Zealand
Thomson Learning
102 Dodds Street
Southbank, Victoria 3006
Australia

Canada
Nelson
1120 Birchmount Road
Toronto, Ontario M1K 5G4
Canada

Europe/Middle East/South Africa
Thomson Learning
High Holborn House
50/51 Bedford Row
London WC1R 4LR
United Kingdom

Latin America
Thomson Learning
Seneca, 53
Colonia Polanco
11560 Mexico D.F.
Mexico

Spain/Portugal
Paraninfo
Calle/Magallanes, 25
28015 Madrid, Spain

PREFACE

This Student Manual is designed to help students use the text, <u>Theories of Psychotherapy and Counseling:</u> <u>Concepts and Cases, Third Edition</u>. Like the text book, this manual focuses on cases. The core of the manual is the opportunity for the student to take the role of a therapist using one theory and try to apply concepts and techniques to a "client." The student can then apply techniques that he or she learns in the chapter by answering multiple choice and (less frequently) open ended questions.

There are several sections of the manual that help students understand the theories and learn significant concepts. The self-inventory assists students in seeing how similar their views of therapy are to theorists. The self-inventory also helps students get a brief overview of the theorists' approaches to helping clients. Background information about the theory is presented in outline form to give students an overview of factors that led to the development of the theory. Concepts that are defined in the glossary are also defined in the personality theory and techniques sections. Case studies illustrate the personality theory and techniques. Students then answer questions about the cases. For difficult questions, immediate feedback is given to students about the correctness of their responses. For other questions, answers are provided at the end of each chapter. In the special topics section, students answer open ended questions about current trends, using a theory with other theories, gender issues, and multicultural issues. To help students think critically about theories, another section asks them to list strengths and limitations of the theory. The final section of most chapters includes 10 true-false and 15 multiple choice questions.

There are several different ways to use the Student Manual. Taking the self-inventory before reading the chapter will help provide an overview of the chapter. Students can read the entire chapter and then skim the concepts in the manual and answer questions about them and about the cases. Another approach is to read each major section in the text and then review the corresponding section in the manual. Some instructors may wish to discuss the cases described in the manual in class. The quizzes at the end of the chapter can be used when students have finished the chapter or they can be saved for review for exams.

ACKNOWLEDGMENTS

In writing this manual, I received the help of several experts who reviewed the manuscript for accuracy and relevance. I would like to thank the following individuals who read the entire Student Manual: Kris Bronson, private practice; Christopher Faiver, John Carroll University; Jodie Janisak, University of Delaware; Beverly Palmer, California State University - Dominquez.

I am very appreciative of the helpfulness of the following individuals who critiqued specific chapters.

Chapter 2. Psychoanalysis. Michele Downie, University of Delaware.
Chapter 4. Adlerian therapy. Michael Maniacci, Adler School of Professional Psychology.
Chapter 6. Person-centered therapy. Douglas Bower, private practice.
Chapter 7. Gestalt therapy. Gary Yontef, private practice.
Chapter 9. Rational emotive behavior therapy. Albert Ellis, The Albert Ellis Institute for Rational Emotive Behavior Therapy.
Chapter 10. Cognitive therapy. Christine Reilly, University of Delaware.
Chapter 11. Reality therapy. Robert Wubbolding, Center for Reality Therapy.

I would also like to thank Lisa Sweder who typed the entire manuscript. Finally, I would like to thank my wife Jane for her proofreading and editorial comments.

Richard S. Sharf   January 30, 2003

TABLE OF CONTENTS

CHAPTER 1

INTRODUCTION

STUDENT MANUAL OUTLINE

The purpose of this manual is to help you learn concepts basic to theories of personality and techniques of change used in a variety of theories of psychotherapy. There are seven major sections in each chapter:

1. A self inventory to compare your views of counseling and psychotherapy to that of the theorist or theorists is at the beginning of all chapters (except this one).

2. There is a chart that summarizes influences on the theorist(s) and important contributions by the theorist or theorists.

3. Basic information about the personality theory is summarized and important concepts are defined. Using multiple choice questions, and occasionally open-ended questions, you are presented with a case study and asked to assess or identify aspects of the client's personality as well as goals of treatment from one theoretical perspective. When multiple choice questions are difficult and require an explanation, answers are given following the question; otherwise they are placed at the end of each chapter.

4. Techniques or methods of change are summarized and defined. You are asked to be the client's therapist and choose the appropriate response that you would make to the client from the point of view of the theory. Sometimes you will be asked to decide on a technique to use or a general therapeutic direction.
This exercise should help you to acquire a clearer understanding of the theory.

5. Open ended questions are asked so that you can summarize and clarify special topics that are discussed in each chapter. Page numbers from the text that contain the answers are given at the end of each question.

6. You will be asked to summarize what you believe are the strengths and limitations of each theory. If you want hints, see the Critique section on page 624 of Chapter 16.

7. In the final section of each chapter, there is a quiz consisting (usually) of 10 true and false questions and 15 multiple choice questions. The quiz is followed by an answer key that includes answers to questions given in case examples and other parts of each chapter as well as to the quiz.

HOW TO USE THIS STUDENT MANUAL

You may choose to use the Student Manual in the same way for each chapter or you may alter your approach. I will give you my suggestions about how to use this guide as you read the text.

1. Before you read each chapter in the text, complete the self inventory at the beginning of each chapter in this guide. The questions will give you a broad idea of what to expect in the chapter and how different the theorist's views are from your own.

2. Skim the definitions of concepts in the Student Manual. This will help you learn the essence of the theory.

3. Read the chapter in the text.

4. Complete the rest of the material in the Student Manual for that chapter. You may want to delay taking the quiz at the end of each chapter until you start to prepare for an exam.

CHAPTER ONE: INTRODUCTION

This chapter explains important concepts such as the meanings of theory, counseling, and psychotherapy. A very brief summary of each chapter is given. Then, I describe the important chapter segments and how the Student Manual will help with each segment. Definitions of concepts that are used throughout the text, such as terms for psychological disorders, are presented here. A 25 item quiz on Chapter 1 of the text concludes the chapter.

THEORY

Theories are a group of related laws or relationships that are used to provide explanations within a discipline. In counseling and psychotherapy, theories provide an understanding of personality and methods that help individuals change behaviors, thoughts, or feelings, as well as gain insights into each of these. The criteria that are used to evaluate theory are defined here.

clarity Rules must be clear and specific. Operational definitions are used to define procedures used in theories.

operational definition An empirical definition that seeks to specify procedures that are used to measure a variable or to distinguish it from others.

comprehensiveness Theories differ in the types of events they make predictions about. Some theories predict many related events; others have a more limited goal.

testability A theory must be able to be verified or confirmed through research.

usefulness A theory should provide methods or concepts that can be applied to problems in the field.

PSYCHOTHERAPY AND COUNSELING

There are many different views on how psychotherapy and counseling are similar. Increasingly, most therapists see a broad overlap between the two. Many of the theorists discussed in this text do not make a distinction between counseling and psychotherapy as it applies to their theory. When there is a distinction, I will describe what the distinction is. Generally, I will use *psychotherapy* and *counseling* interchangeably to describe the process of helping others with emotional or psychological problems.

The terms *patient* and *client* are also used interchangeably in this text. Theories that are derived by psychiatrists and are used in a medical setting tend to use *patient*. Those people seen in a non-medical setting are usually called *clients*. Often, I will use the term that the theorist and practitioners of the theory use.

THEORIES OF PSYCHOTHERAPY AND COUNSELING

Estimates of the number of theories of counseling and psychotherapy suggest that there may be over 400. About 30 of these theories are included in this text. Surveys such as those on pages 4 and 5 of the text indicate the popularity of various theories. Many therapists use more than one theory. Those who apply techniques from a variety of theories are called *eclectic* therapists. Integration of theories is discussed in Chapter 15.

Only those theories that have been used by a number of practitioners and have published information about them are included here. These theories represent a very wide range of approaches. To provide a sense of the wide range of theories, I will summarize each in a sentence. This should give you a broad but incomplete overview of different approaches.

Chapter 2. Psychoanalysis. Psychoanalytic approaches emphasize the importance of unconscious processes and the impact of childhood experiences (prior to the age of 6) on the development of personality.

Chapter 3. Jungian Analysis. Universal patterns that are reflected in the unconscious processes of all people as they affect the patient are brought into consciousness.

Chapter 4. Adlerian Therapy. Early relationships in the family can lead to dysfunctional beliefs which become the focus of therapy.

Chapter 5. Existential Therapy. A philosophy for understanding human existence becomes the basis for helping clients deal with life themes such as death, freedom, responsibility, and meaninglessness.

Chapter 6. Person-Centered Therapy. Client change comes about from understanding the client and communicating that understanding to the client so that an atmosphere of trust can develop which fosters client growth.

Chapter 7. Gestalt Therapy. Therapists emphasize psychological and bodily awareness that leads to greater client self-responsibility and self-awareness.

Chapter 8. Behavior Therapy. Scientific principles of behavior, such as reinforcement and modeling, are used to bring about changes in clients' behaviors or actions.

Chapter 9. Rational Emotive Behavior Therapy. Challenging irrational beliefs through disputing techniques and teaching rational ways of acting and thinking is the focus of this therapy.

Chapter 10. Cognitive Therapy. Clients are taught to recognize a variety of distorted thoughts and replace them with more accurate thoughts.

Chapter 11. Reality Therapy. Individuals learn to be responsible for their lives and to take control over what they do, think, and feel.

Chapter 12. Feminist Therapy. Emphasis is placed on dealing with problems that society creates for clients (especially women) and empowering them to deal effectively with these problems.

Chapter 13. Family Systems Therapy. Viewing the family as a single unit, assessing interactions within the family, and making suggestions for change are the focus of four therapies discussed in this chapter.

Chapter 14. Other Therapies. Five different therapies are explained. Asian therapies emphasize quiet reflection and personal responsibility to others. Body psychotherapies assess and manipulate the body to bring about psychological change. Interpersonal therapy is used with depression and focuses on changes in four areas of problems. In psychodrama, clients and audience or group members play roles to enact their problems, and the therapist directs and facilitates this process. Creative arts therapies include art, dance movement, drama, and music to encourage expressive action and therapeutic change.

Chapter 15. Constructivist and Integrative Theories. Constructivist therapists see their clients as theorists and try to understand clients' problems from the clients' points of view. Integrative theorists combine two or more theories to help their clients.

Chapter 16. Comparison and Critique. This chapter summarizes the theories in this text and critiques them. The chapter should provide help for you when preparing for exams for this course.

ORGANIZATION OF THE CHAPTERS

To help you use this Student Manual in conjunction with the text, I will briefly describe the contents of each. In this way you can see how the Student Manual will help you learn the content of each section of the text. Each major section is described here.

HISTORY OR BACKGROUND

Text. To understand each theory, I describe its development. Usually this includes information about the lives of the theorists and important personal and intellectual influences on the development of their theories as well as their own writings. The theorists' use of specific psychological and philosophical ideas that were available at the time the theorists were developing their theory are explained.

Student Manual. Using tables, I list people who influenced the theorists as well as their significant writings or contributions.

PERSONALITY THEORY

Text. How theorists understand personality is the basis for making therapeutic change. I describe and illustrate each concept that the theorists use to understand individuals' personalities.

Student Manual. The personality theory is briefly described. Most concepts that the theorists use in their theory are defined. In most chapters, I use a case example in which you become the therapist. Using a multiple choice format, you select the personality concept that best fits the client.

THEORY OF PSYCHOTHERAPY

Text. This is the most important section of each chapter. The goals of the theory show the theorists' approach to bringing about change. Assessment methods indicate how theorists plan to assess personality and decide which therapeutic approaches to take. The techniques or methods used by the theorists are described here. Several case illustrations help to explain the techniques and methods.

> *Student Manual.* Goals and approaches to assessment are briefly summarized. For almost all of the techniques, a definition is given. Using the same case that illustrates personality concepts, you pick the therapeutic response or statement that you would use to help the client and is most consistent with the theory. In this way, you can try to put the theory into practice or try it out.

PSYCHOLOGICAL DISORDERS

Text. For each theory, I give between three and five case examples to illustrate the theory. Each example represents a different diagnostic category or problem type. The purpose of these examples is to show how therapists use techniques and methods to bring about positive changes in their clients' lives. You can also compare theories across problem type. For example, you can compare how Adlerian therapists and cognitive therapists help individuals who are depressed.

> *Student Manual.* This Student Manual does not focus on specific psychological disorders but rather on becoming familiar with theories of psychotherapy and counseling. However, throughout the text, reference is made to disorders such as depression, anxiety, phobias, borderline disorders and many others. Chapter 1 explains these terms, giving examples. A textbook on abnormal psychology would give much more detailed explanation. During your course, you may have a need to find a brief definition of one or more of these terms. For that reason, I am listing their definitions in alphabetical order to use as a reference. Like almost all terms defined in this Student Manual, they may also be found in the glossary of the text.

anorexia A disorder in which individuals are unable to eat food, may have a severe decrease in appetite, and have an intense fear of becoming obese even when emaciated. Anorexia is diagnosed when individuals lose at least 25 percent of their normal weight.

anxiety An unpleasant feeling of fear and/or apprehension accompanied by physiological changes such as fast pulse, quick breathing, sweating, flushing, muscle aches, or stomach tension.

borderline personality disorder Characteristics include unstable interpersonal relationships and rapid mood changes in a short period of time. Behavior is often erratic, unpredictable, and impulsive in areas such as spending, eating, sex, or gambling. Emotional relationships tend to be intense, with individuals becoming easily angry or disappointed in the relationship.

bulimia Binge eating and inappropriate methods of preventing weight gain, such as vomiting and use of laxatives, characterize bulimia.

compulsion An irresistible impulse to repeat behaviors continually.

conversion reaction A disorder in which a psychological disturbance takes a physical form, such as when arms or legs are paralyzed and there is no physiological explanation.

delusions Beliefs that are contrary to reality and are firmly held despite evidence that they are inaccurate.

depression An emotional state characterized by deep sadness, feelings of worthlessness, guilt, and withdrawal from others. Other symptoms include difficulty in sleeping, loss of appetite or sexual desire, and loss of interest in normal activities. When not accompanied by manic episodes, it is usually referred to as major depression or unipolar depression.

drug abuse Using a drug to the extent that individuals have difficulty meeting social and occupational obligations.

generalized anxiety disorder One of a group of anxiety disorders, it is characterized by a persistent pervasive state of tension. Physical symptoms may include a pounding heart, fast pulse and breathing, sweating, muscle aches, and stomach upset. Individuals may be easily distractable and fearful that something bad is going to happen.

hallucinations Perceiving (seeing, hearing, feeling, tasting, or smelling) things that are not there.

hysteria A disorder occurring when psychological disturbances take a physical form and there is no physiological explanation, such as an unexplained paralysis of the arms or legs. This term has been replaced by conversion reaction in common usage.

mania (manic episodes) Individuals may demonstrate unfounded elation as indicated by making grandiose plans, being extremely talkative, easily distracted, and engaging in purposeless activity.

narcissistic personality disorder A pattern of self-importance; a need for admiration from others and a lack of empathy for others are common characteristics of individuals with this disorder. Boasting or being pretentious and feeling that one is superior to others and deserves recognition are also prominent characteristics.

neurosis A large group of disorders characterized by unrealistic anxiety, fears, or obsessions. They are contrasted with more severe psychotic disorders.

obsessions Pervasive and uncontrollable recurring thoughts that interfere with day-to-day functioning.

obsessive-compulsive disorder Persistent and uncontrollable thoughts or feelings in which individuals feel compelled to repeat behaviors again and again.

personality disorders These are characterized by being inflexible, lasting many years or a lifetime, and include traits that make social or occupational functioning difficult.

phobia Fear of a situation or object out of proportion to the danger of the situation or the threatening qualities of the object. Examples include fear of heights, rats, or spiders.

posttraumatic stress disorder (PTSD) Extreme reactions to a highly stressful or traumatic event such as being raped, robbed, or assaulted define PTSD. Resulting behaviors may include being easily startled, having recurrent dreams or nightmares, or feeling estranged from or afraid of others.

psychosis A broad term used for severe mental disorders in which thinking and emotion are so impaired that individuals have lost contact with reality.

schizophrenia Severe disturbances of thought, emotions, or behaviors may be evident by observing disorganized speech and obtaining reports of delusions or hallucinations.

sociopathy Also called antisocial personality or psychopathic, this term refers to behavior which shows no regard for others, inability to form meaningful relationships, and a lack of responsibility for one's own actions.

somatoform disorders Physical symptoms are known and present, but there is no physiological cause, and a psychological cause is suspected. Reporting headaches or stomachaches when no physiological cause can be found constitutes an example of somatoform disorders.

BRIEF THERAPY

Text. Sometimes called short-term therapy, brief therapy refers to limiting therapy to a certain number of sessions. Time-limited therapy is a term that refers to a theoretical approach that is designed to be completed in a certain number of sessions. Often several aspects of therapy are to be completed in sessions one through three, and other aspects in sessions four through seven, and so forth. Many therapeutic approaches are brief in their general therapeutic plans. The theory that has developed many different methods of brief or time-limited therapy is psychoanalysis.

Student Manual. Brief therapy is addressed directly in Chapter 2 of this guide and in a few other chapters where there is specific reference to time limits or brief therapy such as Chapters 13 and 14. The Special Topics section of the guide often includes a question about the duration of therapy.

CURRENT TRENDS

Text. Theories are often growing and changing. Depending on research or other factors, theories may be modified or changed. Sometimes they are applied to new client populations. These trends are described in the book. Two specific trends that are addressed for almost all of the theories in the book are treatment manuals and postmodernism. Within postmodernism two important philosophical areas that address psychotherapy are constructivism and social constructionism.

treatment manuals Written guidelines for therapists on how to treat patients with a particular disorder. They describe skills to be used and the specific sequencing of these skills.

postmodernism A philosophical position that does not assume that there is a fixed truth, but rather that individuals have their own perception of reality or the truth.

modernism Modernists take a rationalist view, believing that there is scientific truth which can be achieved through advances in technology and science.

constructivism Believing that individuals create their own views or constructs of events or relationships in their own lives.

social constructionism A constructivist point of view that focuses on the shared meanings that people in a culture or society develop.

Student Manual. In a section called Special Topics, you will be asked to summarize some specific current trends.

USING A THEORY WITH OTHER THEORIES

Text. Theories vary as to how open they are to using methods and techniques of other theories. Also, some theories are more easily incorporated into the methods of other theories. This section describes one theory as it relates to other theories, especially those that are similar to it.

Student Manual. Usually, I will include a question about using one theory with another in the Special Topics section.

RESEARCH

Text. Theories vary widely as to the amount of research that has been done on testing specific concepts or in studying the effectiveness of therapy. I describe recent typical investigations for many of the theories. Also, there have been meta-analyses to examine the results of many studies. Because research is a complex topic, only some of the most basic concepts are discussed in Chapter 1. These concepts are defined here.

factorial design A research method that can study more than one variable at a time.

meta-analysis A method of statistically summarizing the results of a large number of studies.

methodology A systematic application of procedures used in research investigations.

pretest-posttest control group design Comparing a group given one treatment to another group given another treatment or no treatment by testing individuals before and after therapy.

patient focused research Monitors the progress of clients and then uses this information to develop treatment methods.

Student Manual. Because I concentrate on helping you understand personality theory concepts and techniques of change, I do not address research in this guide except briefly in Chapter 16. Also, to further summarize summaries of research tends to give a simplified overview of therapy research. Despite my reservations, I have done this on pages 616 to 618 of the text in Chapter 16.

GENDER ISSUES

Text. Many people have asked whether or not a theory can be applied fairly to both men and women. Chapter 12, Feminist Therapy, addresses the question most thoroughly. However, gender issues have been addressed by therapists who follow each theoretical orientation described in the text. Using these writings, I have described issues as they affect gender for each of the major theories in the text.

Student Manual. In the Special Topics part of each chapter of this guide, I ask a question about how information in this section in the text applies to multicultural issues in the theory.

MULTICULTURAL ISSUES

Text. The consideration of the application of theory to people with diverse cultural backgrounds has been relatively recent (since the 1960s and 1970s). The relationship between culture and therapy has been of particular interest in the 1990s. Psychoanalysis, the theory that was developed first, has been particularly subject to criticism in part due to its origins in 19th century Vienna. Some early theorists such as Carl Jung and Erik Erikson were interested in issues that relate to people living in cultures that were very different than traditional Western culture. Chapter 12, Feminist Therapy, uses a multicultural model and provides some techniques that can be used with individuals from different cultures as well as genders. Each chapter describes how multicultural issues have been addressed within the theory.

Student Manual. In the Special Topics part of each chapter of this guide, I ask a question about how information in this section in the text applies to multicultural issues in the theory.

GROUP THERAPY

Text. All theories that have been applied to individual therapy have also been adapted for group therapy. Therapists as well as theorists differ in terms of the importance that they place on group therapy. This section shows how concepts and methods from the theory can be applied to group therapy.

Student Manual. In the Special Topics section of this guide, I have summarized how each theory can be applied to group therapy. This information can also be found on pages 621 to 623 of the text.

ETHICS

Regardless of their theory of psychotherapy or counseling, all practitioners must adhere to a code of ethics. All therapists, psychiatrists, psychologists, counselors, social workers, psychiatric nurses, pastoral counselors, marriage counselors, and sex therapists must follow their own code of professional ethics. Theories do not have their own code of ethics; rather their principles, concepts, and techniques must be consistent with professional ethical guidelines. Although there are minor differences between ethical guidelines that various mental health professionals adhere to, there are many more similarities.

Many graduate training programs have entire courses that deal with ethical principles. I have chosen not to go into detail about ethics because this subject is handled better elsewhere. Furthermore, theories of psychotherapy follow ethical guidelines; they do not make them. Unethical behavior would not be sanctioned by any theory of therapy discussed in this book.

THE INTRODUCTION: A QUIZ

True or false items. Decide if the following items are more "true" or more "false" as they apply to concepts discussed in the first chapter.

T F Q1. For a theory to be applied to psychotherapy, it should be tested through research.

T F Q2. Operational definitions only apply to medicine, not to psychology or counseling.

T F Q3. Definitions of psychotherapy and counseling overlap so much that they are used interchangeably in the text.

T F Q4. Psychodynamic, dynamic, or psychoanalytic therapies are the most widely practiced forms of therapy.

T F Q5. Two types of depression are unipolar and bipolar depression.

T F Q6. Compulsions are thoughts that cannot be controlled.

T F Q7. Neuroses are more severe in their effects than psychoses.

T F Q8. If a psychological cause is suspected for a physiological problem, then that individual may have a somatoform disorder.

T F Q9. Each theory of psychotherapy has its own ethical code.

T F Q10. Each theory of psychotherapy has its own techniques of research which it applies to testing the effectiveness of its procedures.

Multiple choice items. Select the best answer from the alternatives given.

_____ Q11. Which of the following is the LEAST important characteristic of a theory?

        a. precision
        b. comprehensiveness
        c. simplicity
        d. testability
        e. usefulness

_____ Q12. Operational definitions are useful to a theory because they help establish

        a. clarity.
        b. comprehensiveness.
        c. simplicity.
        d. usefulness.

_____ Q13. An eclectic therapist is one who

        a. is a counselor.
        b. is a psychologist.
        c. draws from more than one theory of therapy or counseling.
        d. appreciates the uniqueness of each client.

_____C_____ Q14. The number of theories of therapy is likely to be more than

        a. 4.
        b. 40.
        c. 400.
        d. 4000.

_____D_____ Q15. The major difference between "patients" and "clients" is that

        a. patients are more deeply disturbed than clients.
        b. patients pay higher fees than clients.
        c. patients are covered by health maintenance organizations and clients are not.
        d. none of the above.

_____B_____ Q16. Muscle tension and restlessness are symptoms associated with

        a. depression.
        b. generalized anxiety disorder.
        c. borderline disorder.
        d. obsessive-compulsive disorder.
        e. somatoform disorder.

_____A_____ Q17. Becoming extremely talkative and "hyper" are sometimes symptoms found in a type of

        a. depression.
        b. generalized anxiety disorder.
        c. borderline disorder.
        d. obsessive-compulsive disorder.
        e. somatoform disorder.

_____C_____ Q18. A pattern of unstable relationships is a characteristic of

        a. depression.
        b. generalized anxiety disorder.
        c. borderline disorder.
        d. posttraumatic stress disorder.
        e. a phobia.

_____D_____ Q19. A reaction to being robbed in your home at gun point may lead to a variety of reactions, but the most common is likely to be

        a. depression.
        b. generalized anxiety disorder.
        c. a borderline disorder.
        d. posttraumatic stress disorder.
        e. a phobia.

_____e_____ Q20. A fear of heights is characteristic of

        a. depression.
        b. generalized anxiety disorder.
        c. a borderline disorder.
        d. posttraumatic stress disorder.
        e. a phobia.

_____ Q21. "Black flack runs in packs, blue, blue." is a statement that is most likely to be made by someone with symptoms of

a. hysteria.
b. borderline disorder.
c. narcissistic personality disorder.
d. schizophrenia.

_____ Q22. Hearing a voice in one's head that is screaming loudly is an example of

a. a delusion.
b. an hallucination.
c. a conversion reaction.
d. psychological dependency

_____ Q23. Going back to check to see if you locked your front door 12 times in a row is called

a. a delusion.
b. an hallucination.
c. a compulsion.
d. an obsession.
e. being thorough.

_____ Q24. The philosophical view that individuals create their own reality as opposed to the existence of a fixed truth is called

a. existentialism.
b. modernism.
c. postmodernism.
d. rationalism.

_____ Q25. A professional group's code of ethics can be applied to the practice of

a. no theories of psychotherapy and counseling.
b. one theory of psychotherapy and counseling.
c. some theories of psychotherapy and counseling.
d. all theories of psychotherapy and counseling.

ANSWER KEY

Q1. T	Q11. c	Q21. d
Q2. F	Q12. a	Q22. b
Q3. T	Q13. c	Q23. c
Q4. T	Q14. c	Q24. c
Q5. T	Q15. d	Q25. d
Q6. F	Q16. b	
Q7. F	Q17. a	
Q8. T	Q18. c	
Q9. F	Q19. d	
Q10. F	Q20. e	

CHAPTER 2

PSYCHOANALYSIS

SPECIAL NOTE ABOUT PSYCHOANALYSIS

WHY IS PSYCHOANALYSIS SO IMPORTANT?

Psychoanalysis was the first approach to therapy. Almost all other psychotherapy theorists have been trained as psychoanalysts. Sometimes their theories are somewhat similar to psychoanalysis; more often they are in reaction to psychoanalysis and very different. Behavior therapy is one of the few therapies not directly influenced by psychoanalysis.

WHY IS THIS CHAPTER SO LONG?

First, psychoanalysis contains many more concepts than any other theory. Second, there are five sub-theories that are described, each with specific concepts. Third, besides Freud, there have been many contributors to psychoanalysis, only some of whom are described in this chapter.

WHY DOES SOME OF THE MATERIAL SEEM DIFFICULT TO GRASP?

Psychoanalysis is concerned with unconscious forces, those aspects of our lives that we are not aware of. It is easier to understand those theories that deal with conscious processes, those parts of our lives that we can directly experience.

PSYCHOANALYSIS SELF-INVENTORY

Directions: By comparing your beliefs about personality to those of psychoanalysis, you should have a clearer idea of how much you will need to suspend your beliefs or change your attitudes to understand the psychoanalytic approaches to personality. You may find it helpful to complete this section before and after you read the chapter. In this way you can see if your views have changed. There are no correct answers, only an opportunity to express your views.

Put an "X" on the line so that it indicates how much you agree or disagree with the statement: A = Agree, D = Disagree.

D _____ A   1. The purpose of therapy is to make the unconscious conscious.

_____   2. To understand human behavior, therapists need to understand the unconscious.

_____   3. Most psychological conflicts have been repressed and contain elements that we are not aware of.

_____   4. Those aspects of our experience that we are not aware of have a great influence on our behavior.

_____   5. It is the first six years of life that have the greatest influence on determining adult personality.

_____   6. Client problems reflect a failure to resolve issues related to childhood psychosexual development.

_____   7. Trust is developed in early childhood through interactions with one's mother.

_____   8. Clients' struggles to control sexual and aggressive impulses are an important aspect of therapy.

_____   9. Children's early parental relationships form the basis of their later adult development.

_____   10. Separating from parents and becoming an independent adult is one of the most important developmental tasks that individuals face.

_____   11. Mothering must be adequate for healthy psychological development to take place.

_____   12. Being too self-absorbed can be an appropriate therapeutic issue.

_____   13. Developing insight and understanding repressed material is an important part of therapy.

_____   14. The type of therapeutic relationship can have an influence on the outcome of therapy.

_____   15. Therapy that meets three or four times a week for five or more years is the best way to resolve problems.

_____   16. Interpretation of dreams is a critical aspect of therapy.

_____   17. Interpretation of the client's resistance to therapeutic change is an important aspect of therapy.

_____   18. Understanding the underlying unconscious motivations that are at the root of a client's problem is essential in bringing about therapeutic change.

_____   19. Therapists should be aware of their own reactions to their patients.

_____   20. Insight into problems will bring about changes in feelings and behaviors.

13

HISTORY OF PSYCHOANALYSIS

Which influences do you think were most important in the development of psychoanalysis?

INFLUENCES ON SIGMUND FREUD

PERSONAL LIFE

Born on May 6, 1856
Austrian parents
Near Vienna
Oldest of 7 children
Father had 2 children from a previous marriage
Encouraged by mother
Very bright student
Graduated high school summa cum laude
1873 - started study of medicine at University of
       Vienna
1879 - one year of military service
1883 - studied neurology and physiology at Viennese
       General Hospital
1885 - studied in Paris with Jean Charcot
1886 - married Martha Bernays - 6 children
       slowly built a private practice
1938 - emigrated to England
1939 - died of throat cancer

PROFESSIONAL LIFE

Influenced by his knowledge of physics, chemistry,
    biology, philosophy, psychology, literature, ideas
    about the unconscious
Nietzsche and Spinoza - philosophers
Wilhelm Wundt and Gustave Fechner - psychologists
Ludwig Borne - free association - writer
Darwin - evolution
Brucke - physiological research
Pierre Janet and Hippolyte Bernheim - psychiatrists
Studies on Hysteria - 1895
The Interpretation of Dreams - 1900
1902 - Wednesday Psychological Society
The Psychopathology of Everyday Life - 1901
Three Essays on Sexuality - 1905
Jokes and Their Relations to the Unconscious - 1905
On Narcissism: An Introduction - 1914
Introductory Lectures on Psychoanalysis - 1917
The Ego and Id - 1923
1909 - G. Stanley Hall Lecture at Clark University in
    Worcester, Massachusetts

FREUD'S DRIVE THEORY OF PERSONALITY

Freud developed many different concepts that cover a wide range of aspects of his theory of personality. Some concepts deal with the importance that he placed on drives or instincts. Other concepts explain terms related to the unconscious. Freud's concepts of id, ego, and superego, and related ideas explain how individuals deal with their basic drives and instincts. In order to cope with unconscious instincts, individuals learn a variety of defense mechanisms. Several are explained in the text and described here. The psychosexual stages (oral, anal, phallic, latency, and genital) describe the part of the body and the developmental sequence in which drives are dealt with in early childhood. Knowing the meaning of the concepts in each of theses areas provides a way of understanding the language of psychoanalysis. Because terms like ego, anal retentive, rationalization, and repression have made their way into normal vocabulary and are sometimes used by other theorists, it is helpful to understand their roots and the theory on which they are based.

CONCEPTS BASIC TO DRIVE THEORY AND INSTINCTS

The following terms describe the basic ideas that Freud uses in explaining his drive theory.

drive A physiological state of tension such as hunger, sex, or elimination that motivates an individual to perform actions to reduce the tension.

instinct Basic drives such as hunger, thirst, sex, and aggression that must be fulfilled in order to maintain physical or psychological equilibrium.

libido The basic driving force of personality which includes sexual energy but is not limited to it.

eros The life instinct, derived from libidinal energy, in opposition to the death instinct (*thanatos*).

thanatos An instinct toward self-destruction and death in opposition to the life instinct (*eros*).

CONCEPTS RELATED TO THE UNCONSCIOUS

Freud believed that many psychological problems that individuals develop occurred outside of their own awareness. He was particularly interested in unconscious forces.

conscious or *consciousness* That portion of the mind or mental functioning that individuals are aware of, including sensations and experiences.

preconscious Memories of events and experiences that can be retrieved with relatively little effort, such as remembering what one said to a friend yesterday. Information is available to awareness but not immediately.

unconscious The part of the mind that people have no knowledge of. It includes memories and emotions that are threatening to the conscious mind and are pushed away.

CONCEPTS THAT DESCRIBE DRIVE THEORY

The concepts of id, ego, and superego help to explain how Freud believed individuals deal with instinctual drives. Most of these concepts are related to regulating id forces or to the way individuals must cope with id forces in order to deal with their external world.

id The biological instincts, including sexual and aggressive impulses, that seek pleasure. At birth, the id represents the total personality.

pleasure principle The tendency to avoid pain and seek pleasure; the principle by which the id operates. It is particularly important in infancy.

cathect Investing psychic energy in a mental representation of a person, behavior, or idea. Infants cathect in objects that gratify their needs.

object cathexis The investment of psychic energy or libido in objects outside the self, such as a person or activity. Such investment is designed to reduce needs.

primary process An action of the id that satisfies a need, thus reducing drive tension, by producing a mental image of an object.

ego A means of mediating between one's instincts or drives and the external world. The ego mediates between the id and the superego.

reality principle A guiding principle of the ego. It allows postponement of gratification so that environmental demands can be met or so that greater pleasure can be obtained at a later time.

secondary process A process of the ego that reduces intrapsychic tension by dealing with external reality. Logic and problem solving skills may be used. It is in contrast with the primary process of the id.

anticathexes The control or restraint exercised by the ego over the id to keep id impulses out of consciousness.

superego That portion of the personality that represents parental values, and more broadly, society's standards. It develops from the ego and is a reflection of early moral training and parental injunctions.

ego ideal A representation in the child of values that are approved by the parents. It is present in the superego as a concern with movement toward perfectionist goals.

DEFENSE MECHANISMS

Freud viewed defense mechanisms as a means that the ego uses to fight off instinctual outbursts of the id or to deal with injunctions by the superego. Ego defense mechanisms are unconscious. They deny or distort reality to reduce stress to the individual. They only become pathological when they are used too frequently. Although Freud and his followers developed a number of defense mechanisms, ten are described in Chapter 2 and are defined here.

repression Threatening or painful thoughts or feelings are excluded from awareness.

denial Individuals may distort or not acknowledge what they think, feel, or see. For example, not believing that a relative has been killed in an auto accident is an illustration of denial.

reaction formation Unacceptable impulses can be avoided by acting in an opposite way. Claiming that you like your occupational choice when you do not can help you avoid dealing with problems that result from not liking your work.

projection People can attribute their own unacceptable desires to others and not deal with their own strong sexual or destructive drives.

displacement Individuals can place their negative feelings about a dangerous object or person, not on that person, but on one who may be safe. For example, it may be safer to express anger at a friend than at a boss who has been angry with you.

sublimation Sexual or aggressive drives can be modified into acceptable social behaviors. For example, anger at others can be sublimated by expressing anger or frustration while being an active spectator at a sports event.

rationalization Individuals can provide a plausible but inaccurate explanation for their failures. An individual who blames her roommate for her own poor performance on an examination may be making excuses for her lack of study and thus rationalizing.

regression When an individual retreats to an earlier stage of development that was both more secure and pleasant, this is referred to as regression. A child hurt by a reprimand of the teacher may suck his thumb and cry, returning to a more secure and less mature time.

identification When individuals take on characteristics of another, often a parent, to reduce their own anxieties and internal conflicts, they are identifying with that person. By identifying with the successful parent, an individual can feel successful even though she has done little that might make her feel productive.

intellectualization Emotional issues are not dealt with directly but rather are handled indirectly by abstract thought.

DEVELOPMENTAL STAGES AND RELATED CONCEPTS

According to Freud, the id, ego, and superego, as well as defense mechanisms, developed over time. Their development could be understood by knowledge of the psychosexual stages. Each psychosexual stage represents a specific area of the body. These stages, along with the Oedipus complex, are defined here.

oral stage The initial stage of psychosexual development lasts about eighteen months. Focus is on gratification through eating and sucking that involves the lips, mouth, and throat.

anal stage The second stage of psychosexual development occurs between the ages of about eighteen months and 3 years. The anal area becomes the main source of pleasure.

phallic stage The third stage of psychosexual development lasts from about the age of three until five or six. The major source of sexual gratification shifts from the anal to the genital region.

latency Following the phallic stage, there is a relatively calm period before adolescence. When Oedipal issues are resolved, the child enters the latency period.

genital stage The final stage of psychosexual development usually starts about the age of twelve and continues throughout life. The focus of sexual energy is toward members of the opposite sex rather than toward oneself.

Oedipus complex The unconscious sexual desire of the male child for his mother, along with feelings of hostility or fear toward the father. This conflict occurs in the phallic stage.

JUNE AS SEEN FROM A FREUDIAN DRIVE PERSPECTIVE

June is a 30-year-old marketing executive living in Albuquerque, New Mexico. She is married and has one seven year old daughter. June has complained of bouts of depression before, but now they seem to stay longer and to become deeper. She complains of having difficulty getting up in the morning. Her interest in spending time with her daughter has also decreased. This is particularly bothering her as June is very concerned about being a good mother. June finds it an effort to help her daughter, Erin, get ready for school. More and more she relies on her husband to take over the child raising functions, which previously she had enjoyed.

At work, June had been known for her enthusiasm and eagerness to take on new projects. Now she is rather quiet in marketing meetings and presents fewer creative ideas. Because of her changing level of interest in work, she worries that her bosses will be critical of her performance. To this point, they have not.

June and her husband, Rob, have been married for ten years and knew each other for a year before that. Since they got married at an early age, June had had relatively little experience with other men. She had come to depend on Rob's protectiveness and his ability to make decisions. Sometimes she found it amusing that she would defer to him so often in questions about home but took on such an independent role at work. Recently, she and Rob have been talking less, and their sexual relationship has been very sporadic.

When June was four, her father, an alcoholic, left the family. He moved from Albuquerque to Los Angeles, and June rarely spoke to him or saw him. When he was employed, which was about half the time, he would send some child support. However, June rarely saw him. When her father visited his brother in a nearby town, he might visit June. However, these visits occurred once or twice a year.

When June's mother was left on her own to deal with June and her sister, two years younger, she had a great deal of difficulty. At first, she was extremely depressed and flustered. She became very irritable and upset. After about a year, she became more involved in a local church. As the years went by, her involvement increased, and June and her sister were very involved with church activities and were influenced by their mother's strict religious upbringing. The bitterness that June's mother felt toward her ex-husband was not lost on June. June learned to distrust men and to be careful of outsiders. It took Rob about two years to really convince June that he was to be trusted. Even when they were first married, June was cautious in her relationship with him. She found that one part of her was trusting and caring of Rob, while the other was worried that somehow he might disappoint or leave.

The following questions about June examine her situation from the point of view of Freudian drive theory.

1. One aspect of June's problems is her diminished

   a. id.
   b. libido.
   c. superego.
   d. unconscious.

2. June's concern about her lack of interest in caring for her daughter is an example of

   a. conscious thoughts.
   b. the preconscious.
   c. the unconscious.
   d. thanatos.

3. When June does care for her daughter, without thinking of herself, this would be an example of

   a. anticathexis.
   b. drive impulse.
   c. object cathexes.
   d. primary process.

4. When June was a young girl and learned from her mother about men and religious values, her mother influenced her about what she should and should not do. Her _____ was developing.

   a. ego
   b. id
   c. superego
   d. all of the above

5. When June was a child, she very much wanted to do well at school. She did not want to be like her father and was concerned about disappointing her mother. In this process June was developing her

   a. ego ideal.
   b. preconscious.
   c. pleasure principle.
   d. primary process.

6. According to Freud, June's basic motivational forces come from her

   a. drives.
   b. ego.
   c. pleasure principle.
   d. reality principle.

7. Although June is spending less time with her daughter, she does not believe that this is true and does not acknowledge this. Which defense mechanism is being used?

   a. denial
   b. displacement
   c. projection
   d. rationalization

8. Sometimes when June is depressed, she starts to sing hymns that she sang in church when she was a little girl. This reminds her of the security she felt being close to her mother and sister. This is an example of

   a. projection.
   b. regression.
   c. repression.
   d. sublimation.

9. Sometimes June blames her problems on the commute to work and the fact that she has a cubicle rather than a private office. This is an example of

   a. intellectualization.
   b. repression.
   c. rationalization.
   d. sublimation.

10. When June was 6, her father took her to a carnival, and then got drunk. On the way home, he shouted and yelled at her, blaming her for the divorce. Although June started to behave differently towards him because of this, she doesn't remember the incident. This is an example of

    a. intellectualization.
    b. repression.
    c. rationalization.
    d. sublimation.

EGO PSYCHOLOGY

In the development of psychoanalysis, Freud focused on psychosexual or id drives. Others who came after him emphasized ego factors in psychoanalysis. His youngest daughter, Anna, was known for her work with children and her development of defense mechanisms. Perhaps the best known ego psychologist is Erik Erikson who extended Freud's psychosexual stages to the entire age range and showed how the psychosexual stages could be modified to focus on developmental personal issues and crises that individuals encounter in their lives.

EGO PSYCHOLOGY CONCEPTS

identification with aggressor This is a defense mechanism in which the individual identifies with an opponent that he or she cannot master, taking on characteristics of that person.

altruism In this defense mechanism, individuals learn to become helpful to avoid feeling helpless. They learn that they can satisfy their own egos as well as the demands of society.

QUESTIONS ABOUT JUNE FROM AN EGO PSYCHOLOGY PERSPECTIVE

11. Which of these psychoanalysts is most likely to use the concept of developmental lines in understanding June's problem?

    a. Anna Freud
    b. Sigmund Freud
    c. Erik Erikson
    d. Heinz Kohut

12. June's early issues of trust with her father would be a concern most clearly articulated by

    a. Anna Freud.
    b. Sigmund Freud.
    c. Erik Erikson.
    d. Heinz Kohut

13. Which of these psychoanalysts might pay the most attention to June's early id development?

    a. Anna Freud
    b. Sigmund Freud
    c. Erik Erikson
    d. Heinz Kohut

14. Which of Erikson's 8 stages best describes June's current problem?

    a. autonomy versus shame and doubt
    b. initiative versus guilt
    c. intimacy versus isolation
    d. integrity versus despair

15. Which of Erikson's 8 stages represents development of Freud's anal stage?

    a. autonomy versus shame and doubt
    b. initiative versus guilt
    c. intimacy versus isolation
    d. integrity versus despair

OBJECT RELATIONS PSYCHOLOGY

Unlike drive theory which focuses on the effects of instincts and drives on child development and ego psychology which is concerned with the adaptive aspects of the ego, object relations deals with the development of relationships between the child and love objects. As children grow older, they internalize their relationships with their parents and use these relationships as a model for interactions with those in their adolescent and adult lives. Although concerned with early childhood development, object relations psychology focuses on relationships with others rather than dealing with biological forces as Freud did. There are at least 15 psychoanalysts who have made important contributions to object relations psychology. In the text, only Donald Winnecott and Otto Kernberg are discussed. Through his work as a pediatrician, Donald Winnecott made significant contributions to object relations psychology by observing healthy and unhealthy mother-child relationships. More recently, Otto Kernberg has taken concepts from object relations and drive theory and applied them to understanding difficult personality disorders such as borderline disorder.

OBJECT RELATIONS CONCEPTS

First, concepts that explain common terms in object relations theory are described. Then concepts associated with specific object relations theorists are defined with their primary theorists or theorist indicated in parentheses.

intrapsychic processes Introduced in the object relations section, this term is used throughout psychoanalysis to refer to impulses, ideas, conflicts, or other psychological phenomenon that occur within the mind.

object A term used in psychoanalytic theory to refer, usually, to an important person in the child's life.

object relations A study of significant others or love objects in the child's life, focusing on how the child views the relationship (usually unconsciously).

separation The process that occurs when children gradually distinguish themselves from their mother and others in their world.

individuation The process of becoming an individual, becoming aware of one's self in relationship to others.

transitional object (Winnicott) An object such as a teddy bear that serves as a transition for infants to shift from experiencing themselves as a center of the world to a sense of themselves as a person among others.

good-enough mother (Winnicott) A mother who adapts to her infant's gestures and needs during early infancy and gradually helps the infant develop independence.

true self (Winnicott) A sense of being real, whole, and spontaneous that comes from the caring of a good-enough mother; used in contrast to the false self.

false self (Winnicott) When good-enough mothering is not available in infancy, children may act as they believe they are expected to. Basically, they adopt their mother's self rather than develop their own. It is used in contrast with the true self.

splitting A process of keeping incompatible feelings separate from each other. It is an unconscious way of dealing with unwanted parts of the self or threatening parts of others. Because of problems of early development adults may have difficulty integrating feelings of love and anger and "split" their feelings by seeing others as all bad or all good.

QUESTIONS

16. From the information available in the case, would June's mother appear to meet Winnecott's definition of the good-enough mother?

   a. Yes
   b. No

17. If June's mother had been controlling, harsh, and not spontaneous, June may have developed

   a. a false self.
   b. an inferiority complex.
   c. a superiority complex.
   d. a true self.

18. If June were to get very angry at her boss for making her stay at work late and all of a sudden see her as hateful and vindictive when there had been no previous problem, June's action would be called

   a. identification.
   b. internalization.
   c. individuation.
   d. splitting.

SELF PSYCHOLOGY

The contribution of Heinz Kohut concentrates on the development of narcissism and how perceived attention, or lack of it, from parents' development can affect adults in later life. Freud had touched on the subject of narcissism in childhood, but Kohut develops this theme fully. For the infant, the world serves to meet his or her needs. Gradually, the child learns to attend to the influence of parents, often idealizing them. In his own therapeutic work, Kohut often worked with clients with narcissistic personality disorders. These were individuals who had difficulty being empathic to others and believed that they were very important and that others were important to the extent that they met the needs of the narcissistic individual.

CONCEPTS RELATED TO SELF PSYCHOLOGY

selfobject Unconscious thoughts, images, or representations of another person in an individual create patterns or themes called the selfobject. This representation of the person may impact the individual's self-esteem.

bipolar self This refers to the tension between the grandiose self ("I deserve to get what I want") and an idealized view of parents forming the two poles of the bipolar self.

mirroring When the parent shows the child that he or she is happy with the child, the child's grandiose self is supported. The mother or father reflects or mirrors the child's view of him or herself.

empathy Kohut used this term in a very specific sense. He believed that the therapist should be empathic with the patient's narcissistic or grandiose self. Therapist interpretations would show that the therapist understood an aspect of the development of narcissism.

19. In working with June, Kohut would attend most to understanding the development of her

    a. ego.
    b. id.
    c. self.
    d. superego.

20. In helping June, Kohut would have been most interested in June's relationship with her

    a. daughter.
    b. co-workers.
    c. husband.
    d. parents.

21. As June discusses her childhood and talks about times when she thought her mother could solve all of June's problems, Kohut would be hearing about

    a. the object.
    b. the ego.
    c. holding.
    d. the idealized parent.

22. When June talks about her view of her father taking her to a carnival when she was 5 years old, her unconscious view of him is called the _____ by self psychologists.

    a. self
    b. object
    c. selfobject
    d. idealized parent

23. If June says, "I need my husband to pay more attention to me. My parents never did. And you certainly don't," you as a self psychology therapist will see this as an illustration of the

    a. grandiose self.
    b. self.
    c. mirroring process.
    d. idealized parent.

RELATIONAL PSYCHOANALYSIS

Relational psychoanalysis builds on the object relations approach and self psychology. The focus is on the therapeutic relationship. The psychoanalyst is no longer seen as the authority but as a partner in the analysis. Rather than a focus on therapeutic neutrality, the therapist is seen as subjective rather than objective. Both therapist and patient have an influence on each other.

intersubjectivity The view that both analyst and patient influence each other in therapy.
one person psychology In psychoanalysis, the view that the patient is influenced by the analyst, but the analyst is not influenced by the patient
two person psychology (similar to intersubjectivity). The idea that both patient and analyst influence each other during therapy

24. If June sees you, her analyst, as an objective authority, June would see analysis from this point of view?
    a. one person
    b. two person
    c. three person
    d. four person

25. In relational psychoanalysis, rather than in other approaches to psychoanalysis, June's analyst would
    a. interpret id impulse
    b. focus on June's grandiosity.
    c. be aware of his/her impact on June, and June's impact on the therapist.
    d. focus on June's development of her bipolar self.

PSYCHOANALYTICAL APPROACHES TO TREATMENT

The different views of personality development and personality structure held by drive, ego, object relations, self psychology and relational theorists can help the therapist understand or assess the patient's problems. Some therapists use one of these perspectives; others use any combination, including all of them. In making assessments of the problems, therapists pay particular attention to material that patients are unaware of (the unconscious). The general goals of treatment and the therapeutic approach or techniques that psychoanalytic therapists use are shared by drive, ego, object relations, self psychology, and relational analysts. They all make use of free association and interpretation of dreams, resistance, and transference as well as countertransference.

THERAPEUTIC GOALS

The major purpose of psychoanalysis and psychodynamic therapy is to help individuals change their personality. By resolving unconscious conflicts within themselves, patients should be able to find more satisfactory ways of dealing with their problems. The goals of therapy are reached by reconstructing, interpreting, and analyzing one's childhood experiences. Although psychoanalysts and psychodynamic therapists of all types focus on unconscious motivations and early childhood development, the five schools of psychoanalysis put different emphases on the importance of understanding different developmental issues. Drive theorists particularly emphasize individuals' awareness of their sexual and aggressive drives. Ego psychoanalysts focus on positive ways of adapting to others and external pressures. They may also focus on understanding one's own defense mechanisms. Object relations therapists listen for problems that may have developed at an early age in the relationship between the patient as a child and his or her parents. Self psychologists also listen for problems that develop in parent-child relationships but do so from the perspective of narcissism. Relational psychoanalysts attend to the effect of therapist and patient on each other.

TYPES OF TREATMENT

There are three broad approaches to treatment which differ in terms of number of meetings per week and length of time. Psychoanalysis, psychoanalytic therapy, and psychoanalytic or psychodynamic counseling are defined here.

psychoanalysis Based on the work of Freud and others, psychoanalysis includes free association, dream analysis, and working through transference issues. The patient usually lies on a couch, and sessions are conducted three to five times per week.

psychoanalytic therapy Free association and exploration of unconscious processes may not be emphasized as strongly as in psychoanalysis. Meetings are usually one to three times per week, and the patient sits in a chair.

psychoanalytic or *psychodynamic counseling* Meetings are usually once a week for a year or two, and the patient sits in a chair. Therapists may use more active techniques than those described in Chapter 2 in the text.

PSYCHOANALYTIC TECHNIQUES

Most psychoanalytic techniques are designed either to elicit information from the patient that may contain unconscious material (free association) or to help the patient develop insights about this material. Most psychoanalytic techniques focus on this latter purpose.

free association The patient relates feelings, fantasies, thoughts, memories, and recent events to the analyst spontaneously and without censoring them. These associations give the analyst clues to the unconscious processes of the patient.

interpretation The process by which the psychoanalyst points out the unconscious meanings of a situation to a patient. Analysts assess their patients' ability to accept interpretations and bring them to conscious awareness.

interpreting resistance Patients may resist uncovering repressed material in therapy. Often, through unconscious processes, patients may show aspects of themselves to the therapist which the therapist then shares with the patient.

interpreting projective identification Patients may take negative aspects of themselves, project them onto someone else, and then identify with or try unconsciously to control that person. In doing so, a part of oneself is "split off" and attributed to another in order to control that other person. When this occurs in therapy, the therapist points this out (interprets it) to the patient.

interpreting transference Transference refers to the patient's feelings and fantasies, both positive and negative, about the therapist. More specifically, it refers to responses by the patient to the therapist as though the therapist were a significant person in the patient's past, usually the mother or father. Where appropriate, the therapist informs (interprets) the patient that this is happening.

interpreting transference psychosis In transference psychosis, patients may act out early childhood destructive relationships with the therapist that they had with their parents. Interpretations are done carefully, considering the patient's ability to deal with this information.

interpreting dreams Dream interpretation may be done rather frequently as dreams represent an excellent source of unconscious material. How the therapist interprets the dream depends on whether the therapist is using a listening perspective from drive, ego, object relations, or self psychology.

countertransference An important concept in psychoanalysis, this term can be defined in three different ways: 1. The neurotic or irrational reactions of a therapist toward the patient, 2. The therapist's conscious and unconscious feelings toward the patient, 3. A way of understanding how people in the patient's past may have felt.

relational responses Comments on issues that arise in the therapeutic hour which reflect the therapist-patient relationship, rather than just making transference and countertransference interpretations.

PSYCHOANALYTIC TREATMENT OF JUNE

In this section, you will be given information about June's work in therapy and asked questions about helping her from a psychoanalytic perspective.

You have been seeing June for therapy three times a week for a year. This is your 145th session with her. June sits across from you in a chair, as your approach can be described as psychoanalytic therapy. At the beginning of the session, June relates this vivid dream that she had. In the questions that follow, you will be asked to determine whether the interpretation given is from a drive, ego, object relations, or self psychology perspective.

"I was in a large church with my mother. We were kneeling next to each other right in front of the pews. There was a large plain wood cross between us with the cross piece over our heads. No one else was there, and we were both praying silently. Sun was coming through the large stained glass windows. They were beautiful. I was aware that there were several themes from the Bible and that Peter, Paul, and the Virgin Mary were there, each in a different theme. All of sudden, out of the corner of my eye right behind my mother, I could see the Virgin Mary. It was like she was a stained glass figure in dark blue, but also three dimensional at the same time. At first I was scared, but it was like at the same time, she and my mother reached out to me. My mother put her arm around me, the cross seemed to disappear, and I felt so much better. It was like the picture of the Virgin Mary seemed to dissolve into us. The feeling was very helpful and lovely. I remember a smile on my face when I woke up. I don't ever remember that happening before in a dream."

Imagine that you have given the following interpretations to the dream; indicate which school of psychoanalysis your interpretation represents.

26. "June, you seem to be returning to a time in your life when you wanted to be close to your mother in a very significant way." This interpretation reflects which of the following viewpoints?

   a. drive theory
   b. ego psychology
   c. object relations
   d. self psychology

27. "You seem to have a sense of your mother of being ideal, perhaps perfect. It may have felt like she was so powerful and you were insignificant. It was like everything in the world revolved around her, not you."
This interpretation reflects which of the following viewpoints?

   a. drive theory
   b. ego psychology
   c. object relations
   d. self psychology

28. "June, having that cross, that symbol of masculinity, removed from you and your mother seemed to help you to develop trust." This interpretation reflects which of the following viewpoints?

   a. drive theory
   b. ego psychology
   c. object relations
   d. self psychology

29. "It seems that first you were afraid of the masculine phallic symbol, the cross. When it disappeared, you were less afraid to express yourself." This interpretation reflects which of the following viewpoints?

   a. drive theory
   b. ego psychology
   c. object relations
   d. self psychology

30. How would you characterize the therapist's comments in Questions 26 through 29?

   a. empathic
   b. therapeutic neutrality
   c. interpretation
   d. countertransference statements

31. After making your interpretive statement, you say to June: "As you think about this dream, I would like you to tell me anything that comes into your mind, a fragment, a thought, an image." Which technique are you using?

    a. free association
    b. eliciting a transference response
    c. providing therapeutic neutrality
    d. interpreting a dream

32. June replies to you saying, "I really don't want to do that. I feel that you are pushing this dream too far. You are trying to make too big a deal of it." You then say, "I wonder if you have some concerns about the progress that we are making in therapy." This would be an example of interpreting the

    a. dream.
    b. resistance.
    c. transference.
    d. countertransference.

33. June says, "You know, we've talked about me being depressed and uncertain, but now I find that my husband is like that. I think he's unsure of himself, and I try to help him gain control over himself. He doesn't seem to appreciate that. He says he's fine and hasn't changed, that it's me. But I really notice that he is depressed and negative like I used to be."
    Being the therapist, you say, "Perhaps you're seeing a part of yourself in your husband, something that you never have seen in him before." Your comment would be an example of

    a. free association
    b. interpreting the resistance.
    c. interpreting the transference.
    d. interpreting projective identification.

34. June now says to you, "I hate it when you say I am unjustly accusing my husband of being depressed. That's what my mother always did. She never believed me and you don't believe me." You reply, "You seem to be getting angry at me just the way you were angry at your mother when you were little. You felt that she was blaming you for not doing enough at home or for not being good enough. Now you seem to be feeling that from me." As a psychoanalytic therapist, you are

    a. interpreting the resistance.
    b. free associating.
    c. interpreting the transference.
    d. providing therapeutic neutrality.

35. Hearing June's comments about you, you start to feel annoyed at her. This kind of attack reminds you of how your own father would criticize you. Your reaction could best be described as

    a. unprofessional.
    b. resistance.
    c. empathic responding.
    d. countertransference.

BRIEF THERAPY

Because traditional psychoanalysis may require meetings three or four times a week for five to eight years, many therapists have been concerned about the cost to patients and the relatively slow progress compared to other theories. More than any other theory, psychoanalysis has been the source of new creative approaches to short term work. Typically short term therapy lasts 12 to 40 sessions. To be successful, short term psychodynamic therapy requires that individuals be motivated, focused on one or two problems, and be experiencing anxiety or depression rather than borderline or narcissistic personality disorders. Techniques tend to be direct rather than indirect. Therapists often ask questions, restate client comments, confront clients, and deal quickly with transference issues. They tend not to use free association and lengthy dream work. In the chart shown here, psychoanalysis is contrasted with the Luborsky's Core Conflictual Theme method.

PSYCHODYNAMIC PSYCHOTHERAPY	LUBORSKY'S CORE CONFLICTUAL THEME METHOD
Free association	Listen to Relationship Episodes
Neutrality or empathy	Determine the Wish The Response From the Other
Interpreting resistance	Response From Self
Interpreting dreams	Communicate the Core Conflictual Relationship Theme
Interpreting transference	
	Use 5-7 Relationship Episodes
Interpreting projective identification and other concerns	Work through Response from Others and Self
	Termination
Countertransference	

OE1. Characterize the difference between long term psychodynamic psychotherapy and Luborsky's method. (60)

_____

_____

_____

_____

_____

SPECIAL TOPICS

OE2. Another current trend in psychoanalysis is that toward shorter therapy. Why is this an important movement within psychoanalysis?

_____

_____

_____

_____

_____

_____

OE3. In analytically informed therapy or counseling (psychodynamic counseling), therapists might use techniques borrowed from other theories. How could that change the practice of psychoanalysis? (63)

_____

_____

_____

OE4. Why has psychoanalytic theory, specifically Freudian drive theory and object relations, been the subject of criticism for its description of the role of the development of women? (67)

_____

_____

_____

OE5. In what ways have psychodynamic writers neglected multicultural issues, and in what ways have they responded to them? (68)

_____

_____

_____

STRENGTHS AND LIMITATIONS

What do you see as the strengths and limitations of psychoanalytic therapy?

Strengths	Limitations

PSYCHOANALYTIC THERAPY: A QUIZ

True/False items: Decide if the following statements are more "true" or more "false" as they apply to psychodynamic or psychoanalytic therapy.

T F Q1. Freud was not influenced by contemporary psychologists, psychiatrists, philosophers, or writers in the development of psychoanalysis.

T F Q2. It is unconscious material, rather than conscious material, that is the focus of psychoanalysis.

T F Q3. In drive theory, the genital stage occurs in adolescence.

T F Q4. Anna Freud is considered to be a drive theorist like her father, Sigmund.

T F Q5. Erik Erikson converted and further developed Freud's psychosexual stages into psychosocial stages.

T F Q6. Donald Winnicott emphasized the early maternal relationship as being important in healthy adult adjustment.

T F Q7. Heinz Kohut developed the term "good enough" mothering which refers to the mother being able to adapt to the infant's needs yet help the infant move toward independence.

T F Q8. The goals of psychoanalytic therapy are designed to bring about changes in a person's personality and character structure.

T F Q9. Psychoanalysts who use a couch do so to allow the patient to free-associate as much as possible. In this way, the therapist is out of view, and there is less interference in the free association process than there would be if the therapist sat across from the patient.

T F Q10. Psychoanalysts and psychodynamic therapists view countertransference as a hinderance to progress in therapy.

Multiple choice items: Select the *best answer* from the alternatives using a psychoanalytic or psychodynamic perspective.

_____ Q11. One of the techniques that Freud used in his early work but later abandoned was

      a. free association.
      b. hypnosis.
      c. behavior modification.
      d. shock therapy.

_____ Q12. Which of these terms fits most closely with Freud's drive theory?

      a. individuation
      b. relational
      c. oral
      d. self

_____ A _____ Q13. Biological forces are most closely associated with which one of these concepts?

      a. id
      b. ego
      c. superego
      d. object

_____ C _____ Q14. If Morris says that it is not a big deal that he is unhappy at school because all his friends are unhappy at school as well, he is most likely using the defense mechanism of

      a. repression.
      b. reaction formation.
      c. projection.
      d. sublimation.

_____ C _____ Q15. When 6-year-old Rachel is scolded by her mother, she curls up into a fetal position and sucks her thumb. She is using the defense mechanism of

      a. repression.
      b. reaction formation.
      c. regression.
      d. sublimation.

_____ D _____ Q16. Ralph has just broken up with his girl friend. Rather than admit that this hurts him, Ralph looks at this event philosophically as just another life event. Ralph is using the defense mechanism of

      a. regression.
      b. reaction formation.
      c. identification.
      d. intellectualization.

_____ A _____ Q17. Which of Erik Erikson's psychosocial stages corresponds to Freud's oral stage?

      a. trust versus mistrust
      b. autonomy versus shame and doubt
      c. initiative versus guilt
      d. industry versus inferiority

_____ D _____ Q18. Which of these theorists developed the idea of the "false self," defined as acting as one is expected to do by parents, rather than acting as one believes or feels?

      a. Sigmund Freud
      b. Otto Kernberg
      c. Stephen Mitchell
      d. Donald Winnicott

_____ D _____ Q19. Self psychology is most concerned with the development of

      a. ego strength.
      b. separation and individuation.
      c. the id.
      d. normal narcissism.

_____ Q20. Seeing the analyst as a subjective rather than objective presence in analysis is associated with

    a. drive theory.
    b. ego psychology.
    c. object relations.
    d. relational psychoanalysis.

_____ Q21. Which school of psychoanalysis is associated with the true self?

    a. drive theory
    b. ego theory
    c. object relations
    d. self psychology

_____ Q22. In psychoanalysis, interpretations help to bring _____ material into consciousness.

    a. id
    b. selfobject
    c. individuated
    d. unconscious

_____ Q23. When the therapist is aware of her reactions to the client, this is typically viewed as

    a. countertransference.
    b. confrontation.
    c. bipolar self.
    d. projective identification.

_____ Q24. Which of these techniques is most likely to be used in psychoanalysis and less likely to be used in psychodynamic therapy?

    a. questions
    b. confrontation
    c. free association
    d. supportive statements

_____ Q25. Intersubjectivity is most closely related to which one of these types of psychoanalysis?

    a. drive theory
    b. ego psychology
    c. object-relations
    d. self psychology
    e. relational psychoanalysis

ANSWERS TO QUESTIONS

1. b	11. a	21. d	31. a
2. a	12. c	22. c	32. b
3. c	13. b	23. a	33. d
4. c	14. c	24. b	34. c
5. a	15. a	25. c	35. d
6. a	16. a	26. c	
7. a	17. a	27. d	
8. b	18. d.	28. b	
9. c	19. c	29. a	
10. b	20. d	30. c	

Q1. F	Q11. b	Q21. c
Q2 T	Q12. c	Q22. d
Q3. T	Q13. a	Q23. a
Q4. F	Q14. c	Q24. c
Q5. T	Q15. c	Q25. e
Q6. T	Q16. d	
Q7. F	Q17. a	
Q8. T	Q18. d	
Q9. T	Q19. d	
Q10. F	Q20. d	

CHAPTER 3

JUNGIAN ANALYSIS
AND THERAPY

JUNGIAN THERAPY SELF-INVENTORY

Directions: By comparing your beliefs about personality to Jung's, you should have a clearer idea of how much you will need to suspend your beliefs or change attitudes to understand Jung's theory of personality. You may find it helpful to complete this section before and after you read the chapter. In this way, you can see if your views have changed. There are no correct answers, only an opportunity to express your views.

Put an "X" on the line so that it indicates how much you agree or disagree with the statement: A=Agree, D=Disagree.

D_____A 1. Becoming more aware of thoughts and feelings that we were previously unaware of (unconscious of) will lead to personal growth.

_____ 2. There are themes and events that are universal for all human beings.

_____ 3. There are important life themes that are played out in different ways in a variety of cultures.

_____ 4. Understanding religious myths and legends of cultures give insights into important life themes.

_____ 5. The concepts of introversion and extraversion are helpful in understanding people's personality.

_____ 6. Knowing how people perceive events and make judgments about these events can help you understand individuals better.

_____ 7. Knowing that some people prefer learning by thinking and others by feeling can help you understand them better.

_____ 8. The important aspect of adolescence is that it is a time where young people discover their own personality.

_____ 9. Middle age is as important a time of life, perhaps more so, than childhood for understanding personality development.

10. Old age is as important a time of life, perhaps more so, as childhood for understanding personality development.

11. An important life goal is to become aware of one's strengths and limitations.

12. An important therapeutic goal is to make previously unconscious material conscious.

13. Dreams are among the most important material that therapists can use to help patients learn about themselves.

14. Insight is an important goal of therapy.

15. Creative methods such as dance, poetry, and artwork provide insight into an individual's personality.

16. Therapy takes time to work, often a year or more.

17. Understanding a patient's culture - religion, myths, and legends - can help the therapist provide useful insight into the patient's personality.

18. When patients understand their dark side, their angry and hostile feelings, they can better understand themselves.

19. Individual therapy is more important than group therapy in understanding oneself as an individual.

20. The therapist's unconscious awareness of a patient can be a useful therapeutic tool.

HISTORY OF JUNGIAN ANALYSIS AND THERAPY

An excellent student, Jung's background was considerably broad. He was very much influenced by his family's history of involvement in theology. His interest in spirituality, ritual, and ceremony can be seen in his childhood and adolescence. His personal experience as well as his broad knowledge of many subjects led him to develop a theoretical perspective that is quite different from any other discussed in the text.

Which influences do you think were most important in the development of Jung's theory?

PERSONAL LIFE

Born in 1875
Kesswil, Switzerland
Childhood dreams and daydreams
Rituals and ceremonies with miniature scrolls
Excellent student - knowledge of Greek and Latin at early age
Later studied philosophy, theology, anthropology, mythology, and science
1895 - started medical training at University of Basel
1903 - married Emma Rauschenbach
1924 - visited the Pueblo of New Mexico
1925 - visited Tanganyika
Studied alchemy, astrology, divination, telepathy, clairvoyance, fortune telling
Built a tower at the end of Lake Zurich
Died June 6, 1961

PROFESSIONAL LIFE

Kant's view of a prioi universal forms of perception
Carl Gustav Carus's view of 3 levels of unconscious including a universal level
Eduard von Hartmann's ideas of a universal unconscious
Gottfried Leibniz (1700's) irrationality of the unconscious
Arthur Schopenhauer's irrational forces based on sexuality
Johann Bachofen - anthropologist symbolism across cultures
1913 - 1919 spiritual suffering, due in part to severing relationship with Sigmund Freud
Adolf Bastian - anthropologist, understanding people by their rites, symbols, and mythology
George Creuzer - anthropology, importance of symbolism in stories

1902 - dissertation - *On Psychology and Pathology of So-called Occult Phenomenon*
Eugen Bleuler and Pierre Janet - psychiatrists
Developed word association test with Franz Riklin
1909 - Lectured at Clark University, along with Freud
1911 - *Symbols of Transformation*
Produced over 20 volumes of writings
Honorary degrees from Harvard, Oxford, and other universities

JUNG'S THEORY OF PERSONALITY

For some students, Jung's theory of personality is the most difficult to grasp of all the theories covered in the text. This is due in part to his emphasis on the importance of the unconscious and understanding symbols of unconscious material. Additionally, his focus on the collective unconscious and its symbolism leads to the labeling of a vast array of archetypes and their symbols. The text focuses only on the most common symbols. Easier to grasp are the attitudes and functions of personality which include the concepts of introvervsion and extraversion. To make the material as clear as possible, I will present these definitions of concepts that help in understanding basic Jungian personality theory. Then, I will return to the dream of June, described in Chapter 2, and ask you some questions about it from a Jungian perspective. Next, I will define concepts important to learning about Jungian personality attitudes and functions. Questions about June's attitudes and functions should help to clarify these terms.

BASIC JUNGIAN PERSONALITY THEORY AND CONCEPTS

Referring to the terms below can help you understand concepts that are most central to the ideas of Carl Jung. To separate Jung's work from that of Freud, it is important to remember that the collective unconscious is a concept used by Jung, but not by Freud. Jung emphasized the universality of the human species, symbolism, and individual development. In contrast, Freud developed a very different personality structure based on his view of the importance of psychosexual drives in early childhood.

psyche Jung's term for personality structure which includes conscious and unconscious thoughts, feelings, and behaviors.

ego An expression of personality which includes thoughts, feelings and behaviors of which we are conscious. Note that this definition is very different from Freud's which describes the ego as a means of mediating between one's instincts or drives and the external world.

individuation The process of integrating opposing elements of personality to become whole. This involves, in part, bringing unconscious contents into relationship with consciousness.

personal unconscious Thoughts, feelings, and perceptions that are not accepted by the ego are stored here. Included are distant memories as well as personal or unresolved moral conflicts that may be emotionally charged.

complex A group of associated feelings, thoughts, and memories that have intense emotional content. Complexes may have elements from a personal and collective unconscious.

collective unconscious This is the part of the unconscious that contains memories and images that are universal to the human species in contrast to the personal unconscious which is based upon individual experience. Humans have an inherited tendency to form representations of mythological motives which may vary greatly but maintain basic patterns. Thus, individuals may view the universe in similar ways by thinking, feeling, and reacting to common elements such as the moon or water.

transcendent function A process which bridges two opposing attitudes or conditions and becomes a third force uniting the two but different from the two.

archetypes Universal images or symbols that are pathways from the collective unconscious to the conscious, such as a mother (Earth Mother) or animal instincts (shadow). They take a person's reactions and put them in a pattern.

symbol The content and outward expression of archetypes. Symbols represent the wisdom of humanity and can be applied to future issues and are represented differentially in a variety of cultures.

persona An archetype representing the roles that people play in response to social demands of others. It is the mask or disguise that individuals assume when superficially interacting with their environment. It may often be at variance with their true identities.

anima The archetype representing the feminine component of the male personality.

animus The archetype that represents the masculine component of the female personality.

shadow The archetype that represents unacceptable sexual, animalistic, or aggressive impulses, usually the opposite of the way we see ourselves.

Self An archetype that is the center of personality and provides organization and integration of the personality through a process of individuation.

mandala A symbolic representation of the unified wholeness of the Self. Usually, it has four sections representing an effort to achieve wholeness in the four sections (such as the four directions of the winds).

BASIC JUNGIAN PERSONALITY THEORY CONCEPTS: A CASE

In Chapter 2 of this manual, we discussed the case of June. In that chapter, one of her dreams was analyzed from four different psychoanalytic points of view. Let us return to that dream and examine it from a Jungian perspective.

In the dream, June was in a church, kneeling next to her mother. There was a large cross between them. No one else was in the church. However, above them were large stained glass pictures of Biblical scenes. The Virgin Mary came out of one of these scenes and appeared behind June and her mother who were facing the altar.

The following questions about this dream deal both with terms referring to important aspects of Jungian personality theory as well as to specific Jungian archetypes.

1. If June has her own thoughts, feelings, and perceptions that are unconscious but are revealed in the dream, these would be referred to as products of the

   a. conscious process.
   b. preconscious.
   c. personal unconscious.
   d. collective unconscious.

2. June's dream is one small part of her entire personality structure, called the _____, which includes both conscious and unconscious thoughts, feelings, and behaviors.

   a. ego
   b. complex
   c. persona
   d. psyche

3. As a result of analyzing the dream, June now sees that the Virgin Mary connects common threads between her and her mother. This common bond gives her a sense of closeness with her mother that feels new. The dream may be said to have served

    a. a transcendent function.
    b. a universal function.
    c. an auxiliary function.
    d. a superior function.

4. As June brings unconscious elements into consciousness, she becomes further integrated as a person. This therapeutic goal is know as

    a. ego mediation.
    b. symbolic clarification.
    c. individuation.
    d. separation.

5. In this dream, the Virgin Mary can be viewed as a (an)

    a. archetype.
    b. anima.
    c. symbol.
    d. transcendent function.

6. If the Virgin Mary is seen as representing the Great Mother, then the Great Mother would be called a (an)

    a. archetype.
    b. religious icon.
    c. symbol.
    d. transcendent function.

7. If in the dream, a warm, caring, older man comes up behind June and gently puts his hands on her shoulders, giving her a sense of strength, one might suspect that this represents the

    a. anima.
    b. animus.
    c. persona.
    d. shadow.

8. When June is interacting with her fellow employees, the archetype that most likely describes her relationship with them and the roles she plays with them would be the

    a. animus.
    b. persona.
    c. Self.
    d. shadow.

9. If in the dream, the Virgin Mary should turn into an aggressive, harmful monster, the archetype that is most represented by this symbol is likely to be the

    a. animus.
    b. persona.
    c. Self.
    d. shadow.

10. As June and her therapist analyze the dream, June develops new insights about her personality. This process is likely to take place in the

   a. conscious part of her psyche.
   b. the preconscious.
   c. the collective conscious.
   d. the collective unconscious.

PERSONALITY ATTITUDES AND FUNCTIONS

The aspect of Jung's theory of personality that is best known are the two attitudes: introversion and extraversion. Less well known are the functions: thinking, feeling, sensing, and intuiting. Inventories such as the Myers-Briggs Type Indicator have been developed to measure these concepts. This aspect of Jungian personality theory has been widely popularized and has been used by non-Jungian therapists. Jungian analysts and therapists see these attitudes and functions as related to the psyche and as expressions of the conscious and the unconscious aspects of the Self.

attitudes Introversion and extraversion are two ways of interacting with the world or two attitudes toward the world.

introversion One of the two major attitudes or orientations of personality, introversion represents an orientation toward subjective experience and focusing on one's own perception of the external world.

extraversion One of the two major attitudes or orientations of personality. Extraversion is associated with valuing objective experience and receiving and responding to the external world rather than thinking about one's own perceptions or internal world.

functions The four ways of receiving and responding to the world (thinking, feeling, sensing, and intuiting) are called functions.

thinking A function of personality in which individuals attempt to understand the world and to solve problems. It is in contrast to feeling.

feeling A function of personality in which individuals attend to subjective experiences of pleasure, pain, anger, or other feelings. Its polar opposite is thinking.

sensing A personality function that emphasizes one's perception of one's self and one's world. Its polar opposite is intuiting.

intuiting A personality function that stresses having a hunch or guess about something, which may arise from the unconscious. Its polar opposite is sensing.

superior function One of the four functions of personality (thinking, feeling, sensing, or intuiting) which is the most highly developed.

auxiliary function The function that takes over when the superior function is not operating. It includes thinking, feeling, sensing, and intuiting.

inferior function This is the function which is least well developed in an individual and may be repressed and unconscious, showing itself in dreams or fantasies.

11. June tells her Jungian analyst that she has a gut feeling that something is about to happen between her and her mother. Which of the following attitudes or functions best describes this reaction?

    a. extraversion
    b. introversion
    c. feeling
    d. intuition

12. While riding the subway to her appointment with her analyst, June was lost in thought about her dream. She couldn't figure out its meaning. Which attitude or function best represents June's way of being at that time?

    a. extraversion
    b. introversion
    c. thinking
    d. feeling

13. June very much enjoys her job because she enjoys interaction with her colleagues. Her analyst has also noticed how expressive June is of her feelings with regard to her family. Which of these is most likely to represent June's attitude towards the world?

    a. feeling
    b. thinking
    c. extraversion
    d. introversion

14. If June's feeling function is well developed, which of these functions is likely to be less well developed?

    a. intuition
    b. sensing
    c. thinking
    d. transcendent

15. Which two functions can be considered irrational functions because they relate to responding to stimuli rather than making judgments about them?

    a. feeling and intuition
    b. thinking and feeling
    c. sensation and intuition
    d. sensation and thinking

JUNGIAN ANALYSIS AND THERAPY

The goal of Jungian analysis and therapy is, broadly speaking, to help individuals bring unconscious material into consciousness. By doing so, patients learn about their strengths and weaknesses, continually learning about new aspects of themselves of which they were previously unaware. This process is called *individuation* (defined previously).

Assessment takes place through the analysis of dreams and other unconscious material. Assessment of personality attitudes and functions can be done through the application of objective personality inventories. The most well known is the Myers-Briggs Type Indicator. Others are the Gray-Wheelwright Jungian Type Survey, and the Singer-Loomis Inventory of Personality. Occasionally projective inventories have been used such as the Rorschach Test and the Thematic Apperception Test. Another assessment technique was developed by Jung and Franz Riklin which is known as word association. Delayed reactions to the patient's response to a word or phrase might indicate an emotional response which may be rooted in the unconscious.

JUNGIAN THERAPY TECHNIQUES

Like Freud and other psychoanalysts, Jungian analysts and therapists use interpretation. They may also make use of transference and countertransference. However, they tend to focus less on transference and countertransference than psychoanalysts. Jung's views of these concepts changed throughout his 50 years of writing. For Jungians, transference and countertransference, like dreams and active imagination, have archetypal components. Other creative techniques such as dance and movement therapy, poetry, art work, and use of the sand tray help unconscious processes enter into consciousness, revealing archetypal material.

JUNGIAN THERAPEUTIC CONCEPTS

amplification A process of using knowledge of the history and meaning of symbols to understand unconscious material, like those that arise from patients' dreams.

dreams Arising from unconscious creativity, "big" dreams represent symbolic material from the collective unconscious; "little" dreams reflect day to day activity and may come from the personal unconscious.

active imagination A technique of analysis in which individuals actively focus on experiences or images (in dreams or fantasy), reporting changes in these images or experiences as they concentrate on them.

sand tray This is a sand box with small figures and forms that individuals can assign meaning to. Jungian therapists may attach archetypal significance to the play or stories that individuals develop as they use the figures and forms.

puer aeternus A man who may have difficulty growing out of adolescence and becoming more responsible.

puella aeterna A woman who may have difficulty accepting the responsibilities of adulthood and is likely to be still attached to her father.

synchronicity Coincidences that have no causal connection. Dreaming of seeing two snakes and then seeing snakes the next day is an example of synchronicity.

A JUNGIAN DREAM INTERPRETATION EXAMPLE

In this example, June will describe a dream that she had. You will play the role of a Jungian analyst and examine and interpret the dream from a Jungian perspective. Because Jungian therapy or analysis is probably the most difficult approach to learn and requires arguably more specific training than any other therapy, the questions that I will present will be followed immediately by answers and an explanation. You may wish to cover the answers as you try to answer the questions.

June comes to the therapy session with notes about a dream that she had two nights ago. As soon as she woke up in the morning, she wrote down as many details as she could remember about different aspects of the dream. However, the part that was most vivid to her was the one in which she had strong emotional reactions. She says: "I don't remember quite how I got there but I was in a hallway behind the stage of a large open air auditorium, I was puzzled by that, but a moment later I was on the stage and I was a musician. I was playing the guitar with the rock band Kiss. They were dressed in their black makeup that they usually wear and their bizarre costumes. The music was very loud, unpleasantly so, and they were screaming into the microphone. The audience of tens of thousands of people were cheering and screaming. I was playing too, more softly, but going along with them, doing what rock musicians are supposed to do. Occasionally, I was yelling too, but then I would find myself surprised at the rage in my voice. That didn't last long; most of the time I just struggled to keep going. There was a feeling of chaos in the dream, and it was confusing. I think the feeling that I had when I woke up was that I was troubled and confused by the dream.

The dream really surprised me. I had grown up with church music. Like my mother, I had been in the choir, and we had sung hymns. Although as a teenager, I listened to other music, my mother really wanted me to only play and listen to church-related music.

I'm not sure about how this is related to my depression. I know I have felt somewhat overwhelmed lately by work and by taking care of my daughter. I worry that I'm not being a good enough mother to her and being there for her when she needs me".

QUESTIONS ABOUT THE DREAM

16. An interpretation of this dream from a Jungian point of view is likely to be

    a. objective.
    b. subjective.

(b. the dream is likely to be a subjective interpretation because members of the audience and the band are not known or important to June.)

17. In the dream, the band, Kiss, may represent a (an)

    a. archetype.
    b. symbol.
    c. neither, because the band is modern and symbols and archetypes refer to myths and fairy tales.

(b. the band is a symbol of an archetype. Symbols may be modern or current characters or events. They do not necessarily have to be mythological or legendary.)

18. The archetype that the band Kiss represents for June is most likely to be

    a. her animus.
    b. the Wise Man.
    c. her persona.
    d. her shadow.

(d. June appears to be a rather restrained, now depressed, person. The aggressive behavior of the band and its loud noise and bizarre appearance represent aggressive impulses in June that are far from her conscious awareness of herself.)

19. As a Jungian therapist, which of the following statements are you most likely to make as you and June interpret her dream?

    a. "Why do you think you might be attracted to the music of Kiss?"
    b. "Perhaps the members of the rock band Kiss represent the fear that you sometimes had of your father after your mother and father divorced."
    c. " Perhaps your discomfort with the band and its loud and raucous music may represent an uncomfortableness with that part of yourself that is sometimes angry or aggressive (the shadow)."
    d. "Have you ever had guitar lessons?"

(c. For June, the band, Kiss, may be a symbol of the archetype of the shadow which may include unacceptable aggressive or sexual feelings. Such a response would help June to explore parts of herself that she was previously unaware of.)

20. June might respond in this way to the therapist's statement in 19.c. "I know that my mother never liked it when I got angry and I try not to. I really want to be a good wife, but sometimes my husband just does things that really irritate me."
    If you were a Jungian analyst or therapist, which of these responses might you choose?

    a. Can you tell me more about that?
    b. Are you aware that your husband also may represent an archetypal symbol for you?

(a. Jungian therapists and analysts are likely to follow up on a new insight that patients have about their feelings, situations, or relationships. Not all comments need be directly related to archetypal imagery. The therapist and June are likely to further explore her relationship with her husband. Her awareness of her strong feelings is prompted by the dream interpretation.)

21. As a Jungian therapist, which of these techniques are you least likely to use in working with June?

    a. acting as if
    b. active imagination
    c. interpretation of transference
    d. the sand tray

(a. Although Jungian therapists and analysts may occasionally use Adlerian techniques, such as "acting as if", they are more likely to use the other three techniques which help to bring unconscious material into awareness.)

22. In interpreting a dream, a Jungian analyst is most likely to ask what does the dream do for the _____?

    a. archetype
    b. dreamer
    c. therapist
    d. patient's parents

(b. Dreams cannot be interpreted without the dreamer. The purpose of understanding the dream is to see what purpose it serves for the dreamer.)

23. Because of the archetypal imagery and new insights that June has developed about an aspect about herself, her dream is most likely to be viewed as a _____ dream?

    a. big
    b. little

(a. The dream might be called a big dream because it comes from June's collective unconscious. A little dream would reflect more day-to-day material. This dream might help June and her analyst explore more aspects of herself than a dream about a movie that she had seen which contained little archetypal material.)

SPECIAL TOPICS

OE1. Why would Jungian therapists find brief therapy inconsistent with Jungian theory? (107)

_____

_____

_____

OE2. One current trend in Jungian therapy is the popularization of Jung's ideas to the general public. Why do you think Jung's ideas have achieved such popularity? (107)

_____

_____

_____

OE3. In terms of using Jung's concepts with other theories, which of his concepts do you believe would be most popular among other theorists or mental health professionals? (108)

_____

_____

_____

_____

OE4. In what way do the concepts of anima and animus help Jungian therapists address gender issues? (110)

_____

_____

_____

_____

OE5. What do Jungian therapists learn in their training that helps them deal with multicultural issues in therapy? (111)

_____

_____

_____

STRENGTHS AND LIMITATIONS

What do you see as the strengths and limitations of Jungian therapy?

STRENGTHS	LIMITATIONS
_____	_____
_____	_____
_____	_____
_____	_____
_____	_____
_____	_____
_____	_____
_____	_____
_____	_____

JUNGIAN THERAPY: A QUIZ

True or false items: Decide if the following statements are more "true" or more "false" as they apply to Jungian therapy and analysis.

T F   Q1.   Much of Jung's life was devoted to exploring the unconscious.

T F   Q2.   Freud and Jung had a friendly collaborative relationship that lasted until Freud died.

T F   Q3.   Jung saw the ego as a way of organizing conscious forces.

T F   Q4.   The collective unconscious refers to an inherited tendency of the human mind to form representations of mythological motifs, representations that vary a great deal without losing their basic pattern.

T F   Q5.   Archetypes are images with form but not content.

T F   Q6.   Symbols are expressions of archetypes and have content.

T F   Q7.   A mandala is an example of an archetype.

T F   Q8.   Like Freud, Jung believed that the most important focus of therapy should be early childhood development.

T F   Q9.   Becoming more aware of previously unconscious forces is an important goal of Jungian therapy and analysis.

T F   Q10. Jungian therapy pays less attention to different cultures than psychoanalysis.

Multiple choice items: Select the *best answer* from the alternatives using a Jungian perspective.

_____ Q11. From the five choices below, choose the concept that Jungian therapists would consider to be most important.

        a. anima
        b. style of life
        c. superego
        d. transference
        e. unconscious

_____ Q12. The tendency of humans to form representations of mythological motifs refers to the

        a. conscious.
        b. preconscious.
        c. collective unconscious.
        d. personal unconscious.

_____ Q13. Which of these is not an archetype?

        a. death
        b. power
        c. the persona
        d. Zeus

_____ Q14. Which of these is not a symbol?

     a. anima
     b. Hitler
     c. Michael Jordan
     d. Queen Elizabeth

_____ Q15. Typical everyday interactions with neighbors would be representative of this archetype.

     a. anima-animus
     b. persona
     c. Self
     d. shadow

_____ Q16. Jung's concept of introversion refers to

     a. being shy and quiet.
     b. being concerned with one's inner world - one's thoughts and ideas.
     c. believing that others are inferior to oneself in any of these three areas: occupation, family, and society.
     d. difficulty in maintaining relationships with others.

_____ Q17. When Harvey decides that he will not take a job offer, he is using which function?

     a. introversion
     b. intuition
     c. sensing
     d. thinking

_____ Q18. To effectively use the process of Jungian analysis, a patient should have at least some of this attitude.

     a. extraversion
     b. introversion
     c. thinking
     d. feeling

_____ Q19. Which of these functions is most likely to exist in an individual's conscious level?

     a. auxiliary
     b. inferior
     c. tertiary
     d. superior

_____ Q20. Which of these is most likely to be a goal of Jungian therapy?

     a. list the archetypes most important to close family members
     b. become more extraverted while still being intuitive
     c. come to terms with unconscious factors, bringing more material into consciousness
     d. become more aware of behaviors, thoughts, and feelings of others.

_____ Q21. Which of these stages of Jungian therapy most closely fits with the contributions made by Carl Jung?

     a. catharsis
     b. elucidation or interpretation
     c. social education
     d. individuation

_____ Q22. Dreaming of a bad experience that one had at a family gathering is most likely classified as a(an) _____.

    a. objective dream.
    b. subjective dream.
    c. inappropriate dream.
    d. nightmare.

_____ Q23. Which of these does NOT directly relate to gender issues in Jungian therapy or analysis?

    a. active imagination
    b. anima
    c. animus
    d. the symbol of Pandora

_____ Q24. Which of these approaches to understanding problems is most closely associated with Jungian theory?

    a. developing better communication skills
    b. establishing a holding environment
    c. using themes developed from cultural knowledge
    d. analysis of the first 5 years of life

_____ Q25. In understanding a patient's psychotic process, a Jungian therapist, more than other therapists, might

    a. take a history of physical problems.
    b. analyze speech fluency.
    c. determine effective communication patterns.
    d. examine symbolism in verbal expression.

ANSWER KEY

1. c	11. d	21. a	Q1. T	Q11. e	Q21. d
2. d	12. b	22. b	Q2. F	Q12 c	Q22. a
3. a	13. c	23. a	Q3. T	Q13. d	Q23. a
4. c	14. c		Q4. T	Q14. a	Q24. c
5. c	15. c		Q5. T	Q15. b	Q25. d
6. a	16. b		Q6. T	Q16. b	
7. b	17. c		Q7. F	Q17. d	
8. b	18. d		Q8. F	Q18. b	
9. d	19. c		Q9. T	Q19. d	
10. a	20. a		Q10. F	Q20. c	

CHAPTER 4

ADLERIAN THERAPY

ADLERIAN THERAPY SELF-INVENTORY

Directions: By comparing your beliefs about personality and therapy to Adler's, you should have a clearer idea of how much you will need to suspend your beliefs or change attitudes to understand Adler's theory of personality and approach to therapy. You may find it helpful to complete this section before and after you read the chapter. In this way, you can see if your views have changed. There are no correct answers, only an opportunity to express your views.

Put an "X" on the line so that it indicates how much you agree or disagree with the statement: A=Agree, D=Disagree.

D_____A 1. Developing an interest in the social welfare of others should be one of several goals of therapy.

_____ 2. Social relationships are more powerful in determining one's personality than sexual factors.

_____ 3. People can be understood by examining what they want to be.

_____ 4. Individuals have a need to overcome inferiority feelings and to strive for success.

_____ 5. Therapists should be able to understand patterns in the way clients lead their lives.

_____ 6. Therapy should focus on thinking patterns that lead to behaviors and feelings. The therapist should not focus on feelings alone.

_____ 7. It is important to understand clients' views of the world.

_____ 8. Although people are influenced by their early childhood experiences, they still may be able to improve and shape their own lives.

_____ 9. To understand clients' problems, it is helpful to ask them about their earliest memories.

_____ 10. Understanding a person's lifestyle is important in understanding his or her problems.

_____ 11. Therapeutic techniques to change beliefs and behaviors are more important than those which bring about insight.

_____ 12. Clients can be seen as discouraged and in need of re-education rather than being unaware of unconscious processes.

_____ 13. Knowing about clients' position in their family helps to understand their problems.

_____ 14. Clients may seek help because they make mistaken assumptions about life.

_____ 15. To bring about therapeutic change, therapy should be directed at the client's thoughts, goals, and beliefs.

_____ 16. Gathering information about the relationships among family members and then summarizing and interpreting this material will help meet therapeutic goals.

_____ 17. Only those past events that are consistent with one's own view of oneself are going to be remembered.

_____ 18. Working with people's conscious memories is more important than trying to bring unconscious memories into current awareness.

_____ 19. Insight by itself is not enough. Clients need help in changing their beliefs.

_____ 20. Therapists and clients cooperate together to help clients change their mistaken beliefs.

HISTORY OF ADLERIAN THEORY

Which influences do you think were most important in the development of Adler's theory?

PERSONAL LIFE

Born February 7, 1870
Hungarian Jewish parents
Near Vienna
Severe illnesses
Traumatic events
Encouragement by father helped his school work
1897 - married
Wife was dedicated to socialism
1902 - joined Freud's Vienna Psychoanalytic Society
1911 - left the Society
Was ophthalmologist and later a practicing physician
in military hospital

PROFESSIONAL INFLUENCES

Kant's approach to helping individuals learn about
themselves and others
Nietzsche's will to power influenced Adler's concept of
superiority
Vaihinger's "as if" - treating values as if they were true
"Fictional finalism" ideas that are not real but help to
deal with reality
Freud's views of the importance of early childhood,
unconscious factors, and dreams

ADLERIAN THEORY OF PERSONALITY

Adler stressed a positive view of human nature. He believed that individuals can control their fate. They can do this in part by trying to help others (social interest). How they do this can be understood through analyzing their lifestyle. Early interactions with family members, peers, and teachers help to determine the role of inferiority and superiority in their lives.

style of life or *lifestyle* A way of seeking to fulfill particular goals that individuals set in their lives. Individuals use their own patterns of beliefs, cognitive styles, and behaviors as a way of expressing their style of life. Often style of life or lifestyle is a means for overcoming feelings of inferiority.

social interest The caring and concern for the welfare of others that can serve to guide people's behavior throughout their lives. It is a sense of being a part of society and taking responsibility to improve it.

superiority The drive to become superior allows individuals to become skilled, competent, and creative.

superiority complex A means of masking feelings of inferiority by displaying boastful, self-centered, or arrogant behavior - inflating one's importance at the expense of others.

inferiority Feelings of inadequacy and incompetence that develop during infancy and serve as the basis to strive for superiority in order to overcome feelings of inferiority.

inferiority complex A strong and pervasive belief that one is not as good as other people. It is usually an exaggerated sense of feelings of inadequacy and insecurity that may result in being defensive or anxious.

birth order The idea that place in the family constellation (such as being the youngest child) can have an impact on one's later personality and functioning.

family constellation The number and birth order, as well as the personality characteristics of members of a family. Important in determining lifestyle.

CASE EXAMPLE

At age 20, Amy is the youngest of four children. Her sister Anne is 22, and her other sister Linda is 24. Bart is 26. Although Bart has been friendly with Amy, they have not been close as Bart spent most of his time as a child with other neighborhood boys and male cousins. Linda and Anne did not get along with each other. Often they would fight for their mother's affection by telling lies about each other or show how they could help their mother. Sometimes, they would try to enlist Amy to be on their side by being nice to her and flattering her. However, when she would borrow their clothes without asking, Anne would yell at and occasionally hit her. Linda would tolerate this behavior. Amy would then cry to her mother about Anne; then her mother would discipline Anne.

Her mother stayed at home with the children until Amy was 13. Then she returned to work as a secretary at a local business. When at home, her mother tried hard to spend time with each of her children. When Anne and Linda were teenagers, she worried about their competitiveness. They were both good students and athletes. Sometimes she would take Amy to their sporting events. She noticed that Amy tried to do as well at sports as her sisters and often she struggled with math at school. Also, Amy lost interest in sports around the time she entered ninth grade. Sometimes Amy's mother would worry about Amy's moping and sullenness.

Amy's father owned a hardware store. Because it was busiest on Saturday, Amy rarely saw him then. During the week when the store closed at 9 p.m., her father didn't get home until 9:30. Often her father would joke with her and treat her differently than the others. He was pleased that she didn't seem to be in trouble. When she was a child, he would tell her stories and play games with her and her stuffed animals. She was happiest when her father, and also her mother, would give her their time or gifts, even if they were small. When she entered high school, her father would talk to her about school work and tell her amusing incidents that happened at work. Although Amy enjoyed his attention and interest, it never seemed enough. She worried about whether her school work would please him. Sometimes she would work at the hardware store because she knew he appreciated that even though she didn't particularly enjoy it. She kept busy both in and out of school, in part to earn money, but also to prove that she could be successful.

2.   The most overriding and important concept in understanding Amy, according to Adlerian theory, is:

    a. birth order.
    b. inferiority.
    c. life style.
    d. social interest.
    e. superiority.

2.   According to Adler, Amy would probably be classified as the

    a. avoiding type.
    b. getting type.
    c. ruling type.
    d. socially useful type.

3.   Adler might question Amy's lack of social interest. This is most likely due to

    a. authoritative parents.
    b. poor relationship between parents.
    c. pampering by parents and siblings.
    d. socially isolating Amy.

4.   According to Adler, Amy seems to be developing many feelings of

    a. inferiority.
    b. industriousness.
    c. introvertedness.
    d. separation anxiety.
    e. superiority.

5.   Adlerian therapists' interest in Amy's relationships with Bart would refer to which of these concepts?

    a. birth order
    b. inferiority
    c. social interest
    d. separation anxiety
    e. superiority

6.   According to Adler, the relationship between Amy and her family can be described by the term

    a. cathartic.
    b. family constellation.
    c. holding environment.
    d. social interest.
    e. style of life.

7.   Examining Amy's relationship with her father, one could conclude that Amy has not sufficiently developed her

    a. inferiority complex.
    b. super ego.
    c. social interest.
    d. superiority complex.

8. According to Adlerians, which of these is not likely to be considered in understanding Amy's life style?

   a. her relationship with her father
   b. her repression of memories of not being as successful as her sisters
   c. her lack of social interest in others
   d. her family constellation

ADLERIAN THERAPY AND COUNSELING

GOALS OF ADLERIAN THERAPY

Amy is depressed and does not feel that her life is going well. She sees other women as being more attractive, more interesting, and brighter. She does not have a boyfriend and is upset that her friends spend too much time with their boyfriends. She feels that her professors do not make her courses interesting enough and that they make the courses too difficult.

9. The *major* focus of counseling or therapy for an Adlerian would be Amy's

   a. feelings of inferiority.
   b. feelings of superiority.
   c. lifestyle.
   d. social interest.

10. Amy seems to expect others to do things for her, but she does not do much for others. Thus, one goal of therapy may be to

   a. explore her feelings of superiority.
   b. explore her feelings of inferiority.
   c. examine her family constellation.
   d. work on her lack of social interest.

11. Which of these is LEAST likely to be a goal of Adlerian therapy or counseling for Amy?

   a. bring unconscious material into conscious awareness
   b. help her resolve problems with her sisters
   c. consider ways to be involved in community service
   d. deal with day to day problems

12. In Adlerian therapy and counseling, most practitioners consider themselves to do

   a. only counseling.
   b. only psychotherapy.
   c. both counseling and psychotherapy.
   d. Adlerian psychoanalysis.

ASSESSMENT IN ADLERIAN THERAPY

Adlerians usually use a lifestyle analysis to assess their clients. Projective techniques, questionnaires, and interviews are a part of this process. Material includes information about the family, early recollection, and dreams. Adlerians determine individuals' strengths and basic mistakes from this material. The following are key concepts to know about assessment:

early recollections Memories of actual incidents that patients recall from their childhood. Adlerians use this information to make inferences about current behavior of children or adults.

basic mistakes Self-defeating aspects of individuals' lifestyle that may affect their later behavior are called basic mistakes. Such mistakes often include avoidance of others, seeking power, a desperate need for security, or faulty values.

assets Assessing the strengths of individuals' lifestyle is an important part of lifestyle assessment, as is assessment of early recollections and basic mistakes.

EXAMPLE OF A LIFESTYLE ANALYSIS

Several lifestyle questionnaires have been developed by Adlerians. A modified version of a lifestyle analysis is presented here. Much of it is adapted from Mosak and Shulman's *Life Style Inventory* (1988). Such a questionnaire could be completed by the client, for the client by the therapist, or both working together.

ADLERIAN LIFESTYLE ANALYSIS OF AMY
(Amy's responses are noted in italics.)

FAMILY CONSTELLATION: BIRTH ORDER AND SIBLING DESCRIPTION

List your brothers and sisters from oldest to youngest and describe them briefly.

Bart +6	Linda +4	Ann +2	Amy
handsome	*aggressive*	*attractive*	*slow*
very social	*athletic*	*sneaky*	*insecure*
rugged	*attractive*	*small*	*loner*
likes outdoors	*independent*	*good in science*	*overprotected*
mature	*well-liked*	*protective sometimes*	*sensitive*
protective	*respected*	*picked on me sometimes*	*exaggerates*
likeable	*looked down on me*	*in trouble with Mom*	*self-critical*

9. Which of your siblings is the most different from you and how? *They all are. Bart maybe, because he's the oldest and a guy. They all seemed to accomplish so much more than me. Linda did the best in school and sports. Bart was ok at school. I'm struggling.*

10. Which of your siblings is most like you? *None really. Maybe Anne as she would get in trouble with Mom for lying. I don't do that, but Anne seemed less perfect than Bart and Linda.*

11. Which played together? *Anne and Linda sometimes. I would get included for some activities.*

12. Which fought each other? *Anne and Linda definitely.*

13. Who took care of whom? *Mainly, Linda took care of me. Once in a while Bart did.*

14. Any unusual achievements? *Bart was an Eagle Scout. Linda was captain of field hockey and softball in high school.*

15. Any accidents or sickness? *Bart had spinal meningitis when he was 12 and almost died. I was in an automobile accident when I was 9 and sprained my neck. Lots of bruises too.*

16. What kind of child were you? *I was lonely sometimes, but I would get my sisters to do things for me. I always seemed to be tagging behind my sisters.*

17. What was school like for you? *It was hard; I didn't feel like I did as well as my sisters. I often went to them for help.*

18. What scared you when you were a child? *I didn't like being alone. I was scared of monsters in my closet. Sometimes I was worried about something bad happening to my mother.*

19. What were your childhood ambitions? *I wanted to be an actress or a singer and be very famous.*

20. What was your role in your peer group? *I had a few friends that I confided in, but we were never a part of the "in" group.*

21. Any significant events in your physical and sexual development? *I wanted to be beautiful like Linda. I was afraid I'd never develop breasts and that I would be flat chested. When I did mature, boys teased me and I didn't like it.*

22. How would you summarize your social development? *I felt slow, shy often. Others seemed to know the right thing to say and I didn't.*

23. What were the most important values in your family? *To be successful, academically and athletically, to make hard work pay off.*

24. What stands out the most for you about family life? *I never seemed to be able to do as well as my brother and sisters even though they would help me out.*

FAMILY CONSTELLATION: PARENTAL FIGURES AND RELATIONSHIPS

	Father	Mother
1. Current age	*55*	*51*
2. Occupation	*Hardware store owner*	*Secretary*
3. Kind of person	*Hardworking, kind, busy*	*Harried, loving*
4. Ambitions for the children	*Go to college, get a prestigious job*	*Stay out of trouble, do well in school*
5. Your childhood view	*I idolized him before I was 9, very fond of him*	*Felt she worried most about my sisters fighting*
6. Relationship to children	*Closest to Bart, then maybe me next*	*Appreciated Linda's accomplishments, seemed to favor her.*
7. Sibling most like	*Bart was very much like my father: looks, behavior*	*Anne was like my mother, often frustrating*

8. Describe your parents' relationship to each other? *Got along well. Not too affectionate. Dad wasn't in the house a lot.*

9. How did your brother and sisters view your parents? *Anne fought, especially with Mom. Bart got along well with both. Sometimes Linda barely noticed them.*

10. What was your parents' relationship to the children? *Dad didn't get too involved in discipline. Very warm. We could drive Mom nuts.*

11. Besides your parents, who was another parental figure in your life? *My grandmother. She often came to visit in the afternoons, and Mom would go out shopping. She was great. She was very loving and had a lot of patience with me.*

EARLY RECOLLECTIONS AND DREAMS

1. What is your earliest single specific memory? *I remember when I was about 4 playing in the snow and then coming into a warm kitchen to lick the pan when my Mom made brownies. My Mom laughed and cleaned me up when I had chocolate all over my face.*

2. What are some other early recollections?
   a. *I was about 5 and I was riding my tricycle. An older boy, maybe 7 or 8, started teasing me and grabbed the handlebars. Bart saw this and made him go home.*
   b. *I had a room next to Anne's. When I was about 6 she took cookies into her room at night. I told on her, and she punched me in the chest.*

3. What feelings are associated with these early memories? *I feel protected by Mom and Bart, but I don't feel confident. I felt hurt by Anne; it seemed she didn't like me.*

4. Any recurring dreams? *I am nominated for an award at the Academy Awards - best supporting actress. My name is mentioned as a nominee, and then the entire audience starts to hoot and jeer. It feels awful.*

LIFESTYLE SUMMARY

1. Summary of Amy's family constellation: Amy is the youngest of four children. She is somewhat like Adler's description of the youngest child. She was taken care of by Linda and Bart but picked on somewhat by Anne. She felt inferior in terms of accomplishments to Bart, Anne, and especially Linda. Amy's family values success, academic and athletic, and now job success. Amy does not feel that she is meeting these values. Amy has tried to show her parents that she can achieve but has not felt that she has done so. She feels somewhat isolated from her family in terms of achievement but has felt loving attention from her father. Amy feels love from her mother but resents that it is shared with her siblings. To get attention, Amy might get hurt or wounded.

2. Summary of Amy's early recollections: Amy enjoys the warmth and protectiveness of family members. She says: "I like the feeling of being cared for, but sometimes I don't think people will care for me or love me because I'm not good at much."

3. Summary of Amy's basic mistake: Amy has some beliefs about herself that cause problems for her in her daily life.

   a. When I set out to do things, I never really do them well enough.

   b. You have to be very bright and talented (like Linda) to be a successful person.

   c. People will see through to my failings and never really care about me.

   d. If I were a stronger person, nothing would bother me.

   Summary of Amy's assets: Some of her assets are not obvious from the lifestyle analysis as Amy tends to be self-deprecating.

   1. Amy is a better than average student. A's and B's in high school.

2. Amy is willing to challenge her beliefs about being inferior to others.

3. She is sensitive to the needs of other people and caring in her relations. Exceptions to this occur when Amy is feeling very inferior to others or afraid she will say the wrong thing.

4. Amy works hard both at school and in her part-time jobs.

5. She takes responsibility when involved in activities like the sociology club or organizing activities for the Student Activities Association.

QUESTIONS

13. Which of Amy's beliefs would you want to help her change? (Select more than one. Answers follow).

   a. Belief that she is inferior to others.
   b. Belief that she won't be successful.
   c. Belief that she will not find someone who cares about her.
   d. Belief that she is better than others.
   e. Belief that if you try hard enough you can do anything you want.

   (*Answer:* a, b, and c because they are consistent with Amy's lifestyle analysis and her feelings of inferiority or lack of self worth. "d" suggests a feeling of superiority that is not evident in the analysis. "e" suggests more confidence than Amy has.)

14. Which of the following are not important in Amy's lifestyle analysis? (Answer follows)

   a. family constellation
   b. early recollections
   c. basic mistakes
   d. assets
   e. all are important

   (e. All are essential to an Adlerian lifestyle analysis. However, information about family constellation and early recollections form the raw data from which inferences about basic mistakes and assets are made.)

TECHNIQUES FOR CHANGE

A lifestyle analysis helps the Adlerian therapist to gain insights into client problems by determining the clients' basic mistakes and assets. These insights are based on assessing family constellation, dreams, and social interest. To help the client change, Adlerians may use a number of active techniques that focus to a great extent on changing beliefs and reorienting the client's view of situations and relationships. These techniques are defined here.

interpretation Adlerians express insights to their patients that relate to patients' goals. Interpretations often focus on the family constellation and social interest.

immediacy Communicating the experience of the therapist to the patient about what is happening in the moment.

encouragement An important therapeutic technique that is used to build a relationship and to foster client change. Supporting clients in changing beliefs and behaviors is a part of encouragement.

acting as if In this technique, patients are asked to "act as if" a behavior will be effective. Patients are encouraged to try a new role, the way they might try on new clothing.

catching oneself In this technique, patients learn to notice that they are performing behaviors which they wish to change. When they catch themselves, they may have an "Aha" response.

Aha response Developing a sudden insight into a solution to a problem, as one becomes aware of one's beliefs and behaviors.

spitting in the client's soup Making comments to the client to make behaviors less attractive or desirable.

avoiding the tar baby By not falling into a trap that the patient sets by using faulty assumptions, the therapist encourages new behavior and "avoids the tar baby."

The Question Asking "what would be different if you were well?" was a means Adler used to determine if a person's problem was physiological or psychological.

paradoxical intention A therapeutic strategy in which clients are instructed to engage and exaggerate behaviors that they seek to change. By prescribing the symptom, therapists make patients more aware of their situation and help them achieve distance from the symptoms. For example, a patient who is afraid of mice may be asked to exaggerate his fear of mice, or a patient who hoards paper may be asked to exaggerate that behavior so that living becomes difficult. In this way individuals can become more aware of and more distant from their symptoms.

homework Specific behaviors or activities that clients are asked to do after a therapy session.

life tasks There are five basic obligations and opportunities: occupation, society, love, self development, and spirituality development. These are used to help determine therapeutic goals.

push-button technique Designed to show patients how they can create whatever feelings they want by thinking about them, the push-button technique asks patients to remember a pleasant incident that they have experienced, become aware of feelings connected to it, and then switch to an unpleasant image and those feelings. Thus patients learn that they have the power to change their own feelings.

QUESTIONS

In the following examples, you are an Adlerian therapist and are using different techniques to help Amy change her beliefs and (sometimes) her behaviors. Identify the techniques.

15. Amy has often gotten her father and also friends to feel sorry for her. Now she is telling you how terrible her week was. Instead of talking to her about the week being really awful, you identify strengths in her behavior. You are

    a. avoiding the tar baby.
    b. spitting in the client's soup.
    c. using paradoxical intentions.
    d. using the push button technique.

16. Amy has met a man that she likes but she is afraid to talk to him because she is afraid he won't be interested in her. You tell her to pretend that she knows he likes her. You are using

    a. the push-button technique.
    b. the acting as if technique.
    c. paradoxical intention.
    d. the "question".

17. Amy says that she has been fighting with her sister Anne a lot. Now when she sees Anne she starts to feel angry even before she talks to her. You tell her to imagine a pleasant time that she has spent with Anne and feel the accompanying feelings. Then she is to imagine an unpleasant scene with Anne and the feelings that go with it. You show Amy how she can create different feelings by changing what she is thinking about. You are using this technique:

    a. catching oneself
    b. avoiding the tar baby
    c. "the question"
    d. the push-button technique

18. Amy has been complaining of stomach aches. You ask her, "What would be different if you were well?" She answers, "I wouldn't be so shy anymore. I would talk to people more easily." You are using

    a. catching oneself.
    b. "the question".
    c. paradoxical intention.
    d. avoiding the tar baby.

19. In the previous example, Amy's problem is most likely

    a. physiological.
    b. psychological.
    c. sociological.

20. Amy comes to a therapy session excited that she has noticed several times that she has felt sorry for herself when she started to complain about all of the homework she had. She was able to see what she was doing and go right to her homework. Which technique did Amy use?

    a. acting as if
    b. avoiding the tar baby
    c. catching oneself
    d. "the question"

21. Being an Adlerian, you are interested in how Amy deals with five important life tasks. Which is NOT an important life task?

    a. love
    b. dreams
    c. work
    d. spiritual development

SPECIAL TOPICS

*OE1. How do Adlerians make therapy briefer? (145)

_____

_____

*OE2. What are current trends in Adlerian therapy? (146)

_____

_____

*OE3.   How are gender issues in Adlerian therapy related to Adler's concept of *masculine protest*? (150)

_____

_____

OE4.   How can multicultural issues affect individuals' family constellation, social interest, and early recollections? (150)

_____

_____

_____

_____

OE5.   What is the Adlerian approach to group therapy? (151)

_____

_____

_____

STRENGTHS AND LIMITATIONS

What do you see as the strengths and limitations of Adlerian therapy?

Strengths	Limitations
_____	_____
_____	_____
_____	_____
_____	_____
_____	_____
_____	_____
_____	_____

ADLERIAN THERAPY: A QUIZ

True/false items: Decide if the following statements are more "true" or more "false" as they apply to Adlerian therapy.

T F Q1.   The Adlerian approach is primarily behavioral.

T F Q2.   Adler was a devoted student of Freud's as reflected by the similarity of his theory to Freud's drive theory.

T F Q3.   Striving for superiority is appropriate for all people.

T F Q4.   Early recollections are helpful to Adlerians in determining life style.

T F Q5.   Confronting and changing faulty beliefs are important aspects of Adler's therapy.

T F Q6.   Adlerians should have a neutral relationship with their clients and not encourage them to change their beliefs.

T F Q7.   Lifestyle is formed in adulthood.

T F Q8.   The "as if" technique can help a client try out a behavior that she may be afraid of.

T F Q9.   Id forces determine an individual's lifestyle.

T F Q10. Assessment is not important in Adlerian therapy.

Multiple choice items. Select the *best answer* from the alternatives using an Adlerian perspective.

_____ Q11. The most comprehensive concept in Adlerian therapy is

        a. birth order.
        b. inferiority.
        c. superiority.
        d. style of life.

_____ Q12. If a person has strong and pervasive feelings of inadequacy which effect his life, he may

        a. have feelings of inferiority.
        b. have an inferiority complex.
        c. have a superiority complex.
        d. lack social interest.

_____ Q13. Which is most important for Adlerians?

        a. changing beliefs
        b. changing behaviors
        c. making unconscious processes concerns
        d. interpreting early childhood family interactions

_____ Q14. Which of these individuals had the least influence on Adler?

        a. Freud
        b. Jung
        c. Kant
        d. Nietzsche

_____ Q15. Which of the following is not a part of lifestyle assessment?

    a. acting as if
    b. dreams
    c. early recollections
    d. mistaken beliefs
    e. family constellation

_____ Q16. Charles has few friends, and he does little but play computer games. An Adlerian goal for Charles would be to increase his

    a. feelings of superiority.
    b. early recollections.
    c. dream activity.
    d. social interest.
    e. aha responses.

_____ Q17. "All men are created equal" is an example of

    a. lifestyle.
    b. fictionalism.
    c. striving for superiority.
    d. an expression of social interest.

_____ Q18. Which of these is NOT an Adlerian life task?

    a. love
    b. lifestyle
    c. occupation
    d. spiritual development

_____ Q19. Which of the following ideas did Adler share with Freud?

    a. Oedipus complex
    b. emphasis on early childhood
    c. educational emphasis in treatment
    d. importance of psychosexual stages

_____ Q20. Allison is scared to talk to her boss but pretends that she can do it. This is called

    a. encouragement.
    b. acting as if.
    c. catching oneself.
    d. immediacy.

_____ Q21. Which Adlerian concept has generated the most research?

    a. lifestyle analysis
    b. the aha response
    c. social interest
    d. masculine protest
    e. birth order

_____ Q22. Which of these is least likely to occur in Adlerian group therapy?

      a. education of clients
      b. interpretation of transference
      c. improving communication style
      d. discussion of family relationships

_____ Q23. Which of these is most likely to be a goal of Adlerian therapy?

      a. modifying behavior
      b. removing symptoms
      c. changing beliefs
      d. developing a holding environment
      e. experiencing feelings as intensely as possible

_____ Q24. Which of these is a basic source of data for Adlerian therapists?

      a. encouragement
      b. lifestyle
      c. early recollections
      d. social interest
      e. aha response

_____ Q25. A lifestyle analysis uses information about

      a. early childhood
      b. relationships with peers
      c. dreams
      d. all of the above

ANSWER KEY

1. c	11. a	Q1. F	Q11. d	Q21. e
2. b	12. c	Q2. F	Q12. b	Q22. b
3. c	13. a, b, c	Q3. T	Q13. a	Q23. c
4. a	14. e	Q4. T	Q14. b	Q24. c
5. a	15. a	Q5. T	Q15. a	Q25. d
6. b	16. b	Q6. F	Q16. d	
7. c	17. d	Q7. F	Q17. b	
8. b	18. b	Q8. T	Q18. b	
9. c	19. b	Q9. F	Q19. b	
10. d	20. c	Q10. F	Q20. b	
	21. b			

OE1*   They may limit time for the lifestyle analysis. They may focus work on one life task.

OE2*   Trends include focusing on social change and issues such as AIDS and family violence; developing educational thrust.

OE3*   Adler believed that some men would focus on masculinity to prove they were superior to women. He was concerned about the social roles that limited women's striving for equality.

CHAPTER 5

EXISTENTIAL THERAPY

EXISTENTIAL THERAPY SELF-INVENTORY

Directions: By comparing your beliefs about personality and therapy to those of existential therapists, you should have a clearer idea of how much you will need to suspend your beliefs or change your attitudes to understand existential therapy. You may find it helpful to complete this section before and after you read the chapter. In this way you can see if your views have changed. There are no correct answers, only an opportunity to express your views.

Put an "X" on the line so that it indicates how much you disagree with the statement: A = Agree, D = Disagree.

D_____A 1. Understanding the qualities of human existence is important in therapy.

_____ 2. Expanding self-awareness and increasing one's potential for making choices in life is an important goal of therapy.

_____ 3. Psychotherapy should concentrate on human relationships rather than on techniques.

_____ 4. It is not techniques themselves that are important in therapeutic change but the resolution of important life issues.

_____ 5. To understand individuals, one must understand how they make important life choices.

_____ 6. The special humanness of the therapeutic relationship is one of the most important determinants in assessing the helpfulness of therapy.

_____ 7. Therapists must truly know themselves, their strengths, and weaknesses to be effective.

_____ 8. Self awareness is one of the most important aspects of humanness. It is this which makes effective therapy possible.

_____ 9. Being responsible for one's choices and actions is an important goal of therapy. To seek freedom and to act responsibly within it is also an important goal of therapy.

_____ 10. A special aspect of being human is the freedom to choose and to be responsible for one's life.

_____ 11. Freedom and responsibility are important issues in therapy. Individuals are thrown into an environment which can be hostile. It is their responsibility to make the best of it.

_____ 12. Relationships with others are one of the most essential qualities of being human.

<u>D</u>   <u>A</u> 13. Individuals, unlike animals, seek meaning and purpose in their life.

_____ 14. To have poor or ineffective relationships in one's life is to experience alienation and isolation.

_____ 15. Anxiety can be normal as well as neurotic.

_____ 16. Being aware of the reality of death helps individuals attribute significance to their own lives and those of others.

_____ 17. An important therapy goal is to strive to be authentic, to be self aware.

_____ 18. An important therapy goal is to try to be all that one is capable of becoming.

HISTORY OF EXISTENTIAL THERAPY

Nineteenth century philosophy forms the basis for existential therapy. A number of philosophers contributed many ideas to the development of existential philosophy. Writers and theologians have also made significant contributions. To help you better understand the basic contributions of these individuals, they are listed along with their most significant contributions.

PHILOSOPHERS

Søren Kierkegaard
  conflicts and problems of
  human existence

Freidrich Nietzsche
  search for a "will to power"

Edmund Husserl
  phenomenology, the study of
  objects as experienced in the
  consciousness of individuals

Martin Heidegger
  emphasized the awareness of
  existence and time

Karl Jaspers
  humans must transcend
  suffering, struggle, and guilt
  through decisions

THEOLOGIANS

Martin Buber
  Jewish; I-thou relationships

Gabriel Marceau
  Catholic; relationships that
  focus on love, hope, and
  faithfulness

Paul Tillich
  Protestant; emphasized
  courage and people's
  capabilities to make life
  meaningful.

WRITERS

Jean-Paul Sartre
  French philosopher, novelist,
  and playwright; humanity is
  freedom, people should find a
  reason to exist

Fyodor Dostoevsky
  Russian novelist; awareness of
  one's actions

Albert Camus
  French novelist and
  philosopher; the absurdity of
  understanding a meaningless
  world

Franz Kafka
  German novelist and essayist;
  despairing and frustrating
  situations that question the
  meaningfulness of existence

1. Which group had the most hopeful view of humanity?

    a. philosophers
    b. theologians
    c. writers
    d. all were similar

2. Which group had the least hopeful view of humanity?

    a. philosophers
    b. theologians
    c. writers
    d. all were similar

ORIGINATORS AND MORE RECENT CONTRIBUTORS TO EXISTENTIAL THERAPY

Unlike many other theories of psychotherapy, there is no single individual who developed existential therapy. The original contributors were the Swiss psychiatrists Ludwig Binswanger and Medard Boss. Other important contributors include Viktor Frankl, Rollo May, Irvin Yalom, James Bugental, R. D. Laing, and Emmy van Deurzen.

ORIGINATORS

Ludwig Binswanger
  Swiss psychiatrist;
  helped patients understand the meaning of their behavior; become authentic

Medard Boss
  Swiss psychiatrist;
  concerned with existential themes and being-in-the-world

Viktor Frankl
  Psychiatrist born in Vienna;
  developed logotherapy; concerned with finding meaning in life

MORE RECENT CONTRIBUTORS

Rollo May
  American psychiatrist;
  author of many books on existential therapy; integrated psychoanalysis and existential therapy

Irvin Yalom
  American psychiatrist;
  influential textbook and casebook on existential therapy; developed existential themes

James Bugental
  American psychiatrist;
  humanistic focus on awareness and self-actualization

R. D. Laing
  English psychiatrist;
  established a therapeutic community for severely disturbed patients' understanding a meaningless world

Emmy van Deurzen
  English psychologist;
  actively involved in writing on existential therapy; developed British School of Existential Psychotherapy

3.   Match the existential therapist with an important contribution.

A. James Bugental
B. Viktor Frankl
C. Medard Boss
D. Rollo May
E. Ludwig Binswanger
F. Emmy van Deurzen
G. R. D. Laing
H. Irvin Yalom

s. developed therapeutic community in England
t. Swiss; helped patients understand meaning of theirs lives
u. Swiss; focused patients on being-in-the-world
v. wrote influential textbook on existential therapy
w. started British School of Existential therapy
x. American; wrote many books on existential themes
y. developed logotherapy
z. humanistic focus on awareness

Answers: A, z, B, y, C, u, D, x, E, t, F, w, G, s, H, v.

EXISTENTIAL PERSONALITY THEORY

Existence and themes related to existence form the core of existential personality theory. Perhaps the most central concept is *Dasein* or *being-in-the-world*. Existential therapists have identified four ways of being in the world: *Ümwelt*, *Mitwelt, Uberwelt,* and *Eigenwelt*. Existing in the world can bring about both normal and neurotic anxiety. Anxiety occurs as individuals deal with important life themes such as living and dying; freedom, responsibility, and choice; isolation and loving; and meaning and meaninglessness. In dealing with these themes, individuals strive for authenticity and self-transcendence.

existentialism A philosophical view that emphasizes the importance of existence, including one's responsibility for one's own psychological existence. Related themes include living and dying, freedom, responsibility to self and others, meaningfulness in life, and authenticity.

being-in-the-world Derived from the German word *Dasein* that refers to examining oneself, others, and one's relationship with the world, thus attaining higher levels of consciousness.

Umwelt Relating to the environment, the objects and living beings within it; attending to the biological and physical aspects of the world.

Mitwelt A way in which individuals relate to the world by interacting socially with others. The focus is on human relationships rather than relationships that are biological or physical Umwelt.

Überwelt Religious or spiritual beliefs about the ideal world, the way an individual wants the world to be.

Eigenwelt A way of relating to one's "own world." It refers to being aware of oneself and how we relate to ourselves.

kairos A Greek word that refers to the critical point at which a disease is expected to get better or worse. In psychotherapy, it refers to the appropriate timing of a therapeutic intervention.

thrown condition Unforseen forces or events in the world that one does not cause.

existential anxiety Anxiety arising from the nature of being human and dealing with unforeseen forces (the thrown condition). Existential anxiety is a significant subset of normal anxiety.

neurotic anxiety Anxiety that is out of proportion to a particular event. It is often an indication that an individual is not living authentically and may fail to make choices and assume responsibility.

boundary situation An urgent experience that compels an individual to deal with an existential situation.

self-transcendence Going beyond one's immediate situation to understand one's being and to take responsibility for that being. Going beyond one's own needs to take responsibility for others or to see the world in different ways.

authenticity Being genuine and real, as well as aware of one's being. Authentic individuals deal with moral choices, the meaning of life, and being human.

EXISTENTIAL CASE STUDY

David is a 28-year old truck driver who makes local deliveries in Las Vegas, the city where he has been living for the last five years. After he graduated high school in Seattle, Washington, he joined the Marines. He received a general discharge from the Marines rather than an honorable discharge due to fights that he had been in with some of his fellow Marines. David finds his truck driving responsibilities routine and boring.

When work is done, David looks forward to spending evenings in the casinos. Gambling and the entertainment that is offered in the casinos takes up his evening and much of his weekend leisure time. In the last year, David has been drinking more heavily. He has been less satisfied with his life and things in general. This is a vague sense which he is aware of only a few times during the week when he is sober and not working, gambling, or being entertained.

Growing up in Seattle, David had an undistinguished high school career. He graduated with C's, while his older brother, an excellent student, became a mechanical engineer. Twice during high school, David was arrested for vandalism and brought before juvenile court. His father, a long-distance truck driver became very angry and distant from David, giving up on him. His mother, who worked in a plastics manufacturing factory, seemed to David to be more concerned about her sisters and their families than about her own family.

About eight months ago, David heard that his father was diagnosed with prostate cancer. He had been complaining of physical problems for months but never went to a doctor. After diagnosis of the problem, David's father learned that the cancer was inoperable. Furthermore, David's father had not responded well to either chemical or radiation therapies.

David had talked to his father a few times, but their conversations had been rather brief. David's view is "stuff happens." He has not returned to Seattle to visit his father.

David had gone out with Melinda for about two years. They broke up about a year ago, as it became evident to Melinda that their relationship would not lead to marriage. Although he has tried to contact her since, she has not been interested in resuming the relationship and has become engaged to someone else.

QUESTIONS ABOUT DAVID FROM AN EXISTENTIAL PERSONALITY THEORY VIEWPOINT

4. Regarding *being-in-the-world*, David would be seen by existential therapists as

   a. barely aware of his existence.
   b. consumed by questions about his existence.
   c. too individuated from his parents.
   d. lacking in social interest.

5. David seems to be most preoccupied with the

   a. Umwelt.
   b. Mitwelt.
   c. Überwelt.
   d. Eigenwelt.
   e. equally present in all four.

6. Existential therapists are particularly concerned with how their patients deal with the

    a. Umwelt.
    b. Mitwelt.
    c. Überwelt.
    d. Eigenwelt.

7. David's relationship with his parents and Melinda occur in the

    a. Umwelt.
    b. Mitwelt.
    c. Überwelt.
    d. Eigenwelt.

8. The fact that David's father unexpectedly developed cancer could be called

    a. Mitwelt.
    b. Überwelt.
    c. kairos.
    d. a thrown condition.

9. David is barely aware of discomforts in his life. As he becomes more aware, then _____ is likely to increase.

    a. kairos
    b. existential anxiety
    c. neurotic anxiety
    d. all of the above

10. For David to take responsibility for his life, to become more involved in family and other relationships, would be to start on the path to

    a. the Ümwelt.
    b. the thrown condition.
    c. self-transcendence.
    d. neurotic anxiety.

11. Which of these existential themes present challenges for David?

    a. living and dying
    b. freedom, responsibility, and choice
    c. isolation and loving
    d. meaning and meaninglessness
    e. all of the above

12. If David were to deal with responsibilities in his life and were to become more genuine, he would become more

    a. authentic.
    b. neurotic.
    c. involved in the Ümwelt.
    d. immersed in his thrown condition.

13. Which of these would help David become more authentic?

    a.   Win $25,000 at poker-slots.
    b.   Get a 20% pay raise.
    c.   Become more self-aware and open to changing his feelings about his father.
    d.   Visit his father.

GOALS OF EXISTENTIAL THERAPY

Existential therapists believe the goals of therapy are to help clients find a purpose to their life, to make it more meaningful. By doing so they become more authentic, more aware of their own being. They become better able to deal with moral choices and decisions.

David is becoming unhappier. His involvement in gambling is not making him richer, nor is it helping him become more satisfied with his life. David is more aware of being lonely. His friendships at work and in the casinos seem superficial and unfulfilling. His phone calls to his mother leave him dissatisfied, whereas in the past he just hung up and went about his business.

14. The goals of David's therapy are likely to focus most on the

    a.   Umwelt.
    b.   Mitwelt.
    c.   Überwelt.
    d.   Eigenwelt.

15. A goal of existential therapy for David is to help him

    a.   become more aware of his need to gamble.
    b.   stop his gambling immediately.
    c.   gradually cut back on his gambling.
    d.   do more for his parents.

16. An existential therapist is most likely to be concerned with how detached David is from

    a.   himself.
    b.   God.
    c.   his parents.
    d.   his work responsibilities.

ASSESSMENT IN EXISTENTIAL THERAPY

Typically assessment in existential therapy takes place throughout the course of therapy. Therapists assess progress on current existential themes or follow the emergence of new themes. For existential therapy to be effective, clients must be willing to work in developing authenticity and dealing with existential themes. Material that is discussed can include dreams and responses or scores on projective or objective tests.

17. If David wants help only on stopping his gambling behavior, an existential therapist is most likely to

    a.   refer him to another type of therapist.
    b.   point out that he is being narrow-minded in his outlook.
    c.   convince him that his issues can only be approached by becoming more authentic.
    d.   none of the above.

18. In using dream material in assessment of patient problems, the important aspect is

    a. the therapist's interpretation of the dream.
    b. the client's experience of the dream.
    c. the thrown conditions in operation at the time.
    d. the therapist's sense of timing.

EXISTENTIAL APPROACH TO THERAPEUTIC CHANGE

The therapist is fully present in the relationship. Her mind does not wander, at least not for long. She brings her attention immediately back to the patient. The relationship is that of therapeutic love - a loving friendship. The therapist genuinely cares for the client and is accepting even though the client may be angry, hostile, or untruthful. The therapist is understanding of client fears that may be expressed as resistance to therapeutic change.

In the following sections, you will be David's existential therapist. Select the response that best fits that of an existential therapist. We will use examples from each of the four existential themes.

LIVING AND DYING

19. David: I'm hearing from my mother that my father's health is getting worse. It bothers me just a little. I wonder why it doesn't bother me more.

    Therapist: a. What bothers you about his illness?
                     b. Are you concerned your mother isn't taking better care of him?
                     c. You may be looking at him from a new point of view. Can you tell me about it?
                     d. You have focused only on yourself, not on him.

20. David: Knowing that he may be dying has helped me to start to look at my life differently.

    Therapist: a. How are you looking at it differently?
                     b. You might be looking not only at how you may be living differently, but also at the possibility of death.
                     c. Your father's dying might make you realize that now is the time to take responsibility for him and your mother.
                     d. How do you know he is dying? Maybe there is a chance for him to live.

21. David: Although we didn't get along, I always assumed my father would be here.

    Therapist: a. You always felt that he would be here and take care of your mother.
                     b. Looking at the possibility of your father's death seems to give you the opportunity to look at your own life differently.
                     c. Do you see this as an opportunity for the two of you to get along better?
                     d. This is an opportunity now for you to change your relationship and try to get along better with him.

FREEDOM, RESPONSIBILITY AND CHOICE

22. **David:** I could change my job. Just because I don't like it, I don't have to change. Lots of people do things they don't like. I can keep it and be bored.

    Therapist:
    a. Your job is really boring you. You don't know what to do.
    b. You may never get another good chance. You're still young, and there are a number of opportunities for you.
    c. Now is the time for you to take responsibility for yourself. Get out of the rut. Go back to school or contact an employment agency. Those actions will pay off for you.
    d. You have the freedom to change your job, but acting on that freedom can be overwhelming.

23. **David:** My job really isn't that bad.

    Therapist:
    a. You've given the job a lot of thought, and it seems right to stay with it.
    b. How do you know what else is out there? Other options might be better.
    c. At times it is really difficult to examine how you react to something, like this job.
    d. When you consider the pay, there are other jobs that are a lot worse.

24. **David:** What should I do?

    Therapist:
    a. Stay at your old job. It's secure. You don't know what's out there.
    b. Look for a new job. There is a bright future ahead of you.
    c. You really don't know what to do, do you?
    d. Making a choice is really difficult. It's hard when two difficult choices present themselves to you.

ISOLATION AND LOVING

25. **David:** I think I really cared for Melinda. When I was with her, I am not sure I wanted her. Now that we've broken up, I miss her.

    Therapist:
    a. Being alone is difficult, and now you're experiencing the loneliness in a way you have not done before.
    b. It is time for you to be decisive. Decide what is best and act on it.
    c. Do you think Melinda wants you back?
    d. When you are indecisive, there is a price to pay. That price is being lonely and being isolated.

26. **David:** It's hard for me to believe anyone cares for me.

    Therapist:
    a. It's hard for me to believe that too. Why would anyone care for you?
    b. You are really wondering why anyone would care?
    c. I know it's hard for you to believe that I care for you, that I really want to help you.
    d. I'm sure your mother and father cared for you. Even though your relationship with your father isn't good, I am sure he cared.

27. **David:** Maybe you could call Melinda. Maybe she'll listen to you if you tell her I've changed.

    Therapist:
    a. Sure. What's her phone number.
    b. You haven't changed much yet. You've got a lot of work to do in therapy.
    c. It's hard being alone, and you really want me to fix things for you.
    d. What makes you think she will listen to me making the request for you?

28. David: Every once in a while when I'm at a casino, I'll stop. I'll look around. Everyone is so busy. And why? Everything starts to look silly.

   Therapist:
   a. That's a special moment. You are aware of yourself, and you can look at yourself as well as the others.
   b. Don't lose your concentration on the cards you're playing.
   c. You've been gambling again. I thought you were going to stop.
   d. You are starting to feel as if gambling is not right for you

29. David: I like the sense I have that I can choose not to gamble and I can leave at that moment.

   Therapist:
   a. Life has meaning at that point. You have the choice to leave or to stay.
   b. There are many questions that present themselves to you.
   c. You can act as if you are not going to gamble.
   d. Why don't you just say "no" to gambling and leave?

30. David: When I decided to leave the casino, I was thinking about my father all the way home in the car.

   Therapist:
   a. You could get into an accident if you aren't careful.
   b. Being aware of yourself at that moment helped you think of your father's life and possible death. It had meaning.
   c. You were really thinking a lot about your father.
   d. Did you decide to call your father?

LOGOTHERAPY: FRANKL

   Viktor Frankl was particularly concerned about the need for individuals to find meaning in their lives. Unlike most existential therapists, he developed a form of therapy that includes specific techniques that the therapist might use with clients.

LOGOTHERAPY CONCEPTS

logotherapy A type of existential therapy that focuses on challenging clients to search for meaning in their lives. It is associated with the techniques of attitude modulation, dereflection, and paradoxical intention.

Socratic dialogue A series of questions designed to help the client arrive at logical answers to and conclusions about a certain hypothesis; also called guided discovery.

dereflection A technique in which clients focus away from their problems instead of on them to reduce anxiety.

paradoxical intention A therapeutic strategy in which clients are instructed to engage in and exaggerate behaviors they seek to change. By prescribing the symptom, therapists make patients more aware of their situation and help them achieve distance from symptoms.

OE1. Most existential therapies do not use specific techniques. What are advantages and disadvantages of this?

_____

_____

_____

_____

OE2. What is your reaction to the specific techniques used in logotherapy?

_____

_____

_____

_____

SPECIAL TOPICS

OE3. Does the Strassers' brief therapy model help to specify existential therapy, or is it too complex? Explain. (187)

_____

_____

_____

_____

OE4. One current trend in existential therapy is Viktor Frankl's logotherapy. Why do you think it has been popular?
(189)

_____

_____

_____

_____

OE5. A second current trend in existential therapy is its similarity to postmodern thought. In what way are the two similar and dissimilar? (190)

_____

_____

_____

_____

OE6. In what ways do you think existential therapy could be integrated with other theories of therapy? (191)

_____

_____

_____

_____

OE7. Do men and women experience death, freedom, responsibility, and choice, loving, and meaningfulness differently? Explain. (192)

_____

_____

_____

_____

OE8. Are the existential themes multicultural? Are the themes universal and relevant for all cultures? Explain. (193)

_____

_____

_____

_____

STRENGTHS AND LIMITATIONS

As you review existential therapy and the concepts that it is based on, what do you view its strengths and limitations to be?

Strengths	Limitations
_____	_____
_____	_____
_____	_____
_____	_____
_____	_____
_____	_____
_____	_____
_____	_____

EXISTENTIAL THERAPY: A QUIZ

True/false items: Decide if the following statements are more "true" or more "false" as they apply to existential therapy.

T F Q1.   Much of existential therapy has its roots in 19th century Western European philosophy.

T F Q2.   As a group, existential therapists focus on techniques to bring about change.

T F Q3.   The goal to become more expert at manipulating others is consistent with existential therapy.

T F Q4.   Existential therapy is based on a thorough grounding on the research into psychotherapy effectiveness.

T F Q5.   Logotherapy is one form of existential therapy.

T F Q6.   The therapist should feel "therapeutic love" for her client.

T F Q7.   The client should feel "therapeutic love" for his therapist.

T F Q8.   Existentialists believe that part of peoples' problems comes from dealing with a world that is not of their making.

T F Q9.   Part of being human is to make choices and take responsibility for them.

T F Q10. Existential therapy is both behavioral and cognitive in its focus.

Multiple choice items: Select the best answer from the alternatives given. Answer each question from the point of view of existential therapy.

_____ Q11. Which of these philosophers could be considered the grandfather of existential therapy?

        a. Søren Kierkegaard
        b. Franz Kafka
        c. Edmund Husserl
        d. Gabriel Marcel

_____ Q12. The "I-thou" relationship was a contribution to existential therapy made by

        a. Karl Jasper.
        b. Martin Buber.
        c. Freidrich Nietzsche.
        d. Jean-Paul Sartre.

_____ Q13. Ludwig Binswanger and _____ could be considered the first existential therapists.

        a. Medard Boss
        b. Rollo May
        c. Paul Tillich
        d. R. D. Laing

_____ Q14. Logotherapy was developed by

        a. Medard Boss.
        b. Ludwig Binswanger.
        c. Rollo May.
        d. Viktor Frankl.

_____ Q15. Which of these is not an important existential theme?

        a. love
        b. death
        c. animosity
        d. meaning

_____ Q16. Existential anxiety can be viewed as a (an)

        a. expression of repressed sexuality.
        b. neurotic symptom.
        c. part of being human.
        d. result of early traumatic childhood experience.

_____ Q17. The basic goal(s) of existential therapy is (are)

        a. to make free choices.
        b. to become more authentic.
        c. to make responsible choices.
        d. to find meaning in life.
        e. all of the above.

_____ Q18. An important issue in existential therapy is

     a. finding meaning in life.
     b. resistance.
     c. countertransference.
     d. separation from parents.

_____ Q19. Which of these most clearly exemplifies existential therapy?

     a. Umwelt
     b. Mitwelt
     c. Überwelt
     d. Eigenwelt

_____ Q20. The existential condition that most concerned Viktor Frankl was

     a. anxiety.
     b. fusion.
     c. judgmentalness.
     d. meaningfulness.

_____ Q21. "Being authentic" is best defined by

     a. a central genuineness and awareness of being.
     b. general agreement about what constitutes the subjective self.
     c. general agreement about what constitutes the objective self.
     d. being able to go beyond the immediate situation.

_____ Q22. In dealing with a patient's problem in making choices, an existential therapist would

     a. point out possible solutions.
     b. show why one solution was better than others.
     c. help the client understand it is important that the client make the decision.
     d. describe decision-making techniques.

_____ Q23. To focus away from one's own problems is

     a. an example of *kairos*
     b. to use dereflection, a logotherapy technique.
     c. to be in the Überwelt.
     d. to be authentic.

_____ Q24. In existential therapy, a therapist might

     a. discuss difficult issues.
     b. conduct a lifestyle analysis
     c. make archetypal interpretations.
     d. use statements highlighting the superego.

_____ Q25. Existential therapy deals with a(an)

     a. objective approach to reality.
     b. subjective approach to reality.
     c. behavioral approach to reality.
     d. cognitive approach to reality.

ANSWER KEY

1. b	16. a	Q1. T	Q16. c
2. c	17. a	Q2. F	Q17. e
3. ___	18. b	Q3. F	Q18. a
4. a	19. c	Q4. F	Q19. d
5. a	20. b	Q5. T	Q20. d
6. d	21. b	Q6. T	Q21. a
7. b	22. d	Q7. F	Q22. c
8. d	23. c	Q8. T	Q23. b
9. b	24. d	Q9. T	Q24. a
10. c	25. a	Q10. F	Q25. b
11. e	26. c	Q11. a	
12. a	27. c	Q12. b	
13. c	28. a	Q13. a	
14. d	29. a	Q14. d	
15. a	30. b	Q15. c	

CHAPTER 6

PERSON-CENTERED THERAPY

PERSON-CENTERED SELF-INVENTORY

Directions: By comparing your beliefs about personality and therapy to the person-centered approach, you should have a clearer idea of how much you will need to suspend your beliefs or change attitudes to understand the person-centered theory of personality and approach to therapy. You may find it helpful to complete this section before and after you read the chapter. In this way, you can see if your views have changed. There are no correct answers, only an opportunity to express your views.

Put an "X" on the line so that it indicates how much you agree or disagree with the statement: A=Agree, D=Disagree.

D_____A   1. Creating a safe atmosphere for clients to express themselves is a major goal of therapy.

_____   2. The answer to problems lies within the client rather than the therapist.

_____   3. People strive to function fully in their world.

_____   4. It is the therapist rather than the therapist's techniques that are important.

_____   5. Clients develop problems in their childhood because of inconsistent or inappropriate relationships with others.

_____   6. As the relationship between the therapist and the client develops, so does progress in therapy.

_____   7. The essential qualities of effective therapy are genuineness, caring, and unconditional positive regard.

_____   8. Empathy is a healing condition.

_____   9. Tests and inventories do not help progress in therapy.

_____   10. The therapist accepts rather than judges the client's experiences.

D_____A 11. Therapeutic change depends on the client's perceptions of experience with the therapist and the therapist's basic attitudes.

_____ 12. Being genuine is essential for therapeutic change.

_____ 13. Giving advice is not consistent with the role of the therapist.

_____ 14. Although the therapist must accept the client, it is not necessary to agree with the client on all or even most issues.

_____ 15. As a result of therapy, individuals learn how to be more open and responsible.

_____ 16. Clients become more creative as a result of the relationship with the therapist.

_____ 17. The client determines the direction of therapy, not the therapist.

_____ 18. Acceptance by the therapist helps to reduce client defenses.

_____ 19. Relating to the therapist in an open manner helps the client relate better to others.

_____ 20. Diagnosis is not an important part of the therapeutic relationship.

HISTORY OF PERSON-CENTERED THERAPY

Person-centered therapy is very much embodied in the work of Carl Rogers. He is mainly responsible for the development of person-centered therapy. His focus on the importance of the client-counselor relationship has had an influence on both theorists and practitioners. The following chart describes the personal and professional development of Carl Rogers. As he changed and developed, so did person-centered therapy.

PERSONAL DEVELOPMENT AND POSITIONS   PROFESSIONAL INFLUENCES

Developmental Stage

Born in 1902 in a suburb of Chicago   Early work influenced by psychoanalysis
Fourth of six children   Rogers was influenced by Rank through his work
Religious fundamental upbringing   with Jessie Taft and Elizabeth Davis. Rank focused
Adolescent interest in agriculture   on the uniqueness of the individual, as did Alfred
Early career goal: the ministry   Adler
Graduated from the University of Wisconsin   Goldstein and Maslow wrote about self-actualization -
Married Helen Elliott   a humanist idea
Attended Union Theological Seminary   Rogers read writings of existentialists
Received Ph.D. from Columbia University Teacher's   *The Clinical Treatment of the Problem Child,* 1939
College in 1931 in clinical psychology
12 years at the Society for Prevention of Cruelty to
Children in Rochester, NY
1940 - academic career at Ohio State University

Non-directive Stage

1945 - worked at the University of Chicago   At Ohio State, started writing about the importance of
                                                         the therapeutic relationship

Client-centered Stage 1945

1957 - University of Wisconsin psychology department,
later psychiatry department

Counseling and Psychotherapy, 1942
*Client-Centered Therapy: Its Current Practice,
Implications and Theory*, 1951
Focus on empathy, genuineness, unconditional positive
regard
APA Distinguished Contribution awarded 1956
Research with hospitalized schizophrenic patients

Person-Centered Stage

1968 - formed the Center for Studies of the Person at
La Jolla, California
Traveled to South Africa, Northern Ireland, and other
countries to help others bring about political change
Died in 1987

On Becoming a Person, 1961
Writings were more philosophical, more concerned
about social issues than before
Concerned about education and global peace; led
encounter groups
Carl Rogers on Personal Power, 1977
A Way of Being, 1980

QUESTIONS

1. Roger's early exposure to theological training led him to

   a. espouse Christian values in his therapy.
   b. train pastoral counselors to be therapists.
   c. a psychology program where he did not have to profess certain beliefs.
   d. become an ordained minister.

2. Rogers was most influenced by the writings of

   a. Freud.
   b. Jung.
   c. Nietschze.
   d. Rank.

3. The development of the philosophical underpinnings of Rogers' work and its subsequent publication occurred during
   the _____ phase of his work.

   a. developmental
   b. nondirective
   c. person-centered
   d. client-centered

4. Rogers was influenced by writings on self-actualization by Kurt Goldstein and

   a. Alfred Adler.
   b. Sigmund Freud.
   c. Abraham Maslow.
   d. Otto Rank.

PERSON-CENTERED THEORY OF PERSONALITY

Carl Rogers was concerned about the way people treated each other and how they cared for or didn't care for each other. This is reflected in his writings on childhood development (which are quite limited). He believed that children would develop a good sense of their own self-worth or self-regard if others (parents, teachers, or friends) treated them as valuable and worthy.

When individuals treated others in a way that was sometimes harsh, manipulative, or self-serving, then the person was treated conditionally. Conditions of worth (conditionality) develop from conditional positive regard from others. Such conditions can make it difficult for a person to become a fully functioning person.

conditionality or *conditions of worth* The process of evaluating one's own experience based on values or beliefs that others hold.

conditional positive regard Receiving praise, attention, or approval from others as a result of behaving in accordance with the expectations of others.

fully functioning person A person who meets his or her own need for positive regard rather than relying on the expectations of others. Such individuals are open to new experiences and not defensive.

Questions about you from a person-centered perspective.

OE 1.   Describe an experience that you have had, in which after a conversation with a person you felt bad about yourself. How does that experience fit with the concept of "conditions of worth?"

_____

_____

_____

OE 2.   Think of a situation in which you only received approval from someone if you did what he or she wanted you to do. How does that experience fit with Rogers' description of conditional positive regard?

_____

_____

_____

PERSON-CENTERED THEORY OF PSYCHOTHERAPY

Rogers' theory of psychotherapy grew out of his experiences with clients. Regardless of their problems, Rogers cared for and accepted his clients. In the process of understanding clients, Rogers helped them to better understand and appreciate themselves. The focus of his work was on the process of therapy not assessment.

GOALS

As the terms "client-centered" and "person-centered" imply, the goals of therapy come from the client. The therapist often helps the client to articulate the goals. Goals typically are consistent with helping an individual become a fully functioning person.

ASSESSMENT

Inventories and tests are not a part of person-centered counseling. In some cases, tests or inventories may be used in career counseling. Assessment is a part of the therapeutic relationship with the client.

NECESSARY AND SUFFICIENT CONDITIONS FOR CHANGE

Rogers believed that therapeutic change could result if six conditions were met. These conditions form the essence of his approach to therapy.

---

1. *Psychological contact* A relationship must exist so that two people may have impact on each other.

2. *Incongruence* For change to take place, a client must be in a state of psychological vulnerability. There is a discrepancy between individuals' views of themselves and their actual experience. Included would be depression, anxiety, or a wide variety of problems. Although individuals may not be aware at first of their incongruence or vulnerability, they will be so if therapy continues.

3. *Congruence and genuineness* Therapists are aware of themselves. They are aware of their feelings, their experiences as they relate to the client, and their general reaction to the client. Therapists are open to understanding their own experiences as well as those of the client.

4. *Unconditional positive regard or acceptance* The therapist does not judge the client but accepts the client for who he or she is. Accepting the client does not mean that the counselor agrees with the client. With acceptance often comes caring and warmth.

5. *Empathy* The therapist enters the world of the client, leaving behind, as much as possible, his or her own values. Since it is not possible to be "value free," the therapist monitors his or her own values and feelings. The therapist tries to understand the experience of the client, what it is to be the client. Caring and warmth are expressed often in statements of empathy.

6. *Perception of empathy and acceptance* Not only must the therapist unconditionally accept and understand the client, the client must perceive that he or she is being understood and accepted. Therapists' voice tone and physical expression contribute to the communication of empathy and acceptance. Thus, they are part of the client's perception of empathy.

PERSON-CENTERED THERAPY: KEY CONCEPTS

The following concepts define the words that Rogers uses in his six necessary and sufficient conditions for client change.

incongruence The disharmony that takes place when there is a disagreement between individuals and their view of themselves and their actual experience.

congruence The harmony that takes place when there is no disagreement between individuals' experience and their views of themselves. For therapists, congruence refers to matching one's inner experiencing with external expressions.

genuineness Similar to congruence, genuineness in the therapist refers to being one's actual self with the client, not phony or affected.

unconditional positive regard Accepting and appreciating clients as they are, regardless of whether the therapist agrees with the person. Positive regard is not contingent on acting or thinking in a specific way. It is essentially appreciating clients for being themselves.

empathy To enter the world of another individual without being influenced by one's own views and values is to be empathic with the individual. The therapist, when being empathic, is attuned to the experience, feelings, and sensitivities of the client.

acceptance Appreciating clients for who they are without valuing or judging them.

A PERSON-CENTERED APPROACH TO RESPONDING TO CLIENTS

Rogers believed that responses to clients should be empathic and genuine. However, non-person-centered therapists who train counselors find it helpful to use exercises to help students learn empathic responding. Because they are exercises, the responses sometimes seem artificial. The exercises here will help you learn some ways of responding empathically.

The responses are sometimes called "reflections". Rogers found that this term sometimes misled counselors into thinking that repeating the essence of a client's statement was adequate. Rogers emphasized the importance of showing the client that he understood the client's experience on feelings.

Read the two examples to get an idea of the exercise. Next, write down the important words or phrases that describe the client's feelings. In the next line, write what situation or event the feeling refers to. Last, put the feeling and event together to make a reflection or empathic response.

Example: A 30-year-old man says: Since my wife left me, I feel all alone. I just go through the motions at work.

   a. What is he feeling? *Lonely. Sad. Uninvolved. Unloved.*

   _____

   b. What is the situation or event? *His wife has left him.*

   _____

   c. Give an empathic response. *You seem to be feeling lonely since your wife left. It's hard to put your*

   heart into your work.

Example: A 43-year-old woman says: My boss really lost his temper and started screaming at me for being a half-hour late for work. Who does he think he is!

   a. What is she feeling? *Angry. Upset. Resentful.*

   _____

   b. What is the situation or event? *Her boss yelled at her for being late.*

   _____

   c. Give an empathic response. *You are really angry that your boss would yell at you for coming to*

   work late.

In the following examples, answer the questions as best you can. Note from the example above that there is often more than one feeling that may be present. In an empathic response you pick the one or two that seem most significant to you. Also notice that the response reflects the client's meaning back to the client. The response does not repeat what the client said. Suggested correct responses are on the last page of this chapter.

*OE3. A girl, 13, says: My father came home from work really drunk. As soon as he came into the house yelling and screaming, he threw a book at my mother. I ran to my room and locked the door.

a. What is she feeling? _____

_____

b. What is the situation or event? _____

_____

c. Give an empathic response. _____

_____

*OE4. An 18-year-old male college freshman says: I am so excited. I just got an A in my biology exam. I really had studied hard for it.

a. What is he feeling? _____

_____

b. What is the situation or event? _____

_____

c. Give an empathic response. _____

_____

*OE5. A 19-year-old female college sophomore says: Here it is 6 weeks into the semester and I haven't gone to classes for 2 weeks. I just haven't felt like leaving my room or doing much of anything.

a. What is she feeling? _____

_____

b. What is the situation or event? _____

_____

c. Give an empathic response. _____

_____

*OE6. A man, 45, says: My wife thinks she is so smart! Like she has all the answers. Whatever I do is wrong.

a. What is he feeling? _____

_____

b. What is the situation? _____

_____

c. Give an empathic response. _____

_____

_____

OE7. An 11-year-old girl says: My mother stinks and she's mean. She won't let me wear makeup to school. Other kids' moms let them do it.

a. What is she feeling? _____

_____

b. What is the situation? _____

_____

c. Give an empathic response. _____

_____

_____

CASE EXAMPLE

Sheila is a 23-year-old secretary working for a trucking firm near Cleveland, Ohio. She is single and lives at home with her mother. When in high school, Sheila was a C student and did not care much for school. She did the minimal amount of homework and spent most of the afternoons and evenings either working at a women's clothing store or with her friends. She has been working for this firm for a year. The work is somewhat boring, but she enjoys the other clerical staff and tolerates her bosses.

When she was seven, Sheila's mother and father were divorced. Her father, a carpenter, moved to California to be closer to his family. When she was younger and in school, she talked to him weekly and visited him for one week per summer. Now, she talks to him about every three months and has not seen him for two years. He has remarried and has two young boys.

Sheila has two older brothers, four years older and six years older. Bob, the oldest, is a roofing supply salesman, and Paul is a plumber. Both are married and live in the Cleveland area.

Sheila's mother has worked in many retail jobs throughout her life. Since the divorce, she has had many boyfriends but has not remarried. Her cocaine abuse is part of the problem that is affecting Sheila. Many of Sheila's mother's boyfriends have also been cocaine abusers and have been the source of cocaine for her mother. Having seen the effects of cocaine on those close to her, Sheila has avoided all drug and alcohol use.

Her current problem is what to do about her mother. Sheila lives at home because the rent is cheap. Sheila's mother does not ask for a specific amount but takes whatever Sheila gives her. However, Sheila has been taking care of her mother since she was in high school. She has prepared the meals and cleaned the house. Sheila is growing resentful of this and is not sure what to do.

Problem: The next set of questions are a dialogue between Sheila and her counselor. You are to be her person-centered counselor and pick the response that most closely fits a person-centered response.

5. Sheila: I don't know what to do. My mother is driving me nuts. She doesn't do anything around the house. I never know which boyfriend is gonna to show up. I can't stand it.

   a. You want to know what to do?
   b. You feel angry at your mother's lack of responsibility in the house.
   c. Your mother has no right to ask more of you than she is willing to give of herself.

6. Sheila: She never has lived up to her end of the bargain. Sometimes it seemed like I was the mother and she was the child. She didn't take care of me or herself.

   a. You're angry at your mother for not being there when you needed her when you were a child.
   b. You know that your mother really loves you and really cares for you.
   c. Sometimes you wonder where your father was in all this.

7. I never knew whether I was doing the right thing at home. Particularly when I was about 14, I had to cook all the meals and have dinner ready when she would get home. If I didn't, nothing would get done.

   a. You felt you were unsure of yourself when you were young. It was so hard to know what to do at home.
   b. Why couldn't your mother take responsibility for the problems that she was making for you at home?
   c. Sometimes you really felt dumb.

8. When she would come home, sometimes she was just really silly. Until I was about 13 or 14, I didn't know what this was about. Later, I got to recognize when she was high and when she wasn't. And when she was high I knew I could get nowhere with her. I couldn't reason with her.

   a. You wondered whether she might get caught for using cocaine.
   b. Being around her was so incredibly depressing.
   c. Sometimes it was so frustrating not being able to talk to her when you really wanted to.

9. When her boyfriend of the week was at the house, it was really bad. Mainly my mother and her boyfriend ignored me, but it was real tense.

   a. You were really scared of your mother's boyfriend.
   b. You wondered where did she get this one now.
   c. You felt tense not knowing this person and yet having him right there in your house.

10. Sheila: The same thing is happening now, and it is really frustrating. I don't know how I can stand it. I want to move out, but I can't afford to.

    a. It's such a difficult struggle for you being caught between dealing with your mother's behavior and the financial responsibility of being on your own.
    b. Living expenses are not so high in the Cleveland area. Have you thought about sharing expenses with a roommate?
    c. Living at home with your mother need not be so bad after all.

The purpose of the above example has been to give you a chance to think like a person-centered therapist. Besides the appropriate person-centered responses listed above, there are many others that could be given. If you want to, see if you can generate some that you think are better than the ones given here.

Students often wonder about using reflections continually in therapy. They may wonder if the client gets bored or if reflections sound repetitious to the client. Many clients are likely to experience therapy differently than this. They may feel understood, value the chance to grow and explore issues, appreciate the safety to explore difficult problems, and feel the opportunity to make positive changes in their lives.

In answering the following questions, try to speculate how a continuing dialogue with Sheila might help her.

OE8. How could person-centered therapy help Sheila take responsibility for herself?

_____

_____

_____

OE9. How might the process of exploring issues dealing with her mother be helpful to Sheila?

_____

_____

SPECIAL TOPICS

*OE10. Why is it difficult for person-centered therapy to be time-limited? (222)

_____

_____

OE11. One current trend of person-centered therapy is its appeal to people of many different cultures. Why do you think this is? (222)

_____

_____

OE12. Would you find Rogers's six necessary and sufficient conditions too restrictive? Explain. (224)

_____

_____

OE13. Why do you think so many therapists find Roger's emphasis on empathic listening so appealing that they want to incorporate his reflecting approach into their theory? (225)

_____

_____

STRENGTHS AND LIMITATIONS

What do you believe are the strengths and limitations of person-centered therapy?

Strengths	Limitations
_____	_____
_____	_____
_____	_____
_____	_____
_____	_____
_____	_____
_____	_____

PERSON-CENTERED THERAPY: A QUIZ

True/false items: Decide if the following statements are more "true" or more "false" as they apply to person-centered therapy.

T F Q1. The influence of Maslow's self-actualization theory can be found in person-centered theory.

T F Q2. Ego formation in childhood determines later functioning.

T F Q3. Conditions of worth bring about ego growth.

T F Q4. Being listened to and understood can give individuals a sense of positive regard.

T F Q5. Therapists choose appropriate goals from the ones that clients present.

T F Q6. Rogers valued assessment instruments for research but not therapy.

T F Q7. An initial assessment is a major part of person-centered therapy.

T F Q8. Advice-giving adds to empathic responding in person-centered therapy.

T F Q9. A feature of person-centered therapy is its brief therapy approach.

T F Q10. Accurate empathy is one of the most significant concepts in person-centered therapy.

Multiple-choice items: Select the best answer from the alternatives given. Answer each question from the point of view of person-centered therapy.

_____Q11.   Person-centered therapy is a form of

        a. psychoanalysis.
        b. humanistic therapy.
        c. behavioral therapy.
        d. reality therapy.
        e. cognitive therapy.

_____Q12.   The founder of person-centered therapy is

        a. Kurt Goldstein.
        b. Abraham Maslow.
        c. Fritz Perls.
        d. Carl Rogers.
        e. Emmy van Deurzen.

_____Q13.   Rogers interest in world peace is reflected in which of these phases?

        a. developmental
        b. nondirective
        c. client-centered
        d. person-centered

_____Q14.   An important developmental issue in childhood in person-centered therapy is the

        a. development of authenticity.
        b. development of the ego.
        c. need for positive regard.
        d. need for incongruence.

_____Q15.   Which one of these concepts is NOT congruent with being a fully functioning person?

        a. being non-defensive
        b. being self-absorbed
        c. being creative
        d. being adaptable

_____Q16.   In person-centered therapy, the goals are chosen by

        a. the client.
        b. the therapist.
        c. neither a nor b.
        d. both a and b.

_____Q17.   Which of these receives the LEAST attention in person-centered therapy?

        a. client-therapist relationship
        b. client goals
        c. diagnosis
        d. all are important

_____Q18. When a therapist is congruent, she is

     a. genuine.
     b. empathic.
     c. reliable.
     d. respectful.
     e. accepting.

_____Q19. A child molester who is in therapy with a person-centered therapist would find that the therapist would _ _____ the child molester.

     a. accept
     b. not accept
     c. agree with
     d. condemn

_____Q20. If a client says, "You know, you really are stupid. You haven't done anything right," the person-centered therapist might respond in this way:

     a. Well, you're not so bright yourself.
     b. You seem angry and disappointed that I haven't been more helpful.
     c. The anger you feel toward your father seems to be directed toward me.
     d. There are several things that I have done right. I have been genuine and empathic.

_____Q21. Unconditional positive regard refers to

     a. accepting the client as a worthy person.
     b. approving of the client's decisions.
     c. agreeing with the client's values.
     d. approving of the client's behavior.

_____Q22. A criticism of person-centered therapy is that

     a. the client is not accepted.
     b. the therapist does not listen to the client.
     c. the client is not shown how to solve her problems.
     d. client feelings are not attended to.

_____Q23. As a result of person-centered therapy, the client should NOT expect to

     a. experience change.
     b. experience the empathy of the therapist.
     c. experience the process of exploration.
     d. experience awareness of contact boundaries.

_____Q24. Which of these concepts is NOT associated with Carl Rogers?

     a. acceptance
     b. emphathy
     c. interpretation
     d. unconditional positive regard

_____Q25. Rogers contributed to

        a. pioneering research in the process and outcome of therapy.
        b. fostering world peace.
        c. understanding the client-therapist relationship.
        d. the development of encounter groups.
        e. all of the above.

ANSWER KEY

1. c	Q1. T	Q11. b	Q21. a
2. d	Q2. F	Q12. d	Q22. c
3. c	Q3. F	Q13. d	Q23. d
4. c	Q4. T	Q14. c	Q24. c
5. b	Q5. F	Q15. b	Q25. e
6. a	Q6. T	Q16. a	
7. a	Q7. F	Q17. c	
8. c	Q8. F	Q18. a	
9. c	Q9. F	Q19. a	
10. a	Q10. T	Q20. b	

ANSWERS TO OPEN ENDED QUESTIONS

The following answers to the Open Ended Questions 3 through 6 may not be exactly like yours. That doesn't mean your responses are wrong. People have different perceptions and will see events differently.

OE3. a. What is she feeling? *Scared. Frightened. Worried about her mother.*

    b. What is the situation or event? *Her father is drunk, angry, and throwing things at her mother. She ran to her room.*

    c. Give an empathic response. *You were so frightened that your father might come after you that you ran to your room. OR You were worried that your father might hurt your mother and you are scared of him.*

OE4. a. What is he feeling? *Excited. Happy. Ecstatic. Happily surprised.*

    b. What is the situation or event? *Getting an A on the biology test. Studying hard for the test.*

    c. Give an empathic response. *An A! That's so exciting to have all your hard work pay off that way!*

OE5. a. What is she feeling? *Very depressed. Despair. Worried.*

    b. What is the situation or event? *Not going to class for two weeks.*

    c. Give an empathic response. *You are feeling so down that you haven't gone to class for two weeks.*

OE6. a. What is he feeling? *Angry. Hurt. Insulted. Lacking in confidence.*

    b. What is the situation? *Wife's criticism of him.*

    c. Give an empathic response. *When your wife criticizes you, it really hurts. Then you may feel bad about yourself.*

OE10. In person-centered therapy, the client chooses the problem and is likely to define the length of therapy. The therapist does not want to artificially restrict the length of the therapeutic exploration process.

CHAPTER 7

GESTALT THERAPY

GESTALT THERAPY SELF-INVENTORY

Directions: By comparing your beliefs about personality and therapy to those of Gestalt therapy, you should have a clearer idea of how much you will need to suspend your beliefs or change attitudes to understand Gestalt therapy. You may find it helpful to complete this section before and after you read the chapter. In this way you can see if your views have changed. There are no correct answers, only an opportunity to express your views.

Put an "X" on the line so that it indicates how much you disagree with the statement: A=Agree, D=Disagree.

D_____A 1. The whole is greater than the sum of its parts.

_____ 2. Relationships between events are important, not just the events themselves.

_____ 3. Focusing on the present in therapy is more important than focusing on the past or the future.

_____ 4. Knowing what is happening and how it happened is more important than knowing why it happened.

_____ 5. Rather than talking about experiences, clients should attempt to relive experiences as though they were happening now.

_____ 6. The past should be viewed in terms of how it affects present functioning.

_____ 7. Dwelling in the past can prevent people from taking responsibility for their own growth.

_____ 8. Self-awareness should be a primary goal of therapy.

_____ 9. Therapy should help clients become less phony.

_____ 10. Unfinished business from the past can result in problems in the present.

_____ 11. Therapeutic support is helpful in encouraging self-support.

_____ 12. Awareness is an important factor in therapy.

_____ 13. Therapy should help clients become more truly alive and aware of their true selves.

14. Awareness of client feelings and feelings within one's body will help clients grow and develop.

_____ 15. The therapist should be empathic as well as help the client gain self awareness.

_____ 16. Diagnosis should focus on present rather than past events or behavior.

_____ 17. Body language and other nonverbal cues are important information for the therapist.

_____ 18. Increased responsibility for client thoughts, feeling, and behaviors are associated with progress in therapy.

_____ 19. Group therapy can be as helpful as individual therapy and can be a useful adjunct to it.

_____ 20. Therapy should help clients become more aware of aspects of themselves that have interfered with their functioning and which they were not aware of previously.

HISTORY OF GESTALT THERAPY

Which influences do you think were most important in Fritz Perls's development of Gestalt therapy?

PERSONAL LIFE

Born in 1893 in Berlin, Germany
German Jewish parents
A sister killed in a concentration camp
Failed seventh grade twice
Worked for a merchant, returned to school at 14
Studied medicine
At 23, volunteered as a medic in World War I
Left Germany for South Africa in 1934
Established South African Institute for Psychoanalysis in 1935
Moved to New York in 1947
Established Gestalt training centers in several cities
Associate psychiatrist in residence at the Esalin Institute, 1964-1969
Died in 1970

PROFESSIONAL LIFE

Assistant to Kurt Goldstein at Institute for Brain Damaged Soldiers
Influenced by Wilhelm Reich, his analyst, who was interested in facial and body position
Trained as a psychoanalyst at the Vienna and Berlin Institute of Psychoanalysis
Sigmund Friedlander's work in polarities
Alfred Korzybiski's work on semantics
Kurt Lewin's field theory
Influenced by several existential therapists
Gestalt psychology background
Influenced by Jan Smut's writings on holism
Ego, Hunger, and Aggression, 1942/1947
Laura Perls, Fritz's wife, influenced Gestalt therapy directly through her emphasis on relationships
Gestalt Therapy Excitement and Growth in the Human Personality, 1951, coauthored with Hefferline and Goodman
Gestalt Therapy Verbatim, 1969
The Gestalt Approach, 1973, was published after his death

GESTALT PERSONALITY THEORY CONCEPTS

Several concepts that are important in the Gestalt theory of personality are related to concepts developed by Gestalt psychologists who then distanced themselves from Gestalt therapy. Other concepts deal with connection or contrast with others. Contact brings with it a sense of self and a differentiation from others. When there are disturbances in the contact boundaries, several difficulties result. Awareness of these disturbances is one focus of Gestalt therapy.

CONCEPTS FROM GESTALT PSYCHOLOGY

Gestalt psychology A psychological approach that studies the organization of experience into patterns or configurations. Gestalt psychologists believe that the whole is greater than the sum of its parts and study, among other issues, the relationship of a figure to its background.

ground The background that contrasts with the figure in the perceptions of a field.

figure That part of a field that stands out in good contour clearly from the ground.

CONCERNS RELATED TO CONTACT

contact The relationship between "me" and others. Contact involves feeling a connection with others or the world outside oneself while maintaining separation from it.

contact boundaries The boundaries that distinguish between one person (or one aspect of a person) and an object, another person, or another aspect of oneself. Examples include body-boundaries, value-boundaries, familiarity-boundaries, and expressive-boundaries.

CONTACT BOUNDARY DISTURBANCES

introjection This occurs when individuals accept information or values from others without evaluating them or without assimilating them into one's personality.

projection When we ascribe aspects of ourselves to others, such as when we attribute some of our own unacceptable thoughts, feelings, or behaviors to friends, projection takes place.

retroflection When we do to ourselves what we want to do to someone else or do things for ourselves that we want others to do for us, then we experience retroflection.

deflection When individuals avoid meaningful contact by being indirect or vague rather than being direct, deflection occurs.

confluence When the separation between one's self and others becomes muted or unclear, we experience confluence. Thus, it can be difficult to distinguish what is one's own perceptions or values from those of another person.

OTHER IMPORTANT PERSONALITY THEORY CONCEPTS

awareness Attending to and observing what is happening in the present. Types of awareness include sensations and actions, feelings, wants, and values or assessments.

unfinished business Unexpressed feelings from the past that occur in the present and interfere with psychological functioning. They may include feelings, memories, or fantasies from earlier life (often childhood) that can be dealt with in the present.

QUESTIONS ABOUT GESTALT PERSONALITY THEORY

1. As you read this question and look at it, this question is the

   a. field.
   b. figure.
   c. ground.
   d. Gestalt.

2. The rest of this page is then called the

    a. field.
    b. figure.
    c. ground.
    d. Gestalt.

3. Which of these terms is the most inclusive?

    a. field
    b. figure
    c. ground

4. Which of these is the weakest Gestalt?

    a. •   •   • •   •
    b. •   •   • •
    c.   •   • •
    d. •   •

5. Greeting a friend on the way to class is an example of this level of contact.

    a. phony
    b. phobic
    c. impasse
    d. implosive
    e. explosive

6. Which of these statements about Gestalt psychology is correct?

    a. Gestalt psychology and Gestalt psychotherapy are one and the same.
    b. Gestalt psychology is based on principles of behavior therapy.
    c. Gestalt psychologists have been critical about the way in which Perls applied Gestalt psychology to Gestalt therapy.
    d. Existential therapists developed Gestalt psychology through focus on authenticity.

7. At this level of contact, individuals are the most authentic.

    a. phony
    b. phobic
    c. impasse
    d. implosive
    e. explosive

8. Wanting to change an aspect of oneself but not being able to do so is likely to be experienced at this level.

    a. phony
    b. phobic
    c. impasse
    d. implosive
    e. explosive

9. Which of these is not a contact boundary?

    a. body
    b. expressive
    c. familiarity
    d. property
    e. value

10. Contact boundary disturbances represent problems that are always significant ones for individuals.

    a. true
    b. false

GESTALT THEORY OF PSYCHOTHERAPY

Gestalt psychotherapy combines a good working relationship with a client and respect for the client with methods that help clients become self aware. Gestalt therapists have developed a number of approaches to helping their clients become more aware of their feelings, attitudes, and verbal and nonverbal behavior. They work in the present, paying attention to changes in the client as therapy progresses.

GOALS

Developing fuller awareness of oneself is the basic goal of Gestalt therapy. Patients should become more aware of their bodies, feelings, experiences, needs and skills, sensations, and their environment. As they do this, they develop the ability to further support themselves and to become more responsible for their actions.

ASSESSMENT

Assessment takes place in the present moment, as Gestalt therapists attend to bodily movements, feelings, sensations, or other aspects of their clients. Therapists' prior experience attending to other clients gives them creative ways of assessing the problems of their clients. Gestalt therapists and those who use a Gestalt approach as a part of their work may include assessment approaches derived from other theories. Some use diagnostic categories and projective or objective tests in their approach to therapy.

GESTALT THERAPY: KEY CONCEPTS

For change to take place in Gestalt therapy, there must be a fully functioning I-Thou relationship. The empathic relationship with the client allows the therapist to use a variety of exercises and experiments that will help the client develop self awareness. Therapeutic approaches include statements and questions that bring about awareness as well as emphasis on behavior or language. Clients not only become more aware of their own feelings and behaviors but become more aware of their relationships with others. Self dialogue through use of the empty chair and enactment are among the more powerful approaches to self-awareness. Awareness is directed not only to what one may be doing but also to what one may be avoiding.

exercises Specific techniques that have been developed to be used in group or individual Gestalt therapy.

experiments Creative approaches or techniques used by the therapist to deal with an impasse in therapy brought about by the client's difficulty in achieving awareness.

empty chair A technique developed by Gestalt therapists and adapted by other theorists in which the patient is asked to play different roles in two different chairs. Dialogues between different aspects of the client or between client and others who are not present can then take place.

enactment In enactment, the patient may act out a previous experience or a characteristic. If the patient says he feels like a rat for cheating on his wife, the therapist may ask him to act like a rat.

CASE EXAMPLE

The purpose of the following case example is to help you become more familiar with Gestalt approaches to enhancing awareness. Helping clients become more aware of themselves is done in a context of a caring relationship. Thus Gestalt therapists may choose less confrontational comments or awareness exercises over more creative ones because of the impact on the relationship. In actual Gestalt therapy, the number and type of awareness experiments that are done vary greatly. To keep this example brief, client statements will be given to you, and then you, playing the role of the Gestalt therapist, will give a response that enhances the client's awareness. Because some of the questions are difficult, answers and explanations will be given after most of the questions.

Juan is a 42-year-old man who has been married for 12 years and has no children. For the past 15 years, he has driven a parcel delivery truck in his city. He daydreams constantly and has had several near misses and one minor accident. He would like to return to school to study to be a nurse but has not felt that he would be successful. His wife is an executive secretary who works for a large packaging company. She often compares Juan's lack of success and ambition to that of her bosses' financial and managerial success.

Whenever possible, Juan spends time watching baseball, basketball, ice hockey, and football on television. He avoids talking to his wife about their relationship. He prefers to talk about sports with her. However, this has only moderate interest for her, and she tolerates it.

Juan's parents and his three sisters live in different parts of the country. His parents, living 40 miles away, are the closest to him. Juan and his wife, Marita, visit his parents about ten times a year. His mother often speaks to Juan about how successful his sisters have been in both their careers and marriages. Juan feels criticized by this and is upset that he has been the one child in the family who has not been successful.

Juan has sought therapy because of his low self-esteem. He is very critical of himself and feels that he has been a failure. He would make changes in his life but feels that nothing will come of them. He does not feel that he will ever be successful. In the last three years, he has become more and more depressed. Marita has become annoyed by his sullenness and irritability. She has started to bring up the subject of a possible divorce, a subject that Juan tries to avoid. The idea of a divorce has frightened Juan very much, and he has sought therapy.

11. Which of the following contact boundary disturbances would best seem to describe Juan's level of awareness about his wife's desire to discuss divorce?

    a. introjection
    b. projection
    c. retroflection
    d. deflection
    e. confluence

(Deflection "d" is a term that can be used to describe his avoidance of dealing with important issues within himself or with his wife.)

12. Which of the following concepts would Gestalt therapists attend to in understanding Juan?

    a. his awareness
    b. his hatching
    c. his inferiority complex
    d. the thrown world

13. In reading the information about Juan, which of these people or events would seem to represent the "figure" for Juan?

    a. his job
    b. his religion
    c. his entire environment
    d. Marita

In the first session, Juan complains of his frustration with his job and his relationship with Marita. He is very upset, to the point of tears, about his failure to be successful. His head is buried in his hands, his elbows are resting on his knees, and he is looking at the floor. He says to you: "Sometimes I can't stand myself. I feel like I am just going through the motions. I want to make progress but I feel so stuck."

14. Which of the following therapeutic comments do you feel would be most appropriate to say in responding to Juan?

    a. Could you please push your face even further into your hands and tell me what you are feeling?
    b. You're so upset with yourself for not having done more with your life that it is hurting you very much.
    c. Could you "go through the motions", make motions now that might express how you feel?
    d. How has your wife been responding to you?

(This is a hard question. At this point in Gestalt therapy, a Gestalt therapist is likely to respond with a relationship-based response such as "b" rather than responses "a" and "c" that call the client's attention to his awareness. At a later time in therapy, such responses may be appropriate. Now is the time to be empathic to Juan's pain.)

Now you are working with Juan about his problems at work. It is the third session, and Juan is trying to make progress in understanding his problems at work and doing something about them.

15. He says to you: "You know, they never give you a break. My bosses, they're always questioning what you do and why you do it." Which of the following responses might be most appropriate in helping Juan develop his awareness in the moment?

    a. Do you think they would talk that way to Marita?
    b. Could you say that again, but use the word "I" instead of "you"?
    c. Can you tell me how you feel your bosses are treating "you"?
    d. Both b and c.

(Both answers "b" and "c" help Juan to take more responsibility for his situation with his bosses. "b" is somewhat more confrontational and direct than "c". Response "c" is more subtle than "b" and redirects Juan's attention to himself.)

In his distress about his boredom with work and his lack of progress, Juan says that it is about time for him to return to school and leave his job.

16. Juan says to you, "I need to do something more meaningful with my life and return to school." Which of these phrases would best replace the word "need"?

    a. have to
    b. must
    c. choose to
    d. am required to

As Juan continues to discuss his frustration with his job, he says to you in a loud voice, while beating his right fist against the arm of his chair: "I've got to stop letting life overwhelm me. Now is the time to do something about it".

17. In response to Juan's emotional frustration to his job situation, which response would seem to be most appropriate?

   a. Could you stop beating on my furniture please?
   b. Could you hit the arm of the chair again with your fist, like you just did? Can you describe what you are aware of?
   c. When you hit your fist against the chair, I believe you are acting out some of the rage that you felt as a child when your parents would not buy you a toy.
   d. Why are you hitting your fist against the arm of the chair?

Now Juan talks about how Marita feels about his job. "When Marita points out that my job is a dead end, I feel like I am all washed out, like I can't do anything. There is just that feeling of helplessness that I really dislike."

18. Respond now to Juan, using a statement that most closely fits a Gestalt awareness approach.

   a. Be that washed out self and talk in a wishy washy voice.
   b. You could tell her that it does not help you to have her complain about your work.
   c. You could say to her, "I am responsible for myself and you are responsible for yourself."
   d. You are projecting your anger at your father onto Marita.

19. As Juan is describing his concern about his job and Marita's interference in his career plans, he says to you, "I'd like to tell Marita to back off and leave me alone." Pick the statement that most closely fits a Gestalt awareness response.

   a. Why don't you tell her to leave you alone, then?
   b. So Marita doesn't seem to think that you're very capable.
   c. Imagine, if you would, that Marita is sitting in this chair across from you; tell her what you would like to say to her.
   d. There are times when husbands and wives don't listen carefully to each other. Perhaps, you can listen more carefully to the underlying meaning of what she has to say.

Juan now describes the conflict that he feels between wanting to take a risk and return to school or being safe and staying with his current job. He describes how often he prefers to be safe, and yet more and more that he is able to take a risk and do something new or different.

20. The conflict that is described in the previous paragraph is seen by Gestalt therapists as representing a (an)

   a. boundary contact disturbance.
   b. exercise.
   c. experiment.
   d. polarity.

(d. Gestalt therapists often become aware of a variety of polarities in their clients' description of their problems.)

In dealing with a polarity such as the one described previously, Gestalt therapists use self-dialogues so that individuals can play out the roles of the polarity.

21. Which of the following roles best describes the polarities that Juan is experiencing now?

   a. bossy self - submissive self
   b. masculine self - feminine self
   c. good boy - bad boy
   d. cautious self - risky self

99

22. In using the empty chair technique to play out the polarity, which choice would be the appropriate Gestalt therapeutic approach?

   a. Free associate to the chair on the other side of the room.
   b. Would you be the cautious self in that chair and express how you feel, then you can respond in the other chair as the risky self?
   c. Tell me more about how you feel when you want to take risks. I think you need to take more risks.
   d. The conflict between the risky and the cautious self is incongruent. In the future, you must compromise between these two. I would like you to play the role of the compromise and express those feelings to the other chair.

Some Gestalt therapists find dreams to be particularly meaningful in understanding issues in one's life. Rather than interpret the dream to the patient, they may ask the patient to enact the dream. Juan reports that he has dreamt about speeding down a highway in the middle of the night. He is going about 80 miles an hour and the scenery is whizzing by him quickly. Behind him he hears a loud siren and in his rear view mirror sees the lights of a police car chasing him. The chase continues through desert scenery. And the sound of the siren grows louder. Finally, the police car crashes into the back of Juan's car with terrible sounds and force.

23. As a Gestalt therapist, you might ask Juan to be (and act the role of)

   a. his car.
   b. the police car.
   c. the road.
   d. the desert scenery.
   e. any or all of the above

The preceding case of Juan should help you to become more familiar with therapeutic approaches or concepts in Gestalt therapy. Because these are presented in a brief amount of space, they can make Gestalt therapy appear gimmicky. When Gestalt therapists make interventions, it is in the interest of helping their patients. Interventions are not made for dramatic effect. They are made to help individuals become more self-aware in a constructive way that helps them become more responsible for themselves, more creative, and less anxious. Respect for the client and the relationship with the client are paramount in Gestalt therapy.

SPECIAL TOPICS

OE1. Why do you think it would be difficult to do Gestalt therapy in a time limited manner? (264)

_____

_____

_____

OE2. An ongoing and current trend in Gestalt therapy is the focus on the client-counselor relationship. Why do you think Gestalt therapists have addressed this topic with so much interest? (265)

_____

_____

_____

OE3. The two theories that have most recently been integrated with Gestalt therapy are person-centered and psychoanalytical theories. What do you believe they have to offer Gestalt therapy? (265)

_____

_____

_____

OE4. How do you think Gestalt therapy can empower women? (268)

_____

_____

_____

OE5. How do Gestalt therapists integrate cultural influences in helping clients to become more aware of themselves? (269)

_____

_____

_____

STRENGTHS AND LIMITATIONS

What do you see as the strengths and limitations of Gestalt therapy?

Strengths	Limitations
_____	_____
_____	_____
_____	_____
_____	_____
_____	_____
_____	_____
_____	_____
_____	_____

GESTALT THERAPY: A QUIZ

True/false items: Decide if the following statements are more "true" or more "false" as they apply to Gestalt therapy.

T   F   Q1. Enhancing awareness is a major goal of Gestalt therapy.

T   F   Q2. The ground encompasses the field.

T   F   Q3. Disturbances in contact boundaries mean that individuals have dysfunctional personality problems.

T   F   Q4. The present, rather than the past, is the focus of Gestalt therapy.

T   F   Q5. Knowledge of archetypes is important in assessment in Gestalt therapy.

T   F   Q6. Awareness, not the therapeutic relationship, is important in Gestalt therapy.

T   F   Q7. Body language and other non-verbal behaviors are important therapeutic data in Gestalt therapy.

T   F   Q8. Interpretation is a major therapeutic technique in Gestalt therapy.

T   F   Q9. Group therapy is highly valued by Gestalt therapists.

T   F   Q10. Enactment is an approach to awareness used by Gestalt therapists.

Multiple choice items. Select the *one best answer* from the alternatives using a Gestalt therapy perspective.

_____ Q11. Gestalt therapy focuses on

        a. early childhood development.
        b. developing rational thinking.
        c. the here and now.
        d. the holding environment.

_____ Q12. Which of the following is NOT important in Gestalt therapy?

        a. awareness
        b. acceptance of responsibility
        c. dealing with impasse
        d. exploring the collective unconscious
        e. unfinished business

_____ Q13. Which of these sentences is least consistent with developing awareness?

        a. I have to do my homework.
        b. I won't do my homework.
        c. I want to do my homework.
        d. I choose to do my homework.

_____ Q14. Which of these statements is most consistent with the goal of Gestalt therapy?

        a. I need to be nicer to my sister.
        b. I can't be nice to my sister.
        c. I want to be nice to my sister.
        d. I have to be nicer to my sister.

_____ Q15. Gestalt therapists work with dreams through

     a. free association.
     b. enactment.
     c. interpretation of contact boundary disturbances.
     d. interpretation of I-thou relationships.

_____ Q16. Gestalt therapists view avoidance as a (an)

     a. active process.
     b. passive process.
     c. resistance to therapeutic love.
     d. transference resistance.

_____ Q17. Gestalt therapists have gone beyond Perl's description of Gestalt therapy to include the study of psychoanalysis in broadening their work with

     a. archetypes.
     b. birth order.
     c. the death instinct.
     d. shame.

_____ Q18. Which of these statements is least consistent with Gestalt therapy?

     a. Could you hold your fist there for a moment?
     b. Could you say that using the word "I" instead of "you".
     c. You should not express your anger to your wife.
     d. You seem to be feeling upset that your wife is angry with you.

_____ Q19. Gestalt therapy can be best characterized as

     a. experiential therapy.
     b. cognitive therapy.
     c. behavior therapy.
     d. therapy focused on the unconscious.

_____ Q20. The process of turning back to ourselves what we would like to do to someone else is called

     a. introjection.
     b. projection.
     c. retroflection.
     d. confluence.
     e. deflection.

_____ Q21. When Joe starts to talk about problems with his wife, he goes from one detail to another without drawing a conclusion. What type of contact boundary disturbance is this?

     a. introjection
     b. projection
     c. retroflection
     d. deflection
     e. confluence

_____ Q22. Mary has had a great level of trouble finding a job. She believes this is due to employers being angry and disdainful. Mary is angry that she has to look for work. What type of contact boundary disturbance is this?

a. introjection
b. projection
c. retroflection
d. deflection
e. confluence

_____ Q23. The focus of Gestalt therapy is on the

a. past.
b. present.
c. future.

_____ Q24. Unfinished business concerns

a. feelings from the past that will impact the future.
b. feelings from the past that are buried and are out of awareness.
c. unexpected feelings from the past that are dealt with in the present.
d. feelings in the present that will be dealt with in the future.

_____ Q25. Gestalt therapy is most concerned with _____ boundaries.

a. borderline
b. depressed
c. I
d. thou

ANSWER KEY

1. b	11. d	21. d	Q1. T	Q11. c	Q21. d
2. c	12. a	22. b	Q2. F	Q12. d	Q22. b
3. a	13. d	23. e	Q3. F	Q13. a	Q23. b
4. d	14. b		Q4. T	Q14. c	Q24. c
5. a	15. d		Q5. F	Q15. b	Q25. c
6. c	16. c		Q6. F	Q16. a	
7. e	17. b		Q7. T	Q17. d	
8. c	18. a		Q8. F	Q18. c	
9. d	19. c		Q9. T	Q19. a	
10. b	20. d		Q10. T	Q20. c	

CHAPTER 8

BEHAVIOR THERAPY

BEHAVIOR THERAPY SELF-INVENTORY

Directions: By comparing your beliefs about personality therapy with those of behavior therapy, you should have a clearer idea of how much you will need to suspend your beliefs and change attitudes to understand behavior therapy's theory of personality and approach to therapy. You may find it helpful to complete this section before and after you read the chapter. In this way, you can see if your views have changed. There are no correct answers, only an opportunity to express your views.

Put an "X" on the line so that it indicates how much you agree or disagree with the statement: A = Agree, D = Disagree.

D_____A 1. Changing and improving symptoms is sufficient to bring about therapeutic change.

_____ 2. Psychotherapy should be based on scientific principles which are supported by research results.

_____ 3. Clients should be informed about the therapy process and be involved in setting treatment goals.

_____ 4 Research on psychotherapy should help to refine concepts and the practice of therapy so that new approaches can be confirmed and developed.

_____ 5. Clients should be informed about the therapy process and be involved in setting treatment goals.

_____ 6. Clients control *what* behaviors are to be changed. Therapists and clients control *how* behavior is to changed.

_____ 7. Past history is important only to the degree that it directly contributes to a client's current difficulties.

_____ 8. A detailed and comprehensive assessment is necessary for behavior change to occur.

_____ 9. Psychotherapy should focus on overt and specific behaviors rather than client's feelings about a situation.

_____ 10. The outcomes of therapy should be assessed to determine the degree of success or failure of treatment.

_____ 11. The focus of psychotherapy should be changing behavior not developing insight into problems.

D_____A 12. Positive reinforcement enhances client learning.

_____ 13. The roles of the therapist should include being a teacher, consultant, facilitator, coach, model, director and/or problem solver.

_____ 14. Client change can take place using imagination or going out into the actual environment.

_____ 15. Both therapist and client can control the pace at which therapeutic change takes place.

_____ 16 Clients should be actively involved in the analysis, planning, process, and evaluation of a treatment program.

_____ 17. Therapy should be made available to all people including those who are severely limited due to psychological or physical functioning.

_____ 18. Therapeutic procedures should be aimed at behavior change.

_____ 19. The client and the therapist should have a good working relationship in order to ensure behavior change.

_____ 20. Cognitive and behavior therapy can compliment each other to bring about therapeutic change.

HISTORY OF BEHAVIOR THERAPY

Which influences do you think were most important in the development of behavior therapy?

PSYCHOLOGISTS AND THEIR CONTRIBUTIONS

CLASSICAL CONDITIONING

Ivan Pavlov - classical conditioning late 19th century
John Watson - applied classical conditioning to the treatment of human behavior, 1910-1926
Mowrer and Mowrer - applied classical conditioning to the treatment of bed wetting using a urine alarm system, 1938

OPERANT CONDITIONING

E. L. Thorndike - studied the learning of new behaviors - Law of Effect - emphasized adaptive nature of learning, 1890s-1920s
B. F. Skinner - selectively reinforced different behaviors - applied behavioral principles to animals and humans, 1930s-1980s

SOCIAL COGNITIVE THEORY

Mary Cover Jones - used models and observation to treat Peter's fear of rabbits, 1924
Albert Bandura - developed social cognitive theory, included beliefs, preferences, self-perceptions, sense of self-efficacy as regulators of behavior, described observations and modeling, 1960

BEHAVIOR THEORY OF PERSONALITY

No single person is responsible for the development of a behavioral theory of personality. Rather, the foundation for a theory of personality is based on principles of behavior that have been developed by the research of many different behavioral psychologists. The principles can be divided into two very broad categories. One category is principles derived mainly from operant conditioning but also classical conditioning. The other is derived from observational learning, the work of Albert Bandura. Behavior therapists build on these principles in developing techniques of behavior change.

OPERANT AND CLASSICAL CONDITIONING CONCEPTS

classical conditioning A type of learning in which a neutral stimulus is presented repeatedly with one that reflexively elicits a particular response so the neutral stimulus will eventually elicit the response itself (also called respondent conditioning).

operant conditioning A type of learning in which behavior is increased or decreased by systematically changing its consequences.

overt behavior Actions that can be directly observed by others.

positive reinforcement The process by which the introduction of a stimulus has a consequence of a behavior that increases the likelihood that the behavior will be performed again.

extinction The process of no longer presenting a reinforcement. It is used to decrease or eliminate certain behaviors.

generalization Transferring the response from one type of stimuli to similar stimuli.

discrimination Responding differentially to stimuli that are similarly based on different cues or antecedent events.

shaping Gradually reinforcing certain parts of a behavior to more closely approximate the desired behavior.

OBSERVATIONAL LEARNING CONCEPTS

observational learning A type of learning in which people are influenced by observing the behaviors of others.

covert behavior Behavior that others cannot directly perceive, such as thinking or feeling.

attentional processes The act of perceiving or watching something and learning from it.

retention processes This basically refers to remembering that which has been observed.

motor reproduction processes This refers to translating what one has seen into action using motor skills.

motivational processes For observations to be put into action and then continued for some time, reinforcement must be present. Reinforcement brings about motivation.

self-efficacy The individuals' perceptions of their ability to deal with different types of events.

QUESTIONS ABOUT BEHAVIORAL PERSONALITY CONCEPTS

1. If Jill is no longer praised for doing her homework, then this process may take place.

    a. positive reinforcement
    b. extinction
    c. generalization
    d. discrimination

107

2. Now that Bradley has been bitten by a dog, he is afraid of all dogs. This process has taken place.

   a. positive reinforcement
   b. extinction
   c. generalization
   d. discrimination

3. The type of learning in which the researcher or experimenter has the most control is

   a. classical conditioning.
   b. operant conditioning.
   c. social cognitive theory.
   d. desensitization.

4. Covert behavior would most closely be associated with which of these concepts?

   a. positive reinforcement
   b. discrimination
   c. shaping
   d. attentional processes

5. When Millie uses self-talk to describe to herself how she is going to visit a friend at her new apartment and not get lost, she is using

   a. attentional processes.
   b. retention processes.
   c. motor reproduction processes.
   d. motivational processes.

BEHAVIORAL APPROACHES TO THERAPY

Methods used for change in behavior therapy have been developed by a variety of practitioners using approaches that are consistent with basic principles of behavior. All aspects of behavior therapy including goals, assessments, and techniques are well defined and specified.

GOALS

There may be several goals in behavior therapy. The client and the therapist work together to develop goals, often referred to as target behaviors.

functional analysis Specifying goals and treatment by assessing antecedents and consequences of a behavior. Analyze what is maintaining the behavior and propose hypotheses about contributors to the behavior. Use this information to guide treatment of the behavior and to further specify goals.

target behavior A part of the client's problem that can be clearly defined and easily assessed. It is the focus of treatment in behavior therapy.

BEHAVIORAL ASSESSMENT

The focus of behavioral assessment is current behavior. Past behavior is useful to the extent that it helps in specifying current behavior. Common methods for assessment are interviews, reports and writings, observations, and physiological measurements.

INTERVIEWS	REPORTS AND RATINGS	OBSERVATIONS	PHYSIOLOGICAL MEASUREMENTS
ask about antecedents and consequences	brief ratings, yes or no or on a scale	naturalistic simulated	blood pressure heart rate respiration

interrater reliability The degree of agreement among raters about their observations of an individual or individuals.

reactivity This occurs when clients change their behaviors because they know that they are being observed.

The fact that behavioral therapists are concerned about interrater reliability and reactivity shows the importance that they place on accuracy, specificity, and scientific principles.

GENERAL BEHAVIORAL TREATMENT APPROACHES

Many behavioral approaches have been developed to reduce fear and anxiety, but they also can be applied to other concerns. Systematic desensitization and implosive therapy are particularly designed to reduce anxiety. Modeling techniques help individuals learn new behaviors. Donald Meichenbaum has developed two approaches that combine cognitive and behavioral methods: Self-instructional training and stress inoculation.

ANXIETY TREATMENT APPROACHES

Several strategies have been developed, such as systematic desensitization and implosive therapy, to reduce fear and anxiety. One useful dimension to examine these approaches determines if the client is to make changes using imagination or in the real situation (in vivo). A second dimension concerns the speed of type of delivery of the approach. Is it to be done gradually or all at once to evoke high levels of anxiety? The following chart describes these dimensions and places systematic desensitization and implosive therapy within the chart.

ANXIETY TREATMENT APPROACHES

	Imagination	In vivo
Gradual	Systematic Desensitization	
Flooding	Implosive Therapy	

systematic desensitization A specific procedure for replacing anxiety with relaxation while gradually increasing the imagined exposure to an anxiety-producing situation.

flooding Prolonged in vivo or imagined exposure to stimuli that evoke high levels of anxiety, with no ability to avoid or escape the stimuli. Implosive therapy uses flooding.

in vivo The Latin term for "in life", which refers to therapeutic procedures that take place in the client's natural environment.

implosive therapy A type of prolonged intense exposure therapy in which the client imagines exaggerated scenes that include hypothesized stimuli.

MODELING TECHNIQUES

Based on Bandura's social cognitive theory, modeling techniques provide an opportunity for clients to observe the behavior of another person (a model) and then use the results of their observations. There are several types of modeling that behavior therapists use:

live Watch a model (can be the therapist).

symbolic Includes films, videotapes, photographs, or pictures.

role playing Acting the part of someone, something else, or oneself under different conditions. Clients may practice different situations. Therapists and clients can play different roles.

participant modeling Therapists model a behavior and guide the client in the use of the behavior.

covert modeling The client imagines a model. The therapist describes the activities of the model which the client follows in her imagination.

COGNITIVE-BEHAVIORAL APPROACHES

Donald Meichenbaum has developed two approaches that combine cognitive and behavioral methods. These are self-instructional training and stress inoculation.

self-instructional training A cognitive-behavioral therapy that teaches patients to instruct themselves verbally so that they may cope with difficult situations.

stress inoculation training Clients use coping skills for dealing with stressful situations and then practice the skills, while being exposed to the situation. In the conceptual phase, the therapist gathers information and educates the client about the problem. In the skills acquisition phase, new cognitive and behavioral skills are taught such as relaxation training, cognitive restructuring, problem-solving skills, and self-reinforcement. In the application phase, clients apply these skills to their problems. Specific homework assignments are given.

THREE OTHER SPECIFIC BEHAVIORAL APPROACHES

exposure and ritual prevention (EXRP) A treatment method used primarily with obsessive-compulsive disorders in which patients are exposed to the feared stimulus for an hour or more at a time. They are then asked to refrain from participating in rituals such as continually checking the door to see if they have closed it.

eye movement desensitization and reprocessing (EMDR) Designed first for post traumatic stress, EMDR requires that the patient visualize a most upsetting memory and accompanying physical sensations. The clients repeat negative self-statements that they associate with the scene. The patient follows the therapist's finger as it moves rapidly back and forth. After completing the eye movements, the client stops thinking about the scene. This procedure is repeated again and again until the client's anxiety is reduced.

acceptance and commitment therapy Behavioral techniques are combined with a focus on clients' use of language to reduce distress. The focus is on accepting a feeling, event, or situation rather than avoiding it. Therapists help clients commit to behaviors that fits with their values.

A CASE STUDY

Judy is a 22-year-old college student majoring in business administration. She is in her senior year at a mid-western university. Except for her freshman year when she received C's and D's , she has been a B+ student. Very conscientious, she worries that her work will not be good enough. There are many things that Judy worries about. Not only is she fearful that she will do poorly on exams, but she worries about how she will be perceived in social situations. About one year ago, she and her boyfriend broke up. Since then, she has dated several times but usually worries about how her date will view her.

Although her concerns about how others see her and her academic performance are important to her, she is most worried about driving. About two years ago, Judy was in a bad accident in which her leg was broken. She was driving near her home when another driver smashed into the driver's side of her car. She was in the hospital overnight and on crutches for about a month. Since that time, she has been very afraid of driving. Living near suburban Chicago, about four hours from her university, Judy often worries about the trips home. She worries even more about driving in the Chicago traffic when she goes to visit friends who live in apartments there.

Judy's father is an orthodontist working in Chicago. Her mother is a computer programmer. When Judy went to college, she was glad to get away. She finds that her mother is overprotective, often asking her if she will be all right when she goes out at night. She worries too about Judy when Judy is driving home. For the last 20 years, Judy's mother has been treated on and off for symptoms of anxiety. For the last four years, she has been taking anti-anxiety medication.

6. Which of Judy's presenting problems would you, as a behavior therapist, most easily be able to define as target behaviors, along with Judy's help?

   a. her academic anxiety
   b. her fear in social situations
   c. anxiety when driving

7. Which of the following questions is most consistent with determining goals in behavior therapy?

   a. What dreams have you had about driving?
   b. What thoughts do you have when you start to drive?
   c. In what type of driving situation are you the most anxious?
   d. How does your mother feel about your driving alone?

8. Which questions seem most appropriate in determining goals for behavior therapy with regard to Judy's driving behavior?

   a. How anxious are you when you are the passenger and a friend is driving?
   b. Are there any driving situations in which you feel little anxiety?
   c. Does the type of car that you are driving affect your problem with driving?
   d. All of the above.

9. Which of the following methods of behavioral assessments will most likely give you the most information in assessing appropriate target behaviors for Judy's concerns about driving?

   a. behavioral interviews
   b. behavioral reports and ratings
   c. behavioral observations
   d. physiological measurements

10. Behavioral observations of Judy's driving could come from

   a. Judy.
   b. her mother.
   c. a friend.
   d. all of the above.

As you and Judy discuss her problems, the two of you decide to devote attention at first to her fear about driving. Judy tells you that she is most fearful when driving alone, slightly less fearful when there is a passenger in the car, and not fearful when she is a passenger. Furthermore, she tells you that it doesn't matter what type of car she is driving, as long as it is not a truck, something she has only driven once. She is most comfortable driving along streets near her college and through small towns. Highway driving isn't as hard for her as driving in downtown Chicago traffic. The more traffic there is, either in the city or on a highway, the more anxious she is.

11. Which of the following treatment approaches that you could discuss with Judy are likely to be the most gentle, yet take the most time?

    a. implosive therapy
    b. in vivo flooding
    c. explosive therapy
    d. systematic desensitization

12. If you and Judy decided to use systematic desensitization, what would be one of the first aspects of treatment?

    a. have her drive her car in downtown Chicago
    b. initiate relaxation training
    c. have Judy imagine a scene that is slightly anxiety producing
    d. have Judy imagine a scene that is very anxiety producing

13. Which of the following instructions fits most closely with a relaxation instruction that you might give to Judy?

    a. Just relax more and more.
    b. Keep relaxing, and tell me when you're done.
    c. Clench both fists together tightly. Feel the tension in both fists. Now tense up your forearms and feel the tension in your forearms.
    d. Think of a lovely day, and just let yourself relax as much as possible.
    e. Tense your biceps. Make your biceps quite hard. Feel the tension in your forearms, upper arms, and into your shoulders. Now let yourself relax. Let your arms become loose and heavy, and feel the relaxation all over your arms.

14. Which of the following items is likely to have the highest rating on Judy's subjective units of discomfort scale (SUDs)?

    a. driving around her college town
    b. driving around home
    c. driving on a highway
    d. driving in downtown Chicago in rush hour

15. Once Judy has learned how to relax, you will ask her to write a number of items on a hierarchy, and then ask her to imagine them. Which item are you likely to have her imagine first?

    a. driving in an unfamiliar city
    b. driving around home
    c. driving on a highway
    d. driving in downtown Chicago in rush hour

16. What type of behavioral treatment would you be using with Judy if you said to her: "Imagine you are in downtown Chicago, driving alone. Your car is stalled at a light and drivers are honking all around you, trying to get you to move. No matter how much you try, the car is still stalled. Someone knocks at you window and asks you to get your car moving."

    a. gradual imagination
    b. gradual in vivo
    c. flooding-imagination
    d. flooding-in vivo

17. If instead of using the preceding approach, you ask Judy to drive with a friend around town for three half hour periods on different days, and then to drive by herself around town for half an hour on three different days, you would be using which of these treatment approaches?

    a. gradual imagination
    b. gradual in vivo
    c. flooding-imagination
    d. flooding-in vivo

Rather than use any of these approaches, you may prefer to use modeling techniques. This would allow Judy to observe someone else driving and make use of her knowledge of others' driving. Judy may reply to that idea, "Well, I drive with others all the time, and that doesn't seem to help." For modeling to work in a situation such as this, Judy would need to watch the other person carefully and learn how she controls her anxiety. Even so, it may not provide sufficient anxiety reduction.

18. If Judy were watching her father drive in Chicago through heavy traffic, while being relatively calm, she would be participating in

    a. live modeling.
    b. symbolic modeling.
    c. role playing.
    d. participant modeling.
    e. covert modeling.

19. If you were to say to Judy: "I want you to imagine your father driving through Chicago. Picture the street he is on and the stores on either side. Notice how relaxed and calm he is as he drives the car. He is breathing slowly and easily. His muscles are relaxed, yet there are cars in front of him at the stop light." Which of the following types of modeling is he likely to be using?

    a. live modeling
    b. symbolic modeling
    c. role playing
    d. participant modeling
    e. covert modeling

Donald Meichenbaum has developed two methods that combine behavioral approaches with a cognitive technique. In using the techniques, clients are often told to give instructions to themselves or to reinforce their own behaviors by saying positive statements to themselves. His two methods are self-instructional training and stress inoculation.

20. If Judy were to practice new skills in the office with you, then plan to apply them in actual traffic situations by repeating instructions to herself, she would be using

    a. self-instructional training.
    b. stress inoculation.
    c. cognitive restructuring.
    d. none of the above.

21. If you teach Judy how to replace a statement such as "I'm afraid I'm going to get into an accident" with "When I am afraid, I will take a breath and be able to handle the traffic," you are using

    a. self-instructional training.
    b. stress inoculation.
    c. cognitive restructuring.
    d. none of the above.

113

22. If Judy said to herself, "I am almost there. I am driving well in Chicago traffic", this statement would be called

    a. classical conditioning.
    b. implosive therapy.
    c. role playing.
    d. self-reinforcement.

SPECIAL TOPICS

OE1. What factors influence the duration of behavior therapy? (302)

_____

_____

_____

OE2. What do you see as the advantages and disadvantages of using treatment manuals in behavior therapy? (303)

_____

_____

_____

OE3. What type of ethical issues face behavior therapists that do not face most other therapists? (305)

_____

_____

_____

OE4. What difficulties would a therapist have in using behavior therapy with psychoanalysis? (306)

_____

_____

_____

OE5. What approaches do behavior therapists use to avoid gender bias in their treatment of clients? (311)

_____

_____

_____

OE6. How can the identification of antecedents and consequences of behavior help therapists avoid cultural bias? (311)

_____

_____

_____

STRENGTHS AND LIMITATIONS

What do you believe are the strengths and limitations of behavior therapy?

Strengths   Limitations

_____   _____

_____   _____

_____   _____

_____   _____

_____   _____

_____   _____

_____   _____

BEHAVIOR THERAPY: A QUIZ

True/false items: Decide if the following statements are "more true" or "more false" as they apply to behavior therapy.

T   F   Q1. Behavior therapy is derived from principles of psychoanalysis.

T   F   Q2. B. F. Skinner studied the process of learning called classical conditioning.

T   F   Q3. Behavior therapy is concerned with changing only visible behaviors.

T   F   Q4. Behavior therapy is based on scientific principles derived from human and animal learning.

T   F   Q5. Newer developments in behavior therapy have focused on cognitive as well as behavioral factors.

T   F   Q6. Client and therapist work together to choose goals of behavior therapy.

T   F   Q7. Questions are an important technique of behavior therapists.

T   F   Q8. Behavioral assessment could include the measurement of the client's blood pressure.

T   F   Q9. The client-therapist relationship is not important in behavior therapy.

T   F   Q10. Clients' sense of self-efficacy is important in social cognitive theory.

Multiple choice items: Select the *one best answer* from those alternatives given. Consider each question within the framework of behavior therapy.

_____   Q11. Behavior therapy is based on

   a. principles of learning.
   b. action oriented techniques.
   c. principles of self-actualization.
   d. classical conditioning.

_____   Q12. Observational learning is a part of

   a. classical conditioning.
   b. operant conditioning.
   c. social cognitive theory.
   d. desensitization.

_____   Q13. The Law of Effect was derived by

   a. Pavlov.
   b. Skinner.
   c. Thorndike.
   d. Bandura.

_____   Q14. When you get an A on an exam, the A serves as

   a. a focus in acceptance and commitment therapy
   b. an unconditioned stimulus.
   c. a positive reinforcer.
   d. an attentional process.

_____   Q15. Which of these terms is most closely associated with social cognitive theory?

   a. positive reinforcement
   b. generalization
   c. shaping
   d. motivational processes

_____   Q16. Which of these is most likely to be a goal of behavior therapy?

   a. increase amount of talking to opposite sex peers
   b. decrease social anxiety
   c. increase awareness of facial movements when anxious
   d. develop a stronger sense of confidence when with peers of the opposite sex

_____   Q17. Which of these is NOT a behavioral assessment technique?

   a. interviews
   b. ratings
   c. observations
   d. flooding
   e. physiological measures

116

_____ Q18. In which of these methods of behavioral assessment is reactivity most likely to be a potential concern?

     a. interviews
     b. reports
     c. measures of physical functioning
     d. observations

_____ Q19. Relaxation training is an important part of

     a. desensitization.
     b. modeling.
     c. implosive therapy.
     d. in vivo flooding therapy.

_____ Q20. Which of these is NOT important in behavior therapy?

     a. assessment
     b. target behaviors
     c. insight
     d. all of the above are important

_____ Q21. Which of these is NOT a modeling technique?

     a. symbolic modeling
     b. role playing
     c. covert modeling
     d. generalization modeling

_____ Q22. Self-instructional training is associated with the work of

     a. Bandura.
     b. Meichenbaum.
     c. Skinner.
     d. Wolpe.

_____ Q23. Which of these disorders can usually be treated more briefly by behavior therapy than can the other disorders?

     a. depression
     b. obsessive-compulsive disorder
     c. general anxiety
     d. phobias
     e. posttraumatic stress disorder

_____ Q24. Exposure and response prevention is a behavioral treatment most commonly applied to

     a. depression.
     b. obsessive-compulsive disorder.
     c. general anxiety.
     d. phobias.
     e. posttraumatic stress disorder.

_____ Q25. Which of these techniques is most likely to be used in behavioral group therapy?

    a. assertiveness training
    b. empathic listening skills
    c. eye movement desensitization
    d. motivational processing
    e. classical conditioning

ANSWER KEY

1. b	11. d	21. c	Q1. F	Q11. a	Q21. d
2. c	12. b	22. d	Q2. F	Q12. c	Q22. b
3. a	13. e		Q3. F	Q13. c	Q23. d
4. d	14. d		Q4. T	Q14. c	Q24. b
5. b	15. b		Q5. T	Q15. d	Q25. a
6. c	16. c		Q6. T	Q16. a	
7. c	17. b		Q7. T	Q17. d	
8. d	18. a		Q8. T	Q18. d	
9. a	19. e		Q9. F	Q19. a	
10. d			Q10. T	Q20. c	

CHAPTER 9

RATIONAL EMOTIVE BEHAVIOR THERAPY

RATIONAL EMOTIVE BEHAVIOR THERAPY SELF-INVENTORY

Directions: By comparing your beliefs about personality and therapy to those of Albert Ellis, you should have a clearer idea of how much you will need to suspend your beliefs or change attitudes to understand REBT's theory of personality and approach to therapy. You may find it helpful to complete this section before and after you read the chapter. In this way, you can see if your views have changed. There are no correct answers, only an opportunity to express your views.

Put an "X" on the line so that it indicates how much you agree or disagree with the statement: A=Agree, D=Disagree.

D_____A 1. Individuals have the potential for both rational thinking and irrational thinking.

_____ 2. Biological factors as well as social factors are important in determining personality.

_____ 3. It is desirable to be loved and accepted but not necessary.

_____ 4. We have irrational ideas without realizing it.

_____ 5. Seeking pleasure and avoiding pain is an appropriate philosophy of life.

_____ 6. Because of their irrational beliefs, individuals largely create their own emotional disturbances.

_____ 7. Therapy preferably should reduce clients' self-defeating outlook, helping them to acquire a rational philosophy of life.

_____ 8. Human interests are more important than theological ones.

_____ 9. Therapy preferably should challenge clients' illogical ideas and teach clients how to think rationally.

_____ 10. Being directive and attacking faulty thinking is an appropriate therapeutic approach.

_____ 11. Being efficient, logical, and flexible can help people get more from life.

D_____A 12. Dysfunctional beliefs can interfere with an individual's enjoyment of life.

_____ 13. Irrational thoughts play a large role in many psychological disorders.

_____ 14. Teaching clients new ways to think can be a valuable tool in therapy.

_____ 15. Problem solving is an appropriate therapeutic technique.

_____ 16. Forceful self-statements that represent rational beliefs are helpful for clients to learn so that they may change self-defeating behaviors.

_____ 17. Understanding the origins of our disturbances can yield insight that will be helpful in solving future problems.

_____ 18. Therapy should attend to clients' thinking, feeling, and behavior.

_____ 19. Disputing clients' irrational thoughts can be a helpful approach to client change.

_____ 20. Although desirable, an empathic relationship between a client and therapist is neither necessary nor sufficient for change in therapy.

HISTORY OF RATIONAL EMOTIVE BEHAVIOR THERAPY

Which influences do you think were most important in the development of Ellis's Rational Emotive Behavior Therapy?

PERSONAL LIFE

Born in Pittsburgh in 1913
Moved to New York City in 1917
Oldest of three children
Hospitalized nine times as a child for kidney disease
Became self-sufficient at an early age
Used rational approaches to deal with rejection as a young man
Undergraduate degree from City College of New York in 1934
Continues to work at the Albert Ellis Institute for Rational Living; very active in professional practice
Many awards and honors

PROFESSIONAL LIFE

Interested in philosophy of the Stoics
Influenced by European philosophers who wrote about happiness and rationality - Spinoza, Nietzsche, Kant
Studied modern philosophers' emphasis on cognition - Dewey, Russell, and Popper.
Influenced by Adler's focus on beliefs.
Started the *Journal of Rational-Emotive Behavior and Cognitive-Behavior Therapy*
Wrote over 725 articles and 65 books, including *Reason and Emotion in Psychotherapy*, 1962, *Humanistic Psychotherapy: The Rational Emotive Approach*, 1973

RATIONAL EMOTIVE THEORY OF PERSONALITY

Philosophical viewpoints as well as attention to biological and social factors have influenced the development of rational emotive behavior's theory of personality. Ellis's A-B-C model is the basis of his personality theory. Ellis believes that it is not the activating event (A) that causes positive or emotional and behavioral consequences (C), but rather it is the individual's belief system (B) that helps cause the consequences (C). When activating events are unpleasant, irrational beliefs may develop. The concepts basic to REBT's theory of personality are defined here.

120

REBT'S PHILOSOPHICAL VIEWPOINTS

Throughout his life, Ellis has had an interest in the study of philosophy. This interest influenced his focus on irrational beliefs as being a major problem for individuals. He encourages patients to consider and adopt a sensible philosophy so that it will help them enjoy their lives. Responsible hedonism, humanism, and rationality are philosophical ideas that can be seen in REBT's approach to psychotherapy.

hedonism A philosophical term referring to the concept of seeking pleasure and avoiding pain. In REBT, responsible hedonism refers to maintaining pleasure over the long-term by avoiding short-term pleasures that may lead to pain, such as alcohol or cocaine.

humanism A philosophy or value system in which human interests and dignity are valued and that takes an individualist, critical, and secular as opposed to a religious or spiritual perspective.

Unconditional Self Acceptance (USA) Individuals have worth. They should accept that they make mistakes and that some of their assets and qualities are stronger than others. Individuals' acts or performances should be criticized, not their personal worth.

rationality Thinking, feeling, and acting in ways that will help individuals attain their goals. This is in contrast to irrationality in which thinking, feeling, and acting are self-defeating and interfere with goal attainment.

FACTORS BASIC TO REBT THEORY OF PERSONALITY

Ellis recognized that individuals' personality development and their emotional disturbances were not independent of biological social aspects. Ellis believes that individuals have a biological tendency to severely disturb themselves and to prolong their emotional dysfunctioning. One reason that Ellis uses such powerful and direct therapeutic techniques is his view of the strength in which individuals hold irrational beliefs. Some of this is due to biological factors. Social factors refer to the effect of interpersonal relationships on beliefs about self. Criticism from others contributes to negative self-beliefs. Likewise, caring too much about what others think of you can negatively affect your own beliefs about yourself.

Being vulnerable to emotional disturbance for both social and biological reasons is a core view of Albert Ellis. Although individuals desire to be successful and happy, many irrational beliefs interfere with these goals. Examples of some of these are irrational beliefs about competence and success, about love and approval, about being treated unfairly, and about safety and comfort.

irrational belief Unreasonable views or convictions that produce emotional and behavioral problems.

THE RATIONAL EMOTIVE BEHAVIOR A-B-C THEORY OF PERSONALITY

Ellis's philosophical viewpoints and his focus on biological and social factors are concepts that support his basic personality theory, the A-B-C model.

    A- ACTIVATING EVENT
    B- BELIEF SYSTEM
    C- CONSEQUENCES

Briefly stated, the A-B-C model refers to what happens when an activating event (A) leads to emotional and behavioral consequences (C). The emotional and behavioral consequences are not caused by (A) the activating event but by the individual's belief system (B). Irrational beliefs occur when the activating event (A) is an unpleasant one. Irrational beliefs (B) can then partly cause difficult emotional and behavioral consequences (C).

According to Ellis, it is bad enough that individuals have irrational beliefs, but they turn these beliefs into new activating events which cause new irrational beliefs. Ellis refers to this as disturbances about disturbances. Thus, if an individual does not get a job promotion that he wants, he may say to himself, "I feel terrible and hopeless," and feels depressed. This consequence can then turn into a new activating event, and the individual can say, "This is really awful that I'm so depressed and hopeless." Now a new consequence is even greater than the original consequence. For Ellis, words such as "have to" and "must" are consequences that lead to more irrational beliefs.

musterbation Albert Ellis's phrase to characterize the behavior of clients who are inflexible and absolutistic in their thinking, maintaining that they must not fail or that they must have their way.

low frustration tolerance Inability or difficulty in dealing with events or situations that do not go as planned, for example, getting very angry because someone does not do as you ask.

RATIONAL EMOTIVE BEHAVIOR THEORY OF PSYCHOTHERAPY

The A-B-C theory of personality affects the way REBT therapists determine goals for their clients, assess their clients, and select therapeutic techniques. Disputing irrational beliefs is a most important therapeutic intervention. Being aware of how vulnerable individuals are to disturbance, Ellis has used a variety of cognitive, affective, and behavioral methods to help clients change.

GOALS

A general goal of REBT is to help clients minimize emotional disturbances, decrease self-defeating behaviors, and become happier. If individuals can think rationally and have fewer irrational beliefs, Ellis believes they will live happier lives. REBT teaches individuals how to deal with negative feelings such as sorrow, regret, frustration, depression, and anxiety. Virtually all client problems are viewed from the perspective of the contribution of their irrational beliefs.

ASSESSMENT

REBT therapists try to assess which thoughts and behaviors create problems for their clients. They may listen for themes that repeat themselves. They can conceptualize these themes more specifically by using the A-B-C theory of personality. Identifying activating events (A), rational and irrational beliefs (B), and emotional and behavioral consequences (C) is the most basic form of assessment in REBT. This assessment continues in each session and is not limited to the first few sessions. The REBT Self-Help Form that is shown in the text provides a specific method for following the A-B-C theory in assessment. Other objective personality inventories may be used, but they yield information that only indirectly applies to the A-B-C theory of personality.

THE A-B-C-D-E THERAPEUTIC APPROACH

Described in detail in the text, the A-B-C-D-E therapeutic approach is briefly summarized here. The therapeutic interventions referred to by D are three parts of disputation. When irrational beliefs are disputed, the client will experience E, a new effect. In essence, the client will have a logical philosophy that allows her to challenge her own irrational beliefs.

A (Activating Event) Therapists often divide activating events into two parts: what happened and what the patient perceived happened. Typically, therapists focus only on a few activating events at a time. Sometimes previous consequences (C) become activating events.

C (Consequences) Sometimes it is difficult for therapists to distinguish between consequences and beliefs. Consequences tend to be feelings such as "I feel so stressed out." Feelings cannot be disputed, but beliefs that bring about feelings can. Changing beliefs (B) can alter consequences (C).

B (Beliefs) Irrational or self-defeating rather than rational or self helping beliefs are the focus of therapy. Changing irrational beliefs can change consequences.

D (Disputing) Disputing irrational beliefs is the major therapeutic technique in REBT. Disputing is often done in three parts.

1. Detecting - the client and therapist detect the irrational beliefs that underlie activating events.
2. Discriminating - the therapist and client discriminate irrational from rational beliefs.
3. Debating - the therapist uses several different strategies to debate the client's irrational beliefs. These include the lecture, the Socratic debate, humor, and self-disclosure.

E (Effect) Developing an effective philosophy in which irrational beliefs have been replaced by rational beliefs is the product of successful REBT.

OTHER THERAPEUTIC APPROACHES

REBT does not limit itself to using disputing methods. Other cognitive approaches, as well as affective and behavioral methods are used. Some of the more common approaches are listed here.

OTHER COGNITIVE APPROACHES	EMOTIVE TECHNIQUES	BEHAVIORAL METHODS
coping self-statements	imagery	activity homework
cost-benefit analysis	role playing	reinforcement and penalties
psychoeducational methods	shame-attacking exercises	skill training
teaching others	forceful self-statements	
problem solving	forceful self-dialogue	

INSIGHT

Three types of insight develop from REBT that can lead to behavioral change.

1. Acknowledging that disturbances largely come from irrational beliefs not from the past.
2. Learning how one has reindoctrinated oneself with irrational beliefs from the past.
3. Accepting 1 and 2, knowing that insight does not automatically change people, and working hard to effect change.

Ellis believes that when clients have achieved all three types of insight, "elegant" change takes place. Clients have thus made changes and know why they have made the changes.

CASE EXAMPLE

Charles is an 11-year-old fifth grade student. His parents have referred him to counseling because Charles seems to be very worried. He reports difficulty sleeping and tries to eat throughout the day. He seems to have very few friends that he plays with either in the neighborhood or at school. When he gets off the bus, he typically goes right to the television set and turns it on, watching soap operas and cartoons.

Charles is a heavy set young man who has been teased because he is overweight. Few things seem to make him happy. When he is watching cartoons, he will laugh as they seem to help him take his mind off his problems.

His younger brother is in third grade and is very active. In fact, his parents think that Jack might have Attention Deficit Disorder. Charles's father is a supervisor in an automobile parts plant, and Charles's mother is an electronics technician in another factory. Neither of Charles's parents have gone to college, but both would like to see their two sons become professionals as they find their own jobs physically and emotionally draining. Charles's mother worries that she has had to leave Jack and Charles in the care of neighbors or occasionally with her mother. Now that both boys seem to be having problems at school, she worries about being an inadequate mother and feels that she may have made a mistake to keep working. However, the family has a high mortgage on their house and are overdue on some of their bills.

Charles has been sent to see you because he is having trouble at school. You will try to help him using the A-B-C-D-E theory of REBT.

When you see Charles, he tells you that he hates school and hates the kids at school. His academic work is at the B level, but he would like it to be higher. He does spend some time helping some of his teachers with tasks like cleaning the blackboard. He tries to stay close to them and worries about being physically beaten by bullies when he goes out onto the playground. His self-esteem is quite low, and he doesn't feel that he is doing well in school at all. In terms of social relationships at school, Charles thinks that the other children consider him to be a nerd and boring. He feels isolated and does not think that other children will want to be with him. He hates when he is teased about his weight, called "fatty" and "big butt."

1. Using rational emotive behavior theory, which of the following statements best describes appropriate goals for Charles to further understand why he is so defensive?

   a. to learn to stand up for himself
   b. to think more rationally about this situation and to act more effectively in achieving goals of living happily
   c. to understand his angry feelings
   d. to speak more assertively to his peers

2. If Charles says to you, "I get so upset when I get a C on a math test at school, I feel like such a moron," a sub-goal that you might have for Charles might be to

   a. change his irrational beliefs about his academic performance.
   b. involve his parents in a parent-teacher conference.
   c. do family therapy with Charles and his parents.
   d. help Charles express his feelings about mistreatment at school.

3. As you try to assess Charles's problems at school and with peers, what types of information are you likely to listen for?

   a. the activating events that cause problems for Charles
   b. the hurtful, angry, and frustrating feelings that are a consequence of the activating events
   c. Charles's belief about the activating events
   d. all of the above

4. When you work with Charles to help him with his problems, which of the following are you most likely to concentrate on helping him change and improve?

   a. the activating events that cause problems for Charles
   b. the hurtful, angry, and frustrating feelings that are a consequence of the activating events
   c. Charles's beliefs about the activating events.
   d. all of the above.

5. In trying to develop a good relationship with Charles, one of the most important things to do is

   a. intervene with his teachers, telling them how to behave with Charles.
   b. let Charles know that you really care for him and want to help him with his problems.
   c. help Charles solve some of his immediate problems as quickly as possible.
   d. help Charles improve his relationship with Jack and his parents.

6. When Charles says, "All of the other boys in my class ignore me except Ralph," his statement refers to a (an)

   a. activating event.
   b. belief.
   c. consequence.
   d. disputing.
   e. effect.

7. His statement, "I feel terrible that nobody but Ralph will play with me" refers to a (an)

   a. activating event.
   b. belief.
   c. consequence.
   d. disputing.
   e. effect.

8. Charles's statement, "I have to have these kids like me" is best described by which of the following terms?
   a. activating event
   b. belief
   c. consequence
   d. disputing
   e. effect

To dispute Charles's negative beliefs, it is helpful first to detect when there is a belief, next to discriminate rational from irrational beliefs and third, to debate the irrational belief.

9. Which of the following would be an appropriate REBT debating statement in reply to Charles saying, "I must do well at school or I'll never be able to do well next year"?

   a. Don't worry, this year has been difficult, but next year will be better.
   b. You really are very conscientious and want to do so well at school, it's admirable.
   c. You are upset that school isn't going well and fearful that next year will be just as bad.
   d. You say you must do well. It would be nice to do well, but you can manage all right, and accept yourself as a person even if you don't live up to your expectations.

The following three statements express irrational beliefs. Write down an appropriate REBT response that debates Charles's belief, and then check it with the answer at the end of the chapter to see how similar your response is.

*OE1. "I have to do well on this book report for English. If I don't, I'll just about die."

_____

_____

*OE2. "If I have to sit by myself at lunch again, I will stand out as the stupidest kid in the cafeteria."

_____

_____

*OE3. "I have to do better at school than Ralph. He really isn't that bright. When he gets a better grade on a paper, I just can't stand it."

_____

_____

The answers that I have given at the end of the chapter are just examples of ways to respond to Charles's irrational beliefs. Your answer does not have to be the same as mine, but it should show that you're disputing Charles's irrational beliefs.

REBT therapists use many other approaches besides disputing. In the following questions, identify the type of approach that an REBT therapist is using with Charles.

10. "Charles, I would like you to learn more about the REBT method so you can apply it yourself when situations come up with other children or at school." This is an example of

    a. imagery.
    b. problem solving.
    c. psycho-educational methods.
    d. cost-benefit analysis
    e. coping self-statements.

11. "Charles, when you are in a situation when you can identify an irrational belief about getting a poor grade at school, say to yourself several times, 'I won't be killed if I get a bad grade. I have done well at school and can do well again.'" This technique is an example of

    a. imagery.
    b. problem solving.
    c. psycho-educational methods.
    d. cost-benefit analysis
    e. coping self-statements.

12. "Charles, when you get upset before a test, say to yourself, 'I want to get an A, *but I don't have to!'* Make that last part of the sentence powerful as you say it to yourself." This is an example of

    a. role playing.
    b. a shame attacking exercise.
    c. a forceful self-statement.
    d. a forceful self-dialogue.

13. "When you don't criticize yourself for doing poorly on an exam, I would like you to reward yourself. What do you think would be a good reward for you?" This method is an example of

    a. imagery.
    b. forceful self-statements.
    c. skill training.
    d. a reinforcement.

14. When Charles realizes that his problems are not from being teased and having difficulty at school but from having irrational beliefs about these events, he is

    a. having insight into his problems from an REBT point of view.
    b. successfully making use of a shame-attacking exercise.
    c. effectively disputing major irrational beliefs that he has encountered.
    d. able to teach others how they too may dispute irrational beliefs.

SPECIAL TOPICS

OE4. What aspects of REBT would tend to make it a brief form of therapy? (344)

_____

_____

_____

_____

OE5. In what ways can REBT be seen as a constructivist approach to therapy? (345)

_____

_____

_____

_____

OE6. In which other theories do you think the REBT disputational technique could be applied? Explain. (346)

_____

_____

_____

_____

OE7. Would REBT be as applicable for women as for men? Explain. (347)

_____

_____

_____

_____

OE8. Would you agree with Ellis that REBT would be applicable to people from all cultures? Explain. (349)

_____

_____

_____

_____

-

STRENGTHS AND LIMITATIONS

What do you believe are the strengths and limitations of REBT therapy?

Strengths   Limitations

_____   _____

_____   _____

_____   _____

_____   _____

_____   _____

_____   _____

_____   _____

_____   _____

REBT THERAPY: A QUIZ

True/false items. Decide if the following statements are more "true" or more "false" as they apply to REBT.

T F Q1. REBT is primarily a cognitive therapy but also attends to feelings and behavior.

T F Q2. To help individuals improve their psychological functioning, therapists should help clients change the activating events rather than their beliefs about the events.

T F Q3. REBT is a mechanistic rather than a humanistic approach.

T F Q4. Vulnerability to disturbance is a factor in determining the extent to which individuals may have psychological problems.

T F Q5. According to REBT, beliefs that individuals hold are all, to some degree, irrational.

T F Q6. Helping individuals minimize emotional disturbance is a major goal of REBT.

T F Q7. REBT has philosophical underpinnings that include responsible hedonism.

T F Q8. Disputation is the most important technique in REBT.

T F Q9. Disputation is the only technique in REBT.

T F Q10. Most REBT techniques have been developed to deal with individuals' irrational beliefs.

Multiple choice items. Select the *best answer* from the alternatives using an REBT perspective.

_____ Q11. Which of the following is not a part of REBT philosophy?

    a. responsible hedonism
    b. humanism
    c. existentialism
    d. rationality

_____ Q12. Activating events can be

    a. pleasant.
    b. unpleasant.
    c. rational.
    d. irrational.
    e. all of the above.

_____ Q13. An individual's vulnerability to disturbance depends on

    a. social factors.
    b. biological factors.
    c. neither a or b.
    d. both a and b.

_____ Q14. "I feel terrible now that my husband left me," is likely to be a (an)

    a. activating event.
    b. belief.
    c. consequence.
    d. all of the above.

_____ Q15. "My husband left me" refers to a (an)

    a. activating event.
    b. belief.
    c. consequence.
    d. all of the above.

_____ Q16. "My husband wouldn't have left me if I weren't so terrible a wife" refers to a (an)

    a. activating event.
    b. belief.
    c. consequence.
    d. all of the above.

_____ Q17. Having disturbances about disturbances refers to turning a (an)

    a. consequence into a new activating event.
    b. activating event into a new consequence.
    c. activating event into a new activating event.
    d. consequence into a new consequence.

_____ Q18. Which of the following words or phrases would turn this statement into an irrational belief? "I _____ go to graduate school."

    a. would like to
    b. would not like to
    c. can afford to
    d. must

_____ Q19. "I have to find the right solution to my marital problems" is an example of a (an)

    a. rational belief.
    b. irrational belief.
    c. low frustration tolerance statement.
    d. disputation.

_____ Q20. In assessing client problems, therapists listen mainly to

    a. clients describing biological factors to determine which are most important.
    b. clients describing social factors to determine which are most important.
    c. clients describing their feelings and behaviors that they feel are caused by specific experiences and the beliefs that clients have about the specific experience.
    d. none of the above.

_____ Q21. In REBT, the goal of therapy may be reached if the client has achieved

    a. A.
    b. B.
    c. C.
    d. D.
    e. E.

_____ Q22. The most important treatment technique in REBT is the use of

    a. coping self-statements.
    b. disputing.
    c. role playing.
    d. forceful self-statements.

_____ Q23. In REBT, skills training is a (an) _____ technique.

    a. behavioral
    b. cognitive
    c. emotive
    d. all of the above

_____ Q24. Which of the following shows that the client has a philosophical understanding of REBT?

    a. imagery
    b. insight
    c. disputing
    d. teaching others

Q25. From a multicultural perspective, REBT can be criticized as placing an overemphasis on

    a. assessment.
    b. beliefs.
    c. existentialism.
    d. self-sufficiency.

ANSWER KEY

1.	b	11.	e	Q1.	T	Q11.	c	Q21.	e
2.	a	12.	c	Q2.	F	Q12.	e	Q22.	b
3.	d	13.	d	Q3.	F	Q13.	d	Q23.	a
4.	c	14.	a	Q4.	T	Q14.	c	Q24.	b
5.	c			Q5.	F	Q15.	a	Q25.	d
6.	a			Q6.	T	Q16.	b		
7.	c			Q7.	T	Q17.	a		
8.	b			Q8.	T	Q18.	d		
9.	d			Q9.	F	Q19.	b		
10.	c			Q10.	T	Q20.	c		

*OE1.   It would be nice to get an A, but you don't *have* to. You won't die. How bad would a B or B+ be?

*OE2.   You say that if you eat alone, others will think you are stupid. Do you believe that's accurate?

*OE3.   How terrible could it be if Ralph does better on a paper than you?

CHAPTER 10

COGNITIVE THERAPY

COGNITIVE THERAPY SELF-INVENTORY

Directions: By comparing your beliefs about personality and therapy to those of cognitive therapy, you should have a clearer idea of how much you will need to suspend your beliefs or change attitudes to understand the cognitive theory of personality and approach to therapy. You may find it helpful to complete this section before and after you read the chapter. In this way, you can see if your views have changed. There are no correct answers, only an opportunity to express your views.

Put an "X" on the line so that it indicates how much you agree or disagree with the statement: A=Agree, D=Disagree.

D_____A 1. People have thoughts that influence their behavior that they are not aware of.

_____ 2. The way individuals think about themselves and their world very much influences how they feel about themselves.

_____ 3. An individual develops a set of beliefs in early childhood that influences later development.

_____ 4. When an individual starts to have strong negative thoughts or distorted thoughts, this thinking can sometimes be seen in the person's facial or bodily movements.

_____ 5. Basic sets of beliefs that individuals have can lead to several types of psychological disorders later on.

_____ 6. Distorted thinking can lead to depression.

_____ 7. Exaggerating an event so that it becomes a catastrophe can contribute to psychological problems.

_____ 8. A basic goal of therapy is to remove biases or distortions in thinking.

_____ . In therapy, it is important to have specific goals and prioritize those.

_____ 10. Goals are developed in collaboration with the client.

D_____A 11. Keeping track of thoughts outside of therapy can be a useful adjunct to therapy.

_____ 12. Scales and questionnaires are very helpful in assessing psychological problems.

_____ 13. Guiding individuals to understand how they distort their thoughts can be helpful in therapy.

_____ 14. Studying the effectiveness of therapy is essential in the development of a theory of psychotherapy.

_____ 15. The best way to change dysfunctional feelings and behaviors is to modify inaccurate and faulty thinking.

_____ 16. Challenging absolutes such as "always" and "never" is a helpful therapeutic technique.

_____ 17. When starting therapy, it is helpful to plan for the end of therapy.

_____ 18. Different cognitive techniques should be used for different psychological disorders.

_____ 19. Putting labels on types of distorted thinking can be useful in therapy.

_____ 20. The therapist's role is to help clients find evidence that either supports or refutes their hypotheses and views.

HISTORY OF COGNITIVE THERAPY

Which influences do you think were most important in the development of Beck's cognitive therapy?

PERSONAL AND PROFESSIONAL LIFE

Born in 1921
1946 - M.D. from Yale
1948 - Internship and Residency at Rhode Island Hospital
Resident in neurology and psychiatry at Cushing VA Hospital in Framingham, Massachusetts
Fellow in psychiatry at Austen Riggs Center in Stockbridge, Massachusetts
1953 - Certified by American Board of Psychiatry and Neurology
Joined Department of Psychiatry of the Medical School of the University of Pennsylvania
1958 - Graduated from Philadelphia Psychoanalytic Institute
Research on depression
Founded Beck Institute for Cognitive Therapy and Research at the University of Pennsylvania

THEORETICAL INFLUENCES

Trained as a psychoanalyst
Freud's emphasis on unconscious processes
Adler's focus on beliefs and ways to change them
Ellis's active and challenging approaches to irrational beliefs
Kelly's theory of personal constructs
Piaget's developmental approach to the study of cognition
Cognitive science models of intellectual functioning

COGNITIVE THEORY OF PERSONALITY

Beck believes that psychological disorders are caused by a combination of biological, environmental, and social factors. Rarely is one of these a cause for a disorder. In understanding psychological disturbance, Beck uses a cognitive model of development that includes the impact of early childhood experiences on the development of cognitive schemas and automatic thoughts. Beliefs and schemas are subject to cognitive distortions, a key concept in cognitive therapy.

133

THE COGNITIVE MODEL OF DEVELOPMENT

As individuals develop, they think about their world and themselves in different ways. Their beliefs and assumptions about people, events, and themselves are cognitive schemas. Individuals have automatic thoughts that are derived from these beliefs that they may not be aware of. How individuals shift from adaptive beliefs to distorted beliefs is referred to as cognitive shifts in Beck's system. These concepts are defined below.

schemas or *cognitive schemas* Ways of thinking that comprise a set of core beliefs and assumptions about how the world operates.

automatic thoughts Notions or ideas that occur without effort or choice, that can be distorted, and lead to emotional responses. Automatic thoughts provide data about core beliefs.

cognitive shift Basically a biased interpretation of life experiences, occurring when individuals shift their focus from unbiased to more biased information about themselves or their world.

negative cognitive shift A state in which individuals ignore positive information relative to themselves and focus on negative information about themselves.

affective shift A shift in facial or bodily expressions of emotion or stress indicating that a cognitive shift has just taken place, often a negative cognitive shift. Often an indication of a hot cognition.

hot cognitions A strong or highly charged thought or idea that produces powerful emotional reactions.

COGNITIVE DISTORTIONS

Automatic thoughts are subject to cognitive distortion. Cognitive therapists have identified a variety of cognitive distortions that can be found in different psychological disorders. Eleven of these are described in the text and are defined here along with "cognitive distortions".

cognitive distortions Systematic errors in reasoning, often stemming from early childhood errors in reasoning; an indication of inaccurate or ineffective information processing.

all-or-nothing thinking Engaging in black-or-white thinking. Thinking in extremes, such as all good or all bad, with nothing in the middle.

selective abstraction Selecting one idea or fact from an event while ignoring other facts in order to support negative thinking.

mind reading Believing that we know the thoughts in another person's mind.

negative prediction Believing that something bad is going to happen even though there is no evidence to support this prediction.

catastrophizing Exaggerating the potential or real consequences of an event and becoming fearful of the consequences.

overgeneralization An example of distorted thinking that occurs when individuals make a rule based on a few negative or isolated events and then apply it broadly.

labeling Creating a negative view of oneself based on errors or mistakes that one has made. It is a type of overgeneralizing which affects one's view of oneself.

magnification A cognitive distortion in which an imperfection is exaggerated into something greater than it is.

minimization Making a positive event much less important than it really is.

personalization A cognitive distortion in which an individual takes an event and relates it to himself or herself when there is no relationship. An example would be, "Whenever I want to go skiing, there is no snow." Wanting to go skiing does not cause a lack of snow.

Discriminating one type of cognitive distortion from another is sometimes difficult. Individuals may present distortions that may fall into more than one category or have elements of more than one distortion.

CASE EXAMPLE

Beth is a 20-year-old college sophomore majoring in marketing. She is very concerned about her grades and her performance in class this semester. Particularly, she is worried about her accounting course which is necessary for her to complete in order to continue with her program in marketing. She dislikes it so much that she finds it difficult to stay in class without being upset.

Throughout her schoolwork, in elementary, middle, and high school, she has been worried about doing well. An only child, she worries about displeasing her parents who would like to see her finish college and have a successful career. Her father is an accountant, and her mother is a chemical engineer. Although neither parent has pressed her to enter a particular career, the pressure seems to come from Beth herself.

Sometimes she gets very upset with herself for not doing well and feels like a failure. Although she maintained a B-average in her first year of colllege, this was not satisfactory to her.

Beth has had trouble making friends at college. Living at school three hours away from home has been difficult for her. She misses her parents and her boyfriend who is at a local community college. Although she was friendly with women on her floor last year, she has not kept up these friendships and has few friendships in her new dormitory. When people ask her to go out with them, she often declines and stays inside. She is feeling lonely and worthless.

1. Beth says to you: "I have to get an A on the economics exam, otherwise, everything is lost." This is an example of

    a. all-or-nothing thinking.
    b. negative prediction.
    c. labeling.
    d. personalization.

2. In talking about her problems, Beth says: "I know my accounting professor doesn't like me. He has never spoken to me, but I can just tell." This is an example of

    a. all-or-nothing thinking.
    b. mind reading.
    c. negative thinking.
    d. catastrophizing.

3. In discussing her schoolwork, Beth says, "I got a D on my first accounting exam. I know I can't do accounting at all." This is an example of

    a. irrational thinking.
    b. selective abstraction.
    c. overgeneralization.
    d. mislabeling.

4. Beth says, "I know when I go home this weekend and see my boyfriend, things will go badly. He's going to tell me I don't spend enough time with him, and I will just get mad at him. I know that I'm going to get furious and things will go terribly." This is an example of

    a. catastrophizing.
    b. all-or-nothing thinking.
    c. minimization.
    d. personalization.

5. Throughout school, Beth has come to believe that she will not do well academically. She believes that other students are smarter that she is. Furthermore, she believes that no matter how hard she works, she won't do well. This set of beliefs can be called a (an)

    a. critical incident.
    b. automatic thought.
    c. cognitive schema.
    d. cognitive shift.

THEORY OF COGNITIVE THERAPY

In cognitive therapy, client and therapist combine to examine thinking patterns and behaviors and change them so that the client can function more effectively. The focus of therapy is often on distorted thinking, such as that shown in the five previous questions. Assessment is quite detailed, more so than in REBT. Techniques challenge the client's distorted thoughts and replace them with more effective thinking.

GOALS OF THERAPY

Cognitive therapy focuses on distorted or biased thinking. Removing such thinking is the goal of cognitive therapy. Since clients often have many negative thoughts, therapists and clients prioritize goals and examine thoughts specifically.

6. Which of these is most likely to be a goal for Beth?

    a. to become a more fully functioning individual.
    b. to identify her catastrophic thinking and overgeneralizations, replacing them with more accurate thinking.
    c. to become more aware of her unconscious motivation to fail.
    d. to be able to relax when studying.

ASSESSMENT IN COGNITIVE THERAPY

Attention to detail is a hallmark of cognitive therapy. In interviews, therapists ask many questions about the presenting problem, past problems, past traumatic experiences, and medical history. Questions elicit details to help therapists make assessments about distorted thinking. Scales and questionnaires, several developed by Aaron Beck, assess for depression, suicide, and other concerns. These may be administered to clients prior to each session. Another method is self monitoring that uses forms such as the Dysfunctional Thoughts Record. Still other methods are used for sampling thoughts.

self-monitoring A method of assessing thoughts, emotions, or behaviors outside of therapy in which clients are asked to keep records of events, feelings, and/or thoughts.

thought sampling A means of obtaining samples of thoughts outside of therapy by asking the client to record thoughts on tape or in a notebook at different intervals.

A cognitive therapist might explain the concept of automatic thoughts to Beth and ask her to write them down on a Dysfunctional Thought Record.

7. Which of these items would not be found on a Dysfunctional Thought Record?

  a. automatic thoughts
  b. actual events
  c. emotions
  d. rational response to the automatic thought
  e. all would be found on the Dysfunctional Thought Record

8. If Beth records her thoughts randomly on a tape recorder and brings them in to discuss with the therapist, she is using the technique of

  a. self-monitoring.
  b. thought sampling.
  c. scaling.
  d. specifying automatic thoughts.

THERAPEUTIC TECHNIQUES

Cognitive therapy techniques are often challenging and specific. Socratic dialogue helps to challenge maladaptive beliefs and assumptions. Basically, it is a series of questions that are designed to help the client arrive at logical answers to and conclusions about a certain hypothesis. The three-question technique is a form of guided discovery. Clients are often asked to specify automatic thoughts by recording them on the Dysfunctional Thought Record or through thought sampling. The client can then bring material to therapy so that the client and therapist can challenge maladaptive assumptions or ineffective beliefs. Several different techniques are used for challenging different distorted beliefs. The ones that are listed in the text are defined here.

challenging absolutes Statements that include words such as "everyone", "never", "no one", and "always" are usually exaggerations which therapists point out to the client.

reattribution Helping clients distribute responsibility for an event (such as an argument) so as to equally place responsibility for the event.

decatastrophizing A "what if" technique, in which clients are asked, "What if X happened, what would you do?" It is designed to explore actual rather than feared events.

scaling A technique of turning a dichotomy into a continuum so that individuals do not see things as "all or nothing." It is used in challenging dichotomous thinking.

cognitive rehearsal A means of using imagination to think about having a positive interaction or experience. For example, to imagine a positive interaction with one's future in-laws.

Some cognitive therapy concepts are associated primarily with certain disorders. For example, the cognitive triad is associated with depression but also may be used to describe negative views or beliefs as they apply to other disorders. Habituation training is a technique that is used most often with obsessive-compulsive disorder and more specifically with obsessional thought.

cognitive triad The negative views that individuals have about themselves, their world, and their future.

habituation training A technique of deliberately evoking a thought, writing the thought down, and focusing on an intrusive or obsessional thought.

In the following questions, you will be Beth's therapist. Pick the statement that fits most closely with cognitive therapy.

9. Beth says to you, "All the other students can learn accounting better than I can."

   a. Why do you think the course is so difficult for you?
   b. Have you considered getting tutoring so that you can do better?
   c. You seem to assume that all the students in the class do better than you. How do you know?
   d. Accounting is so frustrating for you.

10. Beth says to you, "I never understand anything that's going on in class." The cognitive technique that you are most likely to use is

   a. challenging absolutes.
   b. challenging all-or-nothing thinking.
   c. labeling of distortions.
   d. reattribution.

11. Beth says to you, "Whenever I go to accounting class, everything is so blah." You reply to her, "What do you mean by blah? Can you tell me more about how you feel?" You are using the technique of

   a. challenging absolutes.
   b. labeling of distortions.
   c. reattribution.
   d. understanding idiosyncratic meaning.

12. Beth says, "If I fail my accounting exam, I don't know what I will do. There's no reason to stay in school or to keep on living." Which of the following techniques are you most likely to use?

   a. understanding idiosyncratic meaning.
   b. decatastrophizing.
   c. reattribution.
   d. cognitive rehearsal.

13. Which of the following would help Beth decatastrophize her statement in question 12?

   a. Have you ever considered killing yourself before?
   b. You seem to be thinking that things will be all good or all bad.
   c. Getting an F is a big assumption. Let's really take a look at what would happen if you got an F in accounting and what you would do.
   d. What do you mean by "failing?"

14. Beth is planning to talk to her professor about her difficulty in the accounting course. She is very much afraid of his potential criticism of her for doing badly. Which technique are you most likely to use in helping her prepare for her talk with her professor?

   a. challenging absolutes
   b. reattribution
   c. decatastrophizing
   d. cognitive rehearsal

   In working with Beth, you are likely to have an opportunity to challenge her distorted thinking on many occasions. It is not necessary for you to challenge her each time. You would also help her develop new alternative responses to her automatic thoughts. You are also likely to use behavioral techniques such as reinforcing her successes and teaching her new skills. There are also times when you may respond to her empathically using person-centered techniques.

SPECIAL TOPICS

OE1.   What aspects of patients and their problems are likely to make cognitive therapy brief? (385)

_____

_____

_____

_____

OE2.   Why do you think treatment manuals can be effective in cognitive therapy? (385)

_____

_____

_____

OE3.   How are REBT and cognitive therapy different from each other? (385)

   Both approaches try to make changes in the clients' belief system. Ellis focuses on irrational beliefs and uses the A-B-C-D-E theory to challenge irrational beliefs of all types. Beck identifies different types of cognitive distortions (a concept similar to irrational beliefs) and has developed different methods for challenging these distortions. Ellis applies his approach to all disorders. Beck has different suggestions and techniques for different disorders. In many ways, their approaches seem to be quite similar, but the language that they use is rather different. Both tend to challenge the clients' belief system. Beck uses different challenging methods for different disorders, whereas Ellis uses disputing, primarily, for most disorders.

OE4.   How can cognitive therapy help women and sexual minorities dispute their distorted beliefs while at the same time recognizing the value of their own views? (390)

_____

_____

_____

OE5.   How can therapists separate their own cultural beliefs from their view of what constitutes distorted beliefs? (391)

_____

_____

_____

_____

139

STRENGTHS AND LIMITATIONS

What do you believe are the strengths and limitations of cognitive therapy?

Strengths	Limitations
_____	_____
_____	_____
_____	_____
_____	_____
_____	_____
_____	_____
_____	_____
_____	_____

COGNITIVE THERAPY: A QUIZ

True/false items: Decide if the following statements are more "true" or more "false" as they apply to cognitive therapy.

T   F   Q1. Freud's psychoanalysis had an indirect influence on the development of cognitive therapy.

T   F   Q2. Beck's cognitive therapy uses techniques similar to psychoanalysis.

T   F   Q3. Cognitive schemas develop from childhood beliefs about oneself and one's world.

T   F   Q4. Automatic thoughts can be exaggerated or inaccurate.

T   F   Q5. Socratic dialogue is an example of distorted thinking.

T   F   Q6. Removing biases and distortions so that individuals can think more effectively is a major goal of cognitive therapy.

T   F   Q7. The Beck Depression Inventory is used for thought sampling.

T   F   Q8. Different therapeutic techniques are used for different psychological disorders.

T   F   Q9. Habituation training is a technique used for obsessive-compulsive disorders.

T   F   Q10. Cognitive therapists assess patients' thoughts, not their feelings or behaviors.

Multiple choice items. Select the *best answer* from the alternatives using a cognitive therapy perspective.

_____ Q11. A developmental approach to understanding how children think was pioneered by

   a. Ellis.
   b. Kelly.
   c. Liese.
   d. Piaget.

_____ Q12. Beck's cognitive schemas bear a resemblance to the personal construct theory of

   a. Ellis.
   b. Kelly.
   c. Liese.
   d. Piaget.

_____ Q13. Individuals may have a number of different cognitions such as "I run slowly," "I'm uncoordinated," "I can't play baseball," "I am always chosen last for a team." These cognitions may exist without a person being aware of them. These thoughts are called

   a. automatic thoughts.
   b. cognitive schemas.
   c. hot cognitions.
   d. negative prediction.

_____ Q14. When the statements from Question 13 are viewed as a whole and represent a belief such as "I'm no good at sports," this belief may represent

   a.   automatic thoughts.
   b.   cognitive schemas.
   c.   hot cognitions.
   d.   negative prediction.

_____ Q15. Which of the following is NOT a cognitive distortion?

   a.   catastrophizing
   b.   cognitive schema
   c.   magnification
   d.   personalization

_____ Q16. "I know that I will have a bad day today" is an example of which type of cognitive distortion?

   a.   all-or-nothing thinking
   b.   selective abstraction
   c.   negative prediction
   d.   mislabeling

_____ Q17. The Dysfunctional Thought Record is an example of

   a.   an interviewing technique.
   b.   a scale.
   c.   self-monitoring.
   d.   thought sampling.

_____ Q18. Which of the following questions is not used in the three-question techniques?

    a.   What is the evidence for the belief?
    b.   How do you feel about your belief?
    c.   How else can you interpret the situation?
    d.   If it is true, what are the implications?

_____ Q19 Jim: If it hadn't been for me, Bob wouldn't have hit me.
Therapist: You said Bob was very drunk. That would seem to play a large role in Bob hitting you.

What cognitive therapy technique is the therapist using?

    a.   understanding idiosyncratic meaning
    b.   challenging absolutes
    c.   reattribution
    d.   decatastrophizing

_____ Q20. Carla: I can't do anything right.
Therapist: Let's talk about some of the things that you do that work well for you.

Which cognitive technique is the therapist using?

    a.   understanding idiosyncratic meaning
    b.   challenging absolutes
    c.   reattribution
    d.   decatastrophizing

_____ Q21. Mary: My boss criticizes me constantly on all of my projects.
Therapist: I believe you may be overgeneralizing from that one time your boss reprimanded you.

Which cognitive technique is the therapist using?

    a.   challenging absolutes
    b.   reattribution
    c.   labeling of distortions
    d.   cognitive rehearsal

_____ Q22. The cognitive schema of hypervigilance is associated with

    a.   depression.
    b.   general anxiety disorder.
    c.   obsessive-compulsive disorder.
    d.   drug abuse.

_____ Q23. The disorder that has generated the most research from cognitive therapy researchers has been

    a.   depression.
    b.   general anxiety disorder.
    c.   obsessive-compulsive disorder.
    d.   drug abuse.

_____ Q24. Defusing thoughts from actions is a technique used in treating

    a. depression.
    b. general anxiety disorder.
    c. obsessive-compulsive disorder.
    d. drug abuse.

_____ Q25. Which of these techniques is most likely to be used in cognitive group therapy?

    a. Suggest new ways of thinking about a problem
    b. Reflect the silence of group members
    c. Analyze the feelings of the therapist towards group members
    d. Educate members about contact boundary disturbances

ANSWER KEY

1. a	11. d	Q1. T	Q11. d	Q21. c
2. b	12. b	Q2. F	Q12. b	Q22. b
3. c	13. c	Q3. T	Q13. a	Q23. a
4. a	14. d	Q4. T	Q14. b	Q24. c
5. c		Q5. F	Q15. b	Q25. a
6. b		Q6. T	Q16. c	
7. e		Q7. F	Q17. c	
8. b		Q8. T	Q18. b	
9. c		Q9. T	Q19. c	
10. a		Q10. F	Q20. b	

CHAPTER 11

REALITY THERAPY

REALITY THERAPY SELF-INVENTORY

Directions: By comparing your beliefs about personality and therapy to those of reality therapy, you should have a clearer idea of how much you will need to suspend your beliefs or change attitudes to understand the reality theory of personality and approach to therapy. You may find it helpful to complete this section before and after you read the chapter. In this way, you can see if your views have changed. There are no correct answers, only an opportunity to express your views.

Put an "X" on the line so that it indicates how much you agree or disagree with the statement: A=Agree, D=Disagree.

D_____A   1. Understanding how people make choices helps in understanding their personality.

_____   2. A major goal of therapy is for clients to become responsible for their actions.

_____   3. To be responsible means to meet one's own needs so that the needs of others are not interfered with.

_____   4. Individuals are responsible for the choices that they make.

_____   5. Focusing on unconscious motivation gives clients excuses for avoiding responsibility.

_____   6. Clients should evaluate their own behavior and decide what changes to make.

_____   7. Therapy should focus on present behavior rather than past behavior.

_____   8. Our perceptions of the world are more important than reality itself.

_____   9. We choose behaviors that keep us anxious and depressed.

_____   10. The therapist does not judge the client's behavior. This should be left to judges, school administrators, and others.

_____   11. The therapist's role includes teaching and educating.

_____   12. The therapist should take a friendly and involved approach to helping clients.

<u>D</u>_____<u>A</u> 13. The major focus in therapy should be changing behavior rather than thoughts and feelings.

_____ 14. Discussion of transference distracts from the therapeutic focus on clients' choices and plans.

_____ 15. In therapy, clients should evaluate the quality of their behavior.

_____ 16. Planning for actions and following through with plans is an important part of therapy.

_____ 17. Making excuses, blaming, or explaining why a particular plan failed should be minimized or not discussed in therapy.

_____ 18. Focusing on the client's positive aspects is more helpful than focusing on negative aspects.

_____ 19. Punishment is not an effective therapeutic technique.

_____ 20. Positive addictions, like running, can be helpful for some clients.

HISTORY OF REALITY THERAPY

Which influences do you think were most important in the development of William Glasser's reality therapy?

PERSONAL AND
PROFESSIONAL LIFE

Glasser born in Cleveland, Ohio in 1925.
1944 - undergraduate degree in chemical engineering
1953 -MD from Case Western Reserve; Psychiatric residency at VA Center in Los Angeles and the University of California at Los Angeles.
1956 - consulting psychiatrist at a state institution for delinquent adolescent girls
Consulted in the California school system.
1962 - Influenced by Harrington's active approach with chronic and regressed psychotic patients.

BOOKS

1965 - *Reality Therapy*
1969 - *Schools Without Failure*
1981 - *Stations of the Mind*
A book influenced by William Power's *Behavior: The Control of Perception* (1973)
1986 - *Control Theory in the Classroom*
1990 - *The Quality School*
1998 - *Choice Theory: A New Psychology of Personal Freedom*
2000 - *Counseling with Choice Theory*
2000 - *Every Student Can Succeed*
2000 - *Getting Together and Staying Together*

PROFESSIONAL
ORGANIZATIONS

1967 - Institute for Reality Therapy, founded
1968 - Educator's Training Center (a branch of the Institute for Reality Therapy), founded
1973 -Training and certification for reality therapists initiated
1981 - International organization for Reality Therapists started - annual meetings
Current - The William Glasser Institute is now the new name for the Institute for Reality Therapy.

PERSONALITY THEORY: CHOICE THEORY

Glasser believed that individuals have control over their lives and make choices about their lives for which they are responsible. His first theory of personality was called control theory, focusing on the control that individuals have in handling their emotional problems. To differentiate this theory from Powers' control theory and to make clear that he is not talking about controlling other people, Glasser changed the name for his personality theory to Choice Theory with his 1998 book, *Choice Theory: A New Psychology of Personal Freedom*. Glasser believes that individuals have perceptions of reality which determine their behavior - actions, thoughts, and feelings. Perceptions or pictures of our world are used to satisfy needs (belonging, power, freedom, and fun). Individuals make choices to meet their needs. Acting on these choices accounts for an individual's total behavior - doing, thinking, feeling, and physiology. If we have choices about how we behave, why would we choose to behave in ways that make ourselves unhappy? Glasser describes a number of reasons why depression, anxiety, and other disorders serve to meet individual's needs in limiting ways.

PICTURES OF REALITY

The perceptions and images that individuals have of the world around them influences how individuals' needs are met. We cannot know reality itself but only our perceptions which we then can compare to others' perceptions of reality.

NEEDS

To satisfy needs that we have, we develop pictures of our reality. These are perceptions of people, objects, or events. Glasser believes that our perceptions that are used to satisfy our needs are primarily visual. The four basic psychological needs according to Glasser are belonging, power, freedom, and fun.

belonging The need to love, to share, and to cooperate with others.

power The need to control others and be better than others.

freedom How we wish to live our lives, express ourselves, and worship. Included also are choices about who we associate with, what we wish to read or write, and how we wish to create or behave.

fun Included are hobbies and things we do for amusement such as sports, reading, collecting, laughing, and joking.

Needs often conflict with each other. In romantic relationships, the need for belongingness and the need for power are often negotiated so that couples can work out harmonious relationships. In political situations, a person's need for power may conflict with someone else's need for freedom. We meet these needs through our perceptions of the world around us.

CHOICE

Often choices are made without awareness that we are choosing. According to Glasser, we choose to be depressed. He prefers to say a person is not *depressed* but *chooses to depress* or is in the act of *depressing*. These choices are made without awareness. However, Glasser believes individuals can control their choices to depress, to anger, or to be anxious.

BEHAVIOR

For Glasser, behavior is how we act to deal with ourselves and the world around us. Individuals respond in very creative ways, sometimes very positive such as through music or art, and sometimes in negative ways such as through suicide or murder.

total behavior Refers to four components in reality therapy: Doing, thinking, feeling, and physiology.

doing These are active behaviors such as walking, talking, writing or eating.

thinking Voluntary and involuntary thoughts, including daydreams and night dreams, make up this aspect of total behavior.

feelings Included are emotions such as happiness, satisfaction, pleasure, anger, and irritation.

physiology Voluntary and involuntary mechanisms such as sweating and urinating make up this aspect of total behavior.

For Glasser, the key to changing behavior is in changing our doing, in particular, and also our thinking. These will bring about emotional and physiological changes.

CHOOSING BEHAVIOR

Why would someone choose to depress, to be anxious, or otherwise to be miserable?

1. By choosing to depress or anxietize, individuals can keep angering under control.

2. People may choose to depress or anxietize to get others to help them.

3. Choosing pain and misery can excuse an individual's unwillingness to do something more effective.

4. Choosing to depress or anxietize can help individuals gain power or control over others.

Glasser sees hallucinations, delusions, and/or active behaviors as creative ones. These are behaviors that individuals choose (without awareness) to deal with various aspects of their lives.

Should people who are "crazy" be responsible for their actions? Glasser's view is that criminals should not be tried until they have enough control over their lives to stand trial. When they have this control, they should be responsible for their actions.

CHOICE THEORY: A CASE EXAMPLE

Jake is a 16-year-old high school sophomore living in a suburb of Philadelphia. He has been arrested for stealing cars. Although this is his first arrest, it is the fifth time that he has stolen a car with friends. He and three friends have done this for fun. Because none of them are licensed drivers, this has been a way for them to practice their driving. Last week, one of Jake's friends was speeding in a stolen car, and Jake was in the back seat. All four of the young men in the car were arrested.

Jake's parents were very upset. His mother was surprised because Jake had not been in trouble before except for poor grades in school. Although teachers had commented about Jake's not doing homework and not paying attention in class, Jake had never been suspended from school. Jake's father saw Jake as a lazy kid who probably would not amount to much. He thought that all that Jake was interested in was sports. Jake's father is a roofer, and his mother is a chef.

Although Jake does not see a problem with his behavior, his mother does. Jake thinks that he was just unlucky and got caught. His mother is afraid that Jake is headed for more trouble, possibly jail, if something is not done. She makes an appointment for him to see a counselor.

Jake tells the counselor: "I don't see what the big deal is. We'd just been driving around. It's been a lot of fun except for getting caught. I have a hearing next week. My mother really worries. She thinks it's the first time I've been in a stolen car. It's not. We just like to have fun. Visit girls. Stuff like that."

"Anyway, it's not my idea. My friend is really good at hot wiring cars, so I go along with him, so do the other guys. Maybe if I didn't hang around with them I wouldn't get into trouble. Joe is the one with the good ideas. Or maybe I should say the bad ideas. My mother always says, 'Jake, what do you think will happen to you when you grow up? At this rate, you might not even graduate high school.' I don't know. Maybe, she's right. My father never graduated from high school and he's done okay."

147

1. Which of the following four needs are being met by Jake's activities?

   a. belonging
   b. power
   c. freedom
   d. fun
   e. all of the above

(e. Currently all four are being met by Jake's activities. He has a feeling of belonging by being with his friends. There is probably a sense of power in being able to get away with stealing a car and doing things that other people don't do. Also, there is a sense of freedom in being able to do things that other people say is wrong. Finally, he is having fun as he seems to enjoy this activity.)

2. Which of the two following needs is Jake not likely to meet in the near future?

   a. belonging
   b. power
   c. freedom
   d. fun

(b and c. Jake is likely to be arrested, and his freedom and power to do what he wants are likely to be limited in terms of rules and guidelines by a juvenile court. Incarceration is likely to be threatened if he continues to do this activity.)

*OE1. List two choices that Jake has made, probably without being aware of them.

_____

_____

*OE2. Jake says, "It's not my fault; it's the guys that I hang around with." Change Jake's statement so that it shows that he is in control and is aware of his choice.

_____

_____

3. Which of the following does not meet Glasser's criteria for "total behavior"? All are Jake's comments.

   a. I ride in the car.
   b. Joe drives the car.
   c. I'm thinking how fast can we go?
   d. I'm feeling pleasantly excited by this.
   e. I can feel butterflies in my stomach.

(b. "b" represents Joe's behavior, not Jake's. "a" refers to doing, "c" to thinking, "d" to feeling, and "e" to physiology.)

THEORY OF REALITY THERAPY

Reality therapy puts the responsibility of choosing goals and following through with them on clients. A good relationship with clients ensures that clients see that therapists are there to help them make changes which will make positive improvements in their lives. Techniques are directed toward changing behaviors and focusing on strengths and accomplishments.

GOALS OF REALITY THERAPY

The basic goal of reality therapy is to help individuals meet their psychological needs for belonging, power, freedom, and fun. These goals are met in such a way that they do not infringe on the needs of others. The focus is on responsible choices.

4.   Which of the following is most likely to be a reality therapy goal for Jake?

   a. To steal cars without getting caught
   b. To improve relationships with his friends
   c. To get better grades at school
   d. To become more aware of his unconscious anger at his parents

ASSESSMENT

Reality therapists ask their clients what they want, what they "really want." A glib answer is likely to be challenged by reality therapists. They would want clients to consider their future.

For example, if the counselor asks Jake what he wants and Jake replied, "I want to be able to go on a joy ride in other people's cars anytime I want," the counselor is apt to challenge that and ask Jake if it is possible, and look at why that is not possible. Such a discussion can lead to examining "total behavior" so that Jake can look at what he wants to do, how he wants to think, and how he wants to feel emotionally and physiologically. The counselor can talk to Jake about this and examine how his behaviors can change without impinging on the needs of others.

5.   If Jake says, "Riding in stolen cars is fun; I want to keep doing it," you as a reality therapist may reply

   a. What else do you like to do that's fun?
   b. You mentioned sports. What sports do you like?
   c. How does your choice affect the lives of others?
   d. All of the above.

(d. Choices "a" and "b" can help to assess other activities that may meet the need for fun. Choice "c" can help Jake see that his need for fun may interfere with other people's need to keep their cars. Then the therapist can continue to assess what activities may meet Jake's need for fun.)

6.   Which of the following comments by Jake would help the therapist assess that Jake does not see choices in his life?

   a. I can steal cars if I want to.
   b. I can hang out with Joe.
   c. I can make noise in the classroom if I want.
   d. I can just sit in the car, and all of a sudden I get arrested for no good reason.

Assessment of how needs (belonging, power, freedom, and fun) are being met and of total behavior (doing, thinking, feeling, and physiology) are done throughout therapy. This is an on-going assessment that takes place from the first session through the last.

THE PROCESS OF REALITY THERAPY

When changing behavior and making plans to change that behavior, the therapist establishes him or herself as someone wanting to help with that process. A friendly approach that shows that the counselor is concerned and wants to be helpful continues throughout therapy. That provides an opportunity to explore client wants, needs, and perceptions. This then further provides an opportunity to examine total behavior, especially doing. With that as a basis, plans can be made to improve behavior. Then commitment to plans can be obtained.

FRIENDLY INVOLVEMENT

The therapist is open to talking about anything that the client and the counselor can consider changing. There should be an atmosphere of openness, optimism, and honesty. There would be more emphasis on what the client is doing rather than what the client is feeling. However, counselors do attend to the client's feelings and will not ignore them. Friendly involvement builds the relationship and establishes a commitment to counseling and planning.

7. Which of the following statements would you as a reality therapist be least likely to say to Jake when he says, "I'm only here because my mom said I needed to be."

    a. Well, since you're here, let's see what we can do.
    b. I know you don't want to be here, but let's see what I can do to help.
    c. Let's see what your Mom may have had in mind when she said come see me.
    d. You haven't been acting very responsibly, and that's why your mom sent you here.

(d. Although "d" is probably true, it is not going to help set up a relationship between you and Jake in which Jake is willing to listen to you and make changes.)

EXPLORING TOTAL BEHAVIOR

8. In exploring Jake's total behavior, which of the following questions are you most likely to ask?

    a. What did you do when your teacher asked you to get back into your seat.?
    b. How did you feel when your teacher asked you to get back into your seat?
    c. What did you think when your teacher asked you to get back into your seat?
    d. How did you feel physically when your teacher asked you to get back into your seat?

(a. Although a reality therapist might ask any of those questions, when asking about total behavior, the reality therapist is more likely to ask about doing rather than thinking, feeling, or a physiological state.)

9. If Jake says that he got in trouble in school yesterday, which of these questions are you least likely to ask?

    a. Where at school did it happen?
    b. Who did it happen with?
    c. Why did it happen?
    d. When did it happen?

(c. Although the question may be answered, questions such as what, who, and when provide more information about what took place or what the client did.)

Reality therapists will explore thinking, feeling, and physiology but focus on doing. They believe that changes in doing will bring about changes in thinking, emotional feeling, and physical feeling.

EVALUATING BEHAVIOR

Self evaluations are a part of therapy. Clients make value judgments about their own behavior as do therapists. However, it is the therapist's goal to help clients see values that are embedded in their behavior. It is not the role of the therapist to criticize the values of the client. One way in which the therapist's values impact counseling in reality therapy is through the questions that the therapist asks. The reality therapist will ask about how the needs of the client and the needs of others are being met. Also the therapist will ask about how the client's behaviors are helping or hurting the client or others.

The text lists questions that Wubbolding (1988) asks clients to help them evaluate their behaviors. Because they communicate the role of evaluation in reality therapy so well, they are listed here.

Does your behavior help you or hurt you?
By doing what you're doing, are you getting what you want?
Are you breaking the rules?
Are your wants realistic and attainable?
How does it help to look at it like that?

10. If Jake says to you, "I guess stealing a car is against breaking the rule, but it's a stupid rule," you as a reality therapist might reply:

   a. Yes, but rules are meant to be kept.
   b. What do you think the rule does for people you know?
   c. What would your mother say if she knew you broke this rule?
   d. Look what happened to Joe when he got arrested.

MAKING PLANS TO DO BETTER

Making plans provides a way for clients to change what they are doing. The emphasis is on doing rather than thinking, feeling, or physiology. In making plans, clients' needs should be met.

11. Which of these plans would probably work best for Jake?

   a. to behave better in school
   b. to play basketball after school with new friends
   c. to clean his parents' house
   d. to tell the police about the other times he stole a car

(b. Playing basketball should help Jake meet his need for fun. "a" is too vague, as "being better" is not defined. "c" and "d", while being laudable goals, may be plans that fulfill other people's needs, not Jake's. If Jake really wants to do something for his mother or really wants to tell the police what he did before, then these choices will meet a need.)

12. When you and Jake make a plan to help him meet his need for fun by playing basketball, which of these statements would be least effective from a reality therapy point of view?

   a. Meet Dan and Pedro in the front hall of school when the final bell rings.
   b. Sign up for intramural basketball at lunch time today.
   c. Plan to meet on Saturday at 1:00 in the afternoon. Pedro will bring the basketball.
   d. Plan to play basketball after school each day next week.

(d. The plans for "d" are vague, too far in advance. The plans describe what Jake will do but do not describe clearly who he will do them with or exactly when.)

COMMITMENT TO PLANS

For a client to commit to a plan, it should be feasible. In question 12, choices "a", "b", and "c" are more feasible than choice "d". In some instances, it can be helpful to use a verbal or written contract to ensure commitment. Depending on your relationship with Jake, you might ask for a written commitment. An advantage of the written commitment with Jake would be that it is clear, and you can refer to it again in a later session. A disadvantage is that it is formal and such formality may affect the relationship that you have with him.

THERAPIST ATTITUDES

Throughout reality therapy, therapists are consistent about their attitudes toward their work with clients. Because the focus of therapy is on planning and carrying out plans, the therapist takes attitudes that will help him or her deal with clients when they do not follow through on plans.

Don't accept excuses.
No punishment or criticism.
Don't give up.

With Jake, it is likely to expect that he will not follow through on all the plans that you and he come up with.

13. If Jake says, "I talked to Dan but not Pedro about playing basketball, and then I just forgot about it," how might you reply?

a. Why didn't you talk to Pedro?
b. Why didn't you get Dan to talk to Pedro?
c. How did you feel about not following through with your plans?
d. Let's talk about playing basketball with Dan and Pedro soon. When would be a good time.

(d. You don't accept excuses from Jake, nor do you punish or criticize him. You would make another plan with him, not giving up on him.)

REALITY THERAPY STRATEGIES

Reality therapists do not emphasize specific techniques. However, they are more likely to use some techniques than others. Because of the focus on exploring and evaluating behavior, reality therapists are likely to ask many questions. They may also listen to client metaphors and make use of them when talking to clients. Because much of reality therapy focuses on making plans and commitment to them, using humor and being positive can be helpful in encouraging clients. Confrontation helps therapists deal with clients when they do not follow up on plans. Paradoxical techniques are ways to help clients when they may be resistant to carrying out plans.

QUESTIONING

Questions can be used to help clients explore their wants, needs, and perceptions. They are also good approaches to understanding how the client thinks, to gathering information, to giving information and making sure it's understood, and in helping clients take more effective control.

BEING POSITIVE

Reality therapists take many opportunities to reinforce the constructive planning of their clients and their success in following through on the plans. Reality therapists may turn negative occurrences into positive ones by taking advantage of opportunities to communicate hope to clients.

METAPHORS

When clients talk, they sometimes use metaphors such as "When I got caught, the whole world fell apart." Therapists listen to those metaphors and may respond to the metaphor such as, "What happened when the world fell apart?"

HUMOR

Because humor is spontaneous and idiosyncratic, it can only occur at the moment so that it can fit in naturally. Humor is a part of friendly involvement as therapists can sometimes laugh at themselves which encourages clients to do the same.

CONFRONTATION

When clients don't follow through on plans, confrontation is unavoidable. Not accepting excuses, being positive, and using humor can be ways of confronting clients.

PARADOXICAL TECHNIQUES

When clients are reluctant to carry out plans or resist making plans, sometimes paradoxical techniques can be used. They are among the most difficult techniques for therapists to use because they are counter-intuitive. Reframing the way clients think about a topic can help them believe a previously undesirable behavior is desirable. Another paradoxical technique is to prescribe a symptom such as telling an anxious person to schedule times when they are anxious.

To prescribe a paradoxical technique with Jake would be difficult. Encouraging an illegal behavior by saying, "Why don't you steal more cars?" could have disastrous effects if Jake does in fact follow up on your request.

Reframing might work better with Jake. For example, if he says, "My teacher got upset with me for looking out the window during class. I just sat there and listened to him. Then he went on with the math problems." You can reframe this by saying, " You chose to control your behavior and not talk back to your teacher. You showed good restraint."

QUESTIONS

14. If Jake comes in during the following session and says to you, "I played basketball twice with Dan and Pedro. The third time I couldn't do it because Dan was sick, so Pedro and I went to the mall." Which of the following strategies are you most likely to take?

    a. questioning
    b. being positive
    c. using metaphors
    d. humor
    e. confrontation

15. In developing new plans with Jake to go over Spanish vocabulary words with Alice, which techniques are you likely to use most frequently?

    a. questioning
    b. being positive
    c. using metaphors
    d. humor
    e. confrontation

SPECIAL TOPICS

OE3. Why do you think a certification program is a good or bad idea for reality therapy? (427)

_____

_____

OE4. Why do you think reality therapy may be difficult to integrate with other theories? (427)

_____

_____

_____

OE5. Does reality therapy ignore gender issues by focusing on personal choice and responsibility? Explain. (430)

_____

_____

_____

OE6. Does reality therapy ignore individuals' multicultural background by focusing on personal choice and responsibility? Explain (430)

_____

_____

_____

STRENGTHS AND LIMITATIONS

What do you believe are the strengths and limitations of reality therapy?

Strengths	Limitations
_____	_____
_____	_____
_____	_____
_____	_____
_____	_____
_____	_____
_____	_____

REALITY THERAPY: A QUIZ

True/false items: Decide if the following statements are more "true" or more "false" as they apply to reality therapy.

T F Q1. Reality therapy emphasizes the way clients perceive the world rather than reality itself.

T F Q2. The theory of personality that reality therapy is based on is choice theory.

T F Q3. Reality therapy is concerned primarily with changing negative self-concepts.

T F Q4. Use of questioning is discouraged as a technique in therapy.

T F Q5. The Dysfunctional Thought Record is an important assessment tool in reality therapy.

T F Q6. Education on how to be a responsible person is the essence of reality therapy.

T F Q7. Reality therapy is a form of psychodynamic therapy.

T F Q8. Establishing a friendly working relationship is important in reality therapy.

T F Q9. Client excuses for not following through on plans should be challenged.

T F Q10. Written contracts to follow through on plans is one approach in reality therapy.

Multiple choice items. Select the *best answer* from the alternatives using a reality therapy perspective.

_____ Q11. The clients that Reality therapy was originally used with were

    a. alcoholics.
    b. delinquent adolescent women.
    c. depressed clients.
    d. middle-class white men.

_____ Q12. Reality therapy is grounded in

    a. Freud's psychoanalysis.
    b. behavior theory.
    c. person-centered therapy.
    d. Power's control theory.

_____ Q13. According to reality therapy, which of the following is not one of the four basic needs?

    a. belonging
    b. power
    c. freedom
    d. self-actualization
    e. fun

_____ Q14. In describing Harry's depression, which sentence would a reality therapist use?

    a. Harry is depressed.
    b. Harry is experiencing many dysfunctional thoughts.
    c. Harry chooses to depress.
    d. Harry is nuts.
    e. Harry is delusional.

_____ Q15. Which of the following is not a component of "total behavior"?

       a. doing
       b. dreaming
       c. thinking
       d. feeling
       e. physiology

_____ Q16. Which of the following do reality therapists believe is most important in making therapeutic change?

       a. doing
       b. dreaming
       c. thinking
       d. feeling
       e. physiology

_____ Q17. Betty chooses to anxietize. Which of the following is likely to be a reason for choosing to anxietize according to Glasser?

       a. She learned to be anxious from her neurotic mother.
       b. She chooses to anxietize to get others to help her.
       c. She chooses to anxietize to get disability payments.
       d. She chooses to anxietize because it is more interesting than choosing to be depressed.

_____ Q18. Miranda chooses to hit her husband over the head with a frying pan and throw his clothes out the window after she finds out he has cheated on her. Unique to reality therapy would be viewing her behaviors as

       a. creative.
       b. criminal.
       c. excessively jealous.
       d. psychotic.

_____ Q19. Which of these would NOT be a necessary goal of therapy according to reality therapy?

       a. I want to have more fun.
       b. I want to feel loved.
       c. I want to understand my problems.
       d. I want to feel more powerful at work.

_____ Q20. In reality therapy, the basis of a therapeutic relationship is

       a. therapeutic control.
       b. friendly involvement.
       c. therapeutic love.
       d. unconditional positive regard.

_____ Q21. Which of the following is NOT one of Wubbolding's procedures or processes in his model of reality therapy?

       a. wants
       b. direction and doing
       c. evaluation
       d. catharsis
       e. planning

_____ Q22. In evaluating behavior, which of these questions is a reality therapist most likely to ask?

       a. Why did you smoke at school?
       b. What did your mother say when the principal called?
       c. Did you break school rules?
       d. Who else was with you when you got caught smoking?

_____ Q23. Glasser supports the notion of a positive addiction because it

       a. gives access to one's creativity.
       b. provides additional strength to help with problems.
       c. neither a or b.
       d. both a and b.

_____ Q24. Which of the following is not a technique used in reality therapy?

       a. questioning
       b. active imagination
       c. humor
       d. metaphor
       e. confrontation

_____ Q25. Reality therapy is a system which helps clients learn

       a. how to make responsible choices for themselves.
       b. how to make responsible choices for others.
       c. how to control events in their lives.
       d. all of the above.

ANSWER KEY

1. e	11. b	Q1. T	Q11. b	Q21. d
2. b, c	12. d	Q2. T	Q12. d	Q22. c
3. b	13. d	Q3. F	Q13. d	Q23. d
4. c	14. b	Q4. F	Q14. c	Q24. b
5. d	15. a	Q5. F	Q15. b	Q25. a
6. d		Q6. F	Q16. a	
7. d		Q7. F	Q17. b	
8. a		Q8. T	Q18. a	
9. c		Q9. F	Q19. c	
10. b		Q10. T	Q20. b	

*OE1. To steal cars, to act out in school, to not do school work, to pick friends, to spend time with certain friends.

*OE2. I choose to be with friends who steal cars. I choose to go with them when they steal cars.

CHAPTER 12

FEMINIST THERAPY

FEMINIST THERAPY SELF-INVENTORY

Directions: By comparing your beliefs about personality and therapy to feminist therapy, you should have a clearer idea of how much you will need to suspend your beliefs or change attitudes to understand the feminist theory of personality and approach to therapy. You may find it helpful to complete this section before and after you read the chapter. In this way, you can see if your views have changed. There are no correct answers, only an opportunity to express your views.

Put an "X" on the line so that it indicates how much you agree or disagree with the statement: A=Agree, D=Disagree.

D_____A 1. Therapeutic issues are different for men than for women.

_____ 2. Gender can be viewed as a multicultural variable.

_____ 3. The sexism of psychotherapists is a concern in the practice of psychotherapy.

_____ 4. Consciousness-raising groups can bring about productive social change.

_____ 5. Violence to women is much more common than violence to men.

_____ 6. Strong identification with one's gender can limit the way individuals view themselves and others.

_____ 7. Men and women often view moral decision-making from different perspectives.

_____ 8. In general, women tend to focus more on relationships and men more on achievement.

_____ 9. Women are placed in a position in which they are subordinate to men in Western society.

_____ 10. Building self-esteem should be a goal of therapy.

_____ 11. Accepting one's body can be an important goal in therapy.

_____ 12. Social action should be a goal in therapy.

_____ 13. "The person is political."

_____ 14. Psychological classification systems like the DSM-IV, encourage social adjustment to norms, reinforcing stereotypes rather than questioning social injustice.

_____ 15. Gender role interventions can be important therapeutic techniques.

16. Power-role interventions can be important therapeutic techniques.

_____ 17. Therapists and clients should have a relationship in which both are equals, rather than the therapist being in a more powerful position.

_____ . Assertiveness is often an appropriate goal for female clients.

_____ . Openness to homosexuality is an important therapeutic characteristic.

_____ . Therapists should be politically active.

HISTORY OF FEMINIST PERSONALITY THEORY

Which influences do you think were most important in the development of feminist personality theory?

HISTORICAL AND PROFESSIONAL INFLUENCES

Chesler's (1972) criticism of the relationship between the female patient and the male therapist; critical of male therapists' gender bias

Criticisms of gender bias in psychoanalysis

Concerns about the social and political rights of women, as expressed by groups such as the National Organization for Women

Consciousness-raising groups

Encouragement of therapist involvement in social action groups

Many contributors to feminist therapy; no single leader

CONCEPTS BASIC TO FEMINIST THERAPY

sex Biological differences that distinguish females from males used in contrast to gender.

gender Socially determined thoughts, beliefs, and attitudes that individuals hold about men and women.

gender role Referring to behaviors that are generally considered socially appropriate for members of one sex.

consciousness-raising groups (CR) A creation of the women's movement, in which women met regularly to discuss their lives and issues in them.

alpha bias The bias that occurs by separating women and men into two specific categories, running the risk of treating women as unequal to men.

beta bias Bias that occurs when treating men and women as identical, thus ignoring important differences between the lives of women and men.

FEMINIST THEORIES OF PERSONALITY

There is not one theory of personality for feminist therapy. Rather researchers have studied differences between the development of women and men. Theories that deal with a subset of development or personality do exist. These include Bem's gender schema theory, Gilligan's ethic of care, and the relationship model.

GENDER DIFFERENCES AND SIMILARITIES ACROSS THE LIFE SPAN

To understand broad differences between the life experiences of men and women, describe your own development (or those of friends) as it relates to common concerns that children, adolescents, and adults face as they relate to gender issues.

CHILDHOOD - YOURS OR OTHERS

_____

_____

_____

_____

_____

_____

_____

COMMON CHILDHOOD GENDER ISSUES

Parental preference for a son (sometimes a daughter)

Clothing and toys of young children

Sex segregation (playing with children of one's own sex)

Devaluing characteristics of the opposite sex

Adults encouraging independence and efficacy in boys, nurturing in girls

Exposure to stereotypes by peers, movies, magazines

ADOLESCENCE - YOURS OR OTHERS

_____

_____

_____

_____

_____

_____

COMMON ADOLESCENT GENDER ISSUES

Onset of puberty (for girls, breast development and menarche; for boys, voice change, sexual development)

Emphasis on attractiveness and appearance

Dating and regulating sexual activity

Females competing with other females for boys

Focus on academic and athletic accomplishments

Relationships with parents

ADULTHOOD - YOURS OR OTHERS

_____

_____

_____

_____

_____

_____

_____

COMMON ADULT GENDER ISSUES

Child bearing and child raising

Full time vs part time work

Leaving the work force

Sexual harassment at work

Income

Housework

Violence - sexual abuse, rape, and physical attack

Aging process - losing sexual attractiveness

GENDER SCHEMA THEORY

Sandra Bem developed two important concepts that have influenced personality theory in feminist therapy: schema theory and androgyny.

androgyny Possessing both masculine and feminine psychological traits, usually in relatively equal amounts.

gender schema A set of mental associations in which individuals are seen from the point of view of their gender, as opposed to other characteristics.

Bem developed the Bem Sex Role Inventory to measure the degree of masculine or feminine traits. However, she moved from the concept of androgyny to gender schema theory because of a concern that labeling behaviors as masculine or feminine may reinforce stereotypes. In contrast, gender schema theory shows how therapists and researchers can measure the importance of a gender schema as opposed to other schemas in the way individuals view their world. This concept helps therapists learn how their clients view gender in their own lives.

GILLIGAN'S ETHIC OF CARE

Carol Gilligan built upon Lawrence Kohlberg's model of moral development. In Kohlberg's model, a high level of morality of justice is determined by individuals' ability to understand rules and the need to obey them as they relate to a need for social order. Gilligan's morality of care deals with being responsible to self and others. There is an emphasis on compassion and the relationship or interdependence between self and others. Males tend to fit more closely with Kohlberg's model and females with Gilligan's model.

THE RELATIONAL MODEL

Developed by Jean Miller and other writers at the Stone Center at Wellesley College, the relational model emphasizes the importance for women of finding a sense of identity through the context of relationships. Miller and her colleagues believe that women (as well as minorities and poor people) have been subordinate to dominant groups (generally white males). As a subordinate group, they have had to please the dominant group and thus improve their relationships with both men and women by tending to the emotional and physical needs of others. Rather than see the need for relatedness as a weakness, the relational model sees this as a strength that should be valued and appreciated.

The relational model holds that women's sense of self develops in the context of relationships and has three basic components.

1. An interest and ability in forming emotional connections with others.
2. The expectation that a mutually empathic process will lead to improved development of women and others.
3. The belief that being sensitive will lead to increased empowerment and self-knowledge.

FEMINIST PERSONALITY THEORY: AN EXAMPLE

The following example is a conversation between April and her three roommates. April, a 23-year-old secretary in a manufacturing firm, has been date raped and is discussing this with Bonita, Clara, and Denise. At the end of the example, there are questions about feminist personality theory. The purpose of these questions is to help you review your knowledge and understanding of feminist personality theory.

April: Last night Dave and I had been at a party drinking. You know Dave, he's the guy in the transportation department who I sometimes see at lunch. I had known him a little bit but not very well. He seemed like a nice guy. Well, we were at this party, and then he took me home. I was tired and sort of interested in him, but not too. Anyway, he asked if he could come in for a soda. I said sure. Actually, I thought maybe some of you would be there, but nobody was there. So we start to kiss, and all of a sudden, he starts to put his hand down my blouse. So I told him to stop it. He did for a while - like about thirty seconds. Then he started again. So I started to get up and push him away. As I did that, he really leaned into me, pushed my head down into the sofa and my hands under my head and told me, "Shut up, you'll enjoy it." Then he really leaned hard on me, took off my panties and raped me. I didn't know what to do. I was afraid that no one would believe me.

Bonita: You know how men are. You find a cop and they don't believe you. They will think that because you knew him and were kissing him that you were asking for it. They're all jerks.

April: I know. That's what I'm afraid of. I don't know what to do.

Clara: I'm really worried about you. What a terrible thing! You must be feeling awful!

April: I am. I'm in shock. I don't know what to do. Nothing like this has ever happened to me before.

Denise: That's not right. We've got to do something about it. We can call a support hot line and get advice about what to do. This slime ought to go to jail. And we've got to get him charged.

April: I know I need to do something. But I feel at such a loss right now. I just feel dirty.

Bonita: It's not you who are dirty. It's men who are. They do something like this and then they tell themselves "Hey, it's okay. She really wanted it." Real slime.

Clara: Oh April! (She moves next to her and hugs her). How devastating for you to have to experience that last night.

April: I know. (crying)

Denise: Don't worry. We're gonna make sure Dave doesn't get away with this. One way or another, he's going to pay.

1. Which of the four women has the strongest gender schema?

   a. April
   b. Bonita
   c. Clara
   d. Denise

2. Which of the four women is using a frame of reference that is most similar to Kohlberg's view of moral development?

   a. April
   b. Bonita
   c. Clara
   d. Denise

3. Which of the four women most closely resembles Gilligan's views of moral development?

   a. April
   b. Bonita
   c. Clara
   d. Denise

4. The behavior of which of these four women most closely fits the relational model?

   a. April
   b. Bonita
   c. Clara
   d. Denise

5. Of April's three friends, who fits least well with Kohlberg's model of moral development?

   a. Bonita
   b. Clara
   c. Denise

6. If I had written this example using the names of Bill instead of Bonita, Carl instead of Clara, and Dennis instead of Denise, I might be guilty of

   a. alpha bias.
   b. beta bias.
   c. gamma bias.
   d. delta bias.

The answer to question 6 is "a". By separating women and men into two categories, my example would indicate alpha bias. Men do not always respond to situations using Kohlberg's morality of justice, and women do not always use Gilligan's morality of care. Likewise, women are not always relational in their comments, nor are men always non-relational and achievement-oriented. However, these models do provide a means for understanding how social factors tend to impact men and women differently.

THEORIES OF FEMINIST THERAPY

Feminist therapy is a theory that is combined with others rather than used strictly on its own. Feminist goals of therapy are goals that reflect how society's institutions affect women. They are not the only possible goals for therapy. Assessment also reflects the therapist's awareness of social and cultural background and events as they affect their clients. Techniques of feminist therapy tend to reflect an awareness of women's lack of power in society in general and our approaches to resolving problems in effective ways.

GOALS OF FEMINIST THERAPY

The goals that are listed in the text are not the only goals of feminist therapy, but they are ones that put a focus on social change. Unlike other therapies, feminist therapies point out that the problem is often in the culture or society rather than in the client.

1. *Symptom removal* Although symptom removal may be appropriate in therapy and is a traditional goal, feminist therapists are aware that the problem can be with a spouse or boss. If a client has headaches that result from an angry and hostile superior, dealing with the boss is preferable to taking headache medication.

2. *Self esteem* A goal is to help women become independent and self-reliant.

3. *Quality of interpersonal relationships* As noted in the previous section on feminist personality theory, feminist therapists greatly value the nature and quality of interpersonal relationships.

4. *Role performance* Expanding clients' views of social roles for themselves and others is consistent with the feminist view that people exist in a political context.

5. *Body image and sensuality* Because of pressures from men that women should be attractive and the focus of many types of media on attractiveness, accepting one's body and sexuality is a frequent goal of feminist therapy.

6. *Political awareness and social action* These are goals that separate feminist therapy from other therapies. For clients and therapists to work toward making social change that will create fewer problems for people in the future is very consistent with the feminist therapy view that the "person is political."

ASSESSMENT

Feminist therapists have been critical of the major diagnostic system (DSM-IV) because of its absence of consideration of social factors and its development by the dominant group (white men). Feminist therapists are wary of encouraging adjustment to social norms and reinforcing stereotypes.

TECHNIQUES OF FEMINIST THERAPY

Although feminist therapists use many methods and techniques in their work, gender-role analysis and intervention, and power analysis and intervention are methods that reflect the need to help people deal with and overcome social inequalities. These methods will be a focus of this section.

CASE EXAMPLE

To apply gender-role analysis and interventions along with power analysis and interventions, let us continue with the case of April. Let's assume that a month after her conversation with her three friends, April is still very much disturbed by being date raped by Dave. She seeks your help to deal with her feelings of confusion and depression that she has had for the last month. In her first meeting with you, she reveals more information about herself.

She was born in a small town about 50 miles from where you are living now. After graduating high school, she moved to the town or city where you live and took a job as a secretary in a medium-sized firm. Both of her parents were farmers. April grew up with her younger brother and sister on the farm. Neither of her parents had gone to college, and both were raised in farm families.

April went to a fairly small high school where she was active as a cheerleader and in student government. Most of her friends were boys and girls who she met in church or lived on nearby farms. She had relatively little dating experience. During the first few months of her senior year, she dated a boy who she knew in her church. However, that relationship seemed to fall apart and did not distress her. Her sexual experience has been quite limited.

When she came to your area, she had few friends. However, she was able to make friends at work and has appreciated spending time with Bonita, Clara, and Denise after work. She has had few dates in the two years that she has been here. Most of the social functions that she has attended have either been at a church or with large groups of people.

She tells you that she feels very differently than she did before the date rape. She feels dirty and tarnished. She wonders if someone would ever want to marry her. When she was home last weekend, she felt different from her family in a way that she had never felt before.

When returning to work this past week, she found it difficult to concentrate on her assignments. It was hard to pay attention to her colleagues and superiors. After work, she would sometimes go back to her apartment, turn on the television, and cry.

In the following sections, fill out a gender-role analysis and power analysis for April. Use the information that is provided about April for your answers and make up any other information that you need.

GENDER ROLE ANALYSIS	POWER ROLE ANALYSIS
1. Identify three gender role messages that April may have received at home or at school.	1. Have April choose a definition for "power" and apply it to different kinds of power.
_____	_____
_____	_____
_____	_____
_____	_____

2. Identify positive and negative consequences of April's gender-related messages.

_____

_____

_____

_____

3. Identify statements that April says to herself based on gender-related messages.

_____

_____

_____

_____

4. Decide which of April's messages you want to change.

_____

_____

_____

_____

5. Develop a plan to help April make changes in her behavior.

_____

_____

_____

_____

2. Describe ways that April can become more powerful (e.g. financial control, self-defense classes, the legal system).

_____

_____

_____

_____

3. Discuss with April different ways to bring about change in power.

_____

_____

_____

_____

4. Examine gender role messages that interfere with April becoming more powerful.

_____

_____

_____

_____

5. Decide how to be powerful in certain situations. Plan behavioral changes with April.

_____

_____

_____

_____

FEMINIST THERAPY INTERVENTIONS

Many interventions and techniques in feminist therapy empower clients to deal with social and political inequities. They also seek to inform and educate clients about ways of dealing with environmental stresses and events. In doing this, they often seek to create equality between themselves and their clients. One method of doing this is to use appropriate self-disclosures. Feminist therapy interventions and methods are defined here.

gender role intervention Such interventions deal with reinforcing or helping clients' interventions or helping them deal with gender role obstacles in their life. Some interventions provide insight into social or political issues that serve as obstacles to clients.

power intervention Empowering clients can occur in the course of therapeutic discussion. Often encouragement and reinforcement are ways to help clients become more powerful.

assertiveness training A technique to teach clients to effectively express positive and negative feelings to others so that they may achieve desired purposes.

bibliotherapy A therapeutic technique in which the therapist suggests readings for the client for purposes such as gaining insight into problems, learning new information, and increasing self esteem.

reframing Looking at an individual's behavior from a different point of reference. This helps individuals understand how social pressures can affect their problems.

relabeling Attaching a new name to a problem so that therapeutic progress can be made. For example, saying that a client is overwhelmed by an issue rather than "depressed" may allow the client to develop methods to deal with the problem.

self disclosure The process in which therapists or counselors discuss aspects of their own lives in order to enhance therapeutic progress with clients.

QUESTIONS ABOUT THE CASE EXAMPLE

7. April says, "I know girls are supposed to be quiet and not contradict boys. Sometimes it's hard just to sit there and take it." Which of the following would be an appropriate gender role intervention?

   a. How do you know that girls are just supposed to be quiet?
   b. How did you learn that girls are supposed to be quiet?
   c. What would happen if you were not quiet?
   d. All of the above.

(d. All of the answers help April explore her assumptions about gender role. They do so without making her resist further exploration).

8. April says, "Sometimes, I want my mother to listen to me, to see that I am not a little girl any more. I certainly don't feel like one now." Which of the following would be an appropriate power intervention?

   a. Why don't you just tell her what's on your mind?
   b. I would like to hear what you would say to her. Then we might talk about how you could say some of this to her.
   c. You can let her know how difficult it has been to have learned gender roles from her that are not helpful to you.
   d. Don't you think you should respect your mother's views?
   e. All of the above.

(b. For April, this statement may be best as it is a way of being more powerful without alienating her mother. Statements "a" and "c" may backfire on April. They don't encourage her to both listen to her mother and to express herself. Statement "d" does not acknowledge April's power.)

9. Which of these techniques is most likely to directly help April with her passivity?

   a. assertiveness training
   b. bibliotherapy
   c. reframing
   d. therapy-demystifying

10. Which of the following methods of feminist therapy is most likely to help April learn new approaches to relationships, sexual violence, and the importance of women's achievement?

   a. assertiveness training
   b. bibliotherapy
   c. reframing
   d. therapy-demystifying

11. April says to you, "My roommates drink and they pressure me to drink. I really don't like it. I'm afraid of getting out of control, and I'm afraid of being with guys who might get out of control with me when they're drinking." Which would be an appropriate feminist therapy response?

   a. You can ignore them and do whatever you want.
   b. Let's examine the pressures on women to drink and how drinking could affect you.
   c. If a guy is too drunk and starts to get obnoxious, mace him.
   d. You seem to be worried about losing control of yourself and being vulnerable to being hurt.

(b. The therapist takes an opportunity to educate April about options having to do with alcohol use and abuse. She also supports April's decision.)

12. Response "b" in question 11 is called

   a. assertiveness training.
   b. bibliotherapy.
   c. reframing.
   d. therapy-demystifying.

("c" is a way of framing the reference for looking at April's behavior. It shifts the focus from April to look at society and alcohol as a social issue.)

13. When April introduces herself to you, she says, "I am April Smith." In introducing yourself, you would use your

   a. first name.
   b. first and last name.
   c. Mr. or Ms. followed by your first and last name.
   d. Dr. followed by your first or last name.

(b. An equal relationship between client and therapist is important in feminist therapy. A feminist therapist would not call herself Dr. and call the client April.)

14. April says, "Sometimes I'm so angry at what Dave did to me that I want to make sure that it doesn't happen to anyone else or at least help decrease the chances that other women will experience that."

Would it be an appropriate feminist therapy response for you to say, "I am glad to hear of your interest and commitment to trying to prevent date rape. Let me give you the number of the local chapter of the National Organization for Women. You may want to contact them as they are working on education about rape?"

    a. yes
    b. no

(a. yes. Empowering clients and getting them involved in social action would be an appropriate feminist therapy technique.)

SPECIAL TOPICS

OE1. How do feminist therapists suggest that the following theories can be modified to be consistent with feminist therapy principles?

a. psychoanalytic theory (457)_____

_____

_____

b. behavioral and cognitive therapy (457)_____

_____

_____

c. Gestalt therapy (458)_____

_____

_____

OE2. Why is it difficult to determine the length of feminist therapy? (459)

_____

_____

OE3. How are the principles of social constructionism consistent with feminist therapy? (465)

_____

_____

OE4. Do you think the advocacy of social action has a place in therapy? (466)

_____

_____

OE5. How can feminist therapy be helpful for the treatment of men? (468)

_____

_____

0E6. How does feminist therapy address these two concepts? (469)

homophobia The dislike, fear, or hatred of homosexual people.

heterosexism The view that being heterosexual is more normal and better than being homosexual thus devaluing the lifestyle of homosexual individuals.

_____

_____

_____

OE7. In what ways is feminist therapy a good and a poor model for counseling people with a variety of multicultural backgrounds? (470)

_____

_____

_____

STRENGTHS AND LIMITATIONS

What do you see as the strengths and limitations of feminist therapy?

Strengths	Limitations
_____	_____
_____	_____
_____	_____
_____	_____
_____	_____
_____	_____
_____	_____
_____	_____
_____	_____

FEMINIST THERAPY: A QUIZ

True/false items. Decide which of the following statements are more "true" or more "false" as they apply to feminist therapy.

T   F   Q1. Feminist therapy should be applied to women, not men.

T   F   Q2. Feminist therapy is independent from multicultural therapy.

T   F   Q3. Feminist therapists are concerned with social injustice.

T   F   Q4. The stronger a person's gender schema is, the more gender aware he or she is.

T   F   Q5. Kohlberg's work on morality is concerned with the ethics of care.

T   F   Q6. Relational theory focuses on finding a sense of identity through the context of relationships.

T   F   Q7. Assertiveness training teaches women how to be more aggressive.

T   F   Q8. Power interventions may be used in feminist therapy.

T   F   Q9. Feminist therapists are concerned with the need to regulate who can call themselves a *feminist therapist*.

T   F   Q10. Feminist therapists work to help both female and male homosexuals combat societal discrimination.

Multiple choice items: Select the best answer from the alternatives given. Answer each question from the point of view of feminist therapy.

_____ Q11. Which of these is a major issue of consideration for feminist therapists?

        a. cultural differences
        b. diagnosis of psychopathology
        c. objectivity
        d. unconscious factors

_____ Q12. In her study of therapy, Chesler pointed to concerns about

        a. male therapists working with female patients.
        b. the destructiveness of therapists' sexual relations with patients.
        c. sex-biased values of therapists.
        d. all of the above.

_____ Q13. Therapists have been particularly concerned about sex-biased values in

        a. cognitive therapy.
        b. Gestalt therapy.
        c. psychoanalytic therapy.
        d. all of the above.

_____ Q14. According to _____ feminist therapists, men cannot be feminist therapists.

        a. biased
        b. liberal
        c. non-sexist
        d. radical

Q15. In which period of life do gender role pressures tend to be the most severe?

    a. childhood
    b. adolescence
    c. adulthood
    d. old age

Q16. Gender schema theory is based on the earlier work on

    a. androgyny.
    b. the ethic of care.
    c. the morality of justice.
    d. the relational model.

Q17. Which of these goals are feminist therapists most cautious about?

    a. symptom-removal
    b. self-esteem
    c. quality of personal relationships
    d. role performance
    e. body image

Q18. Which of these is NOT a technique of feminist therapy?

    a. gender-role analysis
    b. power analysis
    c. biological analysis
    d. therapist demystifying strategies

Q19. Which of the following responses would feminist therapists see as appropriately assertive?

Statement: "Would you mind working late for me now? I want to go home early."

    a. Sure. I would be glad to.
    b. I would be glad to work for you, but later I would like for us to arrange a time for you to do the same.
    c. Don't ask me at the last minute to work for you. Show some consideration.

Q20. Feminist therapists seek to

    a. enhance the feminine mystique in therapy.
    b. demystify therapy for clients.
    c. educate male clients about social injustice.
    d. reframe therapy as consciousness-raising.

Q21. Societal pressures are likely to cause women to be more prone to _____ than men.

    a. anorexia
    b. bulimia
    c. depression
    d. all of the above

_____ Q22. Feminist therapy with men is likely to include observations about

    a. men abusing their power with their wives.
    b. the Oedipus complex.
    c. societal effects on men's behavior.
    d. men's body boundaries.

_____ Q23. Feminist therapists tend to be sensitive to gender issues as well as to

    a. cultural views.
    b. existential issues.
    c. choice theory.
    d. the use of problem solving methods.

_____ Q24. _____ groups were responsible for the development of other groups for women.

    a. Alcoholics anonymous
    b. Body image
    c. Consciousness-raising
    d. Male/female

_____ Q25. Which of these issues are feminist therapists most concerned with?

    a. literary
    b. psychodynamic
    c. political
    d. organizational

ANSWER KEY

1. b	11. b	Q1. F	Q11. b	Q21. d
2. d	12. c	Q2. F	Q12. d	Q22. c
3. c	13. b	Q3. T	Q13. c	Q23. a
4. c	14. a	Q4. F	Q14. d	Q24. c
5. b		Q5. F	Q15. b	Q25. c
6. a		Q6. T	Q16. a	
7. d		Q7. F	Q17. a	
8. b		Q8. T	Q18. c	
9. a		Q9. T	Q19. b	
10. b		Q10. T	Q20. b	

CHAPTER 13

FAMILY THERAPY

This chapter has a different format from the others. Four different family systems therapies are presented along with brief information about several others and information about early work leading to the development of systems therapy. A brief inventory that is general in nature will be presented first. One case will be explained, and then you will have the opportunity to answer questions about it from different family systems points of view. The sections will focus on basic concepts, goals, and therapeutic techniques.

FAMILY SYSTEMS THERAPY SELF-INVENTORY

Put an "X" on the line so that it indicates how much you agree or disagree with the statement: A = Agree, D = Disagree.

D_____A 1. Individuals should be viewed from the perspective of their family rather than from the perspective of a single individual.

_____ 2. Individuals' problems can best be understood by understanding their family problems.

_____ 3. Change in one part of a family system is likely to result in changes in other family members.

_____ 4. Changes within a person can only be made if significant others do not interfere with these changes.

_____ 5. A family therapist should be a teacher and coach as well as a therapist.

_____ 6. The major goal of family therapy is to help the family to solve the presenting problems.

_____ 7. To understand a family's problems, therapists should attend to who says what to whom and how they communicate.

_____ 8. Being active and often directive is a part of the therapist's role in family therapy.

_____ 9. Attending to both verbal and nonverbal communications within the family are important aspects of family therapy.

_____ 10. An important goal of family therapy is the growth of individuals, not just the growth of the family.

BASIC FAMILY THERAPY CONCEPTS

The following terms distinguish types of work with families. Family therapy that is described in other chapters is distinguished from family systems therapy described in this chapter.

family therapy Any psychotherapeutic treatment of the family to improve psychological functioning among its members. Most major theories of psychotherapy have applications to family therapy.

family systems therapy A type of family therapy in which the entire family is seen as a unit or as a system. Focus is often on the interaction of family members.

conjoint therapy A type of couples therapy in which one therapist sees both members of the couple at the same time.

identified patient The person who other members of the family identify as having the problem for which treatment is sought.

HISTORY OF FAMILY THERAPY

EARLY APPROACHES TO FAMILY COUNSELING

Before the 1930s advice was provided by clergy, friends, doctors, and lawyers
The first centers for marriage counseling were in New York and Los Angeles
In 1930s and 1940s different therapists saw different members of the family or couple
Conjoint therapy in the 1950s became more common
Children often were dealt with in guidance clinics separately from the parents
Some blaming of parents for the child's problems
In the 1950s a shift to helping parents and children relate better to each other

EARLY PSYCHOANALYTIC INFLUENCES

Sigmund Freud's work with five-year-old Hans and other children using a drive theory perspective
Anna Freud's work with children in a clinic in England
Donald Winnicott was a pediatrician and object relations therapist who made recommendations to parents as well as working with children
Erikson specialized in working with children
Alfred Adler developed and was involved with child guidance clinics in Vienna
Harry Stack Sullivan studied how children and their families behaved in interpersonal situations
Nathan Ackerman was the first to treat children and families as a single unit, making use of psychoanalytical techniques

CASE EXAMPLE

The following case will be used for each of the next four sections. By using the same example, you will be able to see the different perspectives of different family therapists. You will be asked questions about the Green family from each of the perspectives.

Sara and her husband, Ron, have sought help for Charles, their 12-year-old son. Charles is in the sixth grade at a local public elementary school. The principal at the school asked Sara and Ron to meet with him because of his concern about Charles' behavior with his classmates. Basically, Charles is described as a bully. He picks fights with his classmates and argues with them. Recently, he hit Jonnie so hard that Jonnie suffered a concussion. He also has been fighting with other children at recess and on the way home from school.

This has not come as a surprise to Sara and Ron as they received a call from Jonnie's father's lawyer about paying the cost of his injuries and possible civil charges against Charles as well as a complaint to be filed regarding Charles in juvenile court.

Sara and Ron have talked to Charles about his behavior which is not limited to school. His nine-year-old sister, Vivian is terrified of Charles. When Charles is angry and upset with Vivian, he swats her rather than talks to her. This behavior has been going on for two years.

Although he does not respond physically to his parents, he is surly and sullen. They have had difficulty getting Charles to clean up his room and put away toys or sports equipment that he uses. Similarly, Charles does little of his homework on time. He does write English papers when prodded. Surprisingly, he does his math homework. His A's in math contrast with C's and D's in other subjects. His behavior has not always been like this. As Sara points out, Charles used to have a more gentle disposition although he has always been rather physical and rough with toys and other children.

Charles is large for his age. He is about 5'6" tall and weighs almost 170 pounds. His large, sloppy appearance tends to put off other children. His athletic skills are average for his age. In sports, like baseball or tennis, he has more difficulty than in football and running.

Vivian is a third grader who is doing well at school. She enjoys playing with friends who live across the street. On weekends she can be found at her friends' houses. At home she is quiet, often going up to her room to play with her dolls. She avoids the conflict that exists between Charles and her parents.

Sara is a manager of a small jewelry store in their town. This puts strong time demands on her as the store is open until 9 PM every evening except Sunday. She works until 9:30 three evenings a week. She has arranged for an after school program for Vivian and Charles. Because she grew up in a situation where her mother took care of her two brothers and sisters while her father traveled frequently, she feels guilty about having made such arrangements . Her father was a wholesale auto parts salesman.

Ron is a lawyer, working mainly with wills and estates. His father died when he was seven. His mother, a seamstress, raised Ron and his older brother by herself. She was a religious woman who believed that one of her main goals in life was to see that her children were educated. Both Ron and his brother, a surgeon, worked their way through college and professional school.

INFLUENCES ON FAMILY SYSTEMS THERAPY

There have been two major influences on family systems theory that are more specific in nature than the influence of psychoanalysis. The first is observations of communication styles in schizophrenic families. The second influence is general systems theory.

COMMUNICATION PATTERNS IN SCHIZOPHRENIC FAMILIES

Although most family therapists believe that physiological factors play a much greater role in schizophrenia than was believed to be the case in the 1950s, work on family communication patterns has had a lasting contribution. Some of the most important concepts are defined here.

double bind A view that when an individual receives an important message with two different meanings and is unable to respond to it, the individual is in an impossible situation. If such messages are repeated over time, individuals may begin to show signs of schizophrenia.

marital schism A situation in which one parent tries to undermine the worth of another by competing for sympathy or support from the children.

marital skew A situation in which the psychological disturbance of one parent dominates the family's interactions. An unreal situation for family members is created so that the family can deal with one member's disturbance.

pseudomutuality Presenting an appearance of open relationships in a family so as to conceal distant or troubled relationships within the family. Members develop roles that they play rather than relating honestly.

GENERAL SYSTEMS THEORY

Systems theory is based on the work of Wiener, a mathematician, and Bertalanffy, a biologist. Systems theory provides several concepts that deal with changes in the system. In the case of family systems therapy, this refers to how changes in one family member can bring about changes in another. Thus, general systems theory has helped therapists look at the entire family as a unit. All of these concepts deal with changes in the system.

systems theory A study of the relationship of parts in their context, emphasizing their unity and their relationship to each other. It is applied to biology, medicine, and other fields and is a basis for family systems therapy.

feedback A communication pattern in which information about the consequences of an event is reintroduced into the system.

negative feedback Information that flows back to a system to reduce behavior that causes disequilibrium.

positive feedback Information that leads to deviation from the system's norm, bringing about change and a loss of stability.

equifinality The ability of a system to arrive at the same destination from different paths or conditions.

homeostasis Balance or equilibrium in a system. Such a balance can bring about a stable environment in the system.

QUESTIONS

1. If Sara says to Charles in a very exasperated voice, "Now, Charles you are such a nice boy," there is evidence that Charles may be experiencing

    a. a double bind.
    b. marital schism.
    c. marital skew.
    d. pseudomutuality.

2. If Ron were to become very depressed, then we might expect _____ to occur in the family.

    a. a double bind
    b. marital schism
    c. marital skew
    d. pseudomutuality

3. The family member who is most likely to behave in a way that demonstrates pseudomutuality is

    a. Ron.
    b. Sara.
    c. Charles.
    d. Vivian.

4. The identified patient in this case example is

    a. Ron.
    b. Sara.
    c. Charles.
    d. Vivian.

5. When Ron gets mad at Charles for getting in trouble at school and this argument escalates into a shouting match, then _____ is occurring in the system.

   a   homeostasis
   b. positive feedback
   c. negative feedback
   d. equifinality

6. Which of these concepts refers to the many ways that Ron could interact with Charles to discuss the problems that he is having at school?

   a. homeostasis
   b. positive feedback
   c. negative feedback
   d. equifinality

BOWEN'S INTERGENERATIONAL APPROACH

Murray Bowen developed a system that is based on an individual's ability to differentiate his or her own intellectual functioning from his or her feelings. He examined relationships among family members. One concept not shared by other family systems theories is his view of passing psychological characteristics from one generation to another.

THEORY OF FAMILY SYSTEMS

Bowen's view of how families interact is shown in his development of significant concepts. Perhaps the key concept is *differentiation of self*. A major problem in families can occur when there is fusion, indicating a lack of differentiation.

fusion A merging or meshing of thoughts and feelings in a family member; the opposite of differentiation.

differentiation The process of differentiating one's thinking from one's feeling; the opposite of fusion.

pseudoself An expression of values or opinions that other family members may find acceptable rather than one's own values or opinions.

triangulation A process in which two people who are in conflict involve a third person in order to reduce the tension in the relationship between the original two people.

family projection process A means of projecting or transmitting a parental conflict to one or more children.

emotional cut-off Given too much stress in a family due to over involvement of parents, children may withdraw or cut themselves off emotionally from the family.

GOALS OF BOWENIAN THERAPY

Bowen tried to help family members become more differentiated and thus reduce their general stress level. He felt that it was helpful to try to get family members to detriangulate.

TECHNIQUES OF BOWENIAN FAMILY THERAPY

In Bowenian therapy, taking a history of the family and using a genogram is a part of the evaluation interview. Later, interpreting information from the genogram and from observations about dynamics in the family takes place. Detriangulation and the use of genograms are among the most important of Bowenian therapeutic approaches.

detriangulation The process of withdrawing from a family member or therapist, so as not to be drawn into alliances of one person against another.

genogram A method of charting a family's relationship system. It is essentially a family tree in which ages, sex, marriage dates, and similar information may be diagrammed.

QUESTIONS

7. As a Bowenian therapist, you would ask for information about Ron and Sara's

   a. parents.
   b. grandparents.
   c. aunts and uncles.
   d. all of the above.

8. The individual in the family who is probably least differentiated is

   a. Ron.
   b. Sara.
   c. Charles.
   d. Vivian.

9. When Vivian is challenged by Charles, she tries to involve her mother as soon as possible. This is called

   a. differentiation of self.
   b. triangulation.
   c. family projection process.
   d. emotional cutoff.

10. The family member most likely to experience an emotional cut off is

   a. Ron.
   b. Sara.
   c. Charles.
   d. Vivian.

11. As a Bowenian therapist, a goal that you might have for this family is to

   a. help the parents deal with their own emotional stress that they feel from dealing with Charles.
   b. help Vivian become more emotional when dealing with Charles.
   c. help the principal become more effective in dealing with Charles.
   d. become more aware of alignments and coalitions within the family.

12. Which of these comments are you most likely to make to Charles when he says: "If the kids at school don't behave the way I like, I push them around"?

   a. It is the teacher's role to discipline the other children, not yours.
   b. When you act as angry as you like, where does it get you?
   c. What do you feel when other children don't do as you ask?
   d. Try something different next time. Pick a child that you might like just a little bit, and say something nice to him or her.

STRUCTURAL FAMILY THERAPY

One of the most influential therapies, Minuchin's structural family therapy deals with alignments and coalitions within the family. Observing and changing relationships in the family is a focus of this system of family therapy.

CONCEPTS OF STRUCTURAL THERAPY

Minuchin was an astute observer of family interactions. He would observe their verbal and nonverbal behavior. He would also inquire about subsystems, smaller units within the family such as the husband and wife. He would learn about the circumstances under which members of the family would join with one another. He would also try to learn the rules within the family. His focus was on current functioning rather than past relationships.

family structure The rules that have been developed in the course of family life to determine which members interact with which other members and in what way.

boundary permeability The degree to which boundaries are flexible among family members, and the nature of the contact that family members have with each other.

enmeshed A reference to families in which members are overly concerned and overly involved in each other's lives. Boundaries are highly permeable.

disengaged A reference to families, where members are isolated or feel unconnected to each other. Boundaries are rigid and non-permeable.

alignment The way where family members join or oppose each other in dealing with events.

coalitions Alliances or affiliations between family members against another family member.

GOALS OF STRUCTURAL THERAPY

Structural therapists try to bring about changes in the family that will alter coalitions and change alliances to help a family function more effectively.

TECHNIQUES OF FAMILY THERAPY

Structural therapists often join with the family to focus on present issues. They may accommodate to family customs to better understand the family and to be accepted by them. Enacting a problem helps the therapist observe coalitions and alliances which they then may map using diagrams to describe the ways that the family relates. Techniques are often active, sometimes subtle, sometimes directive. The intensity of an intervention may be varied in order to bring about a certain reaction.

mimesis A process by which a therapist appears similar to family members by imitating body language, styles, or other features. A way of joining a family system and getting cooperation from a family.

tracking Staying attuned to a family's style of relating and understanding symbols of a family's life.

enactment A therapeutic procedure in which families are asked to act out a conflict so that the therapist can work with the actual conflict rather than a report of it.

boundary marking A technique to change boundaries or interactions among individual family members. An example would be to change the seating of family members in therapy.

reframing Giving a new or different explanation for an event so that constructive change can occur in the family.

13. The relationship between Charles and Vivian can be viewed as a

    a. family structure.
    b. family subsystem.
    c. family boundary.
    d. family coalition.

14. When all four members of the family are together, Ron tends to give orders, and the others are expected to follow. Sara is often expected to see that the orders are carried out. This is an example of a(an) _____ family.

    a. fused
    b. coalesced
    c. enmeshed
    d. disengaged

15. As you talk to and observe the family, you notice that they all sit up very straight in their chairs. You also decide to do this. This is an example of

    a. family sculpting.
    b. enactment.
    c. mimesis.
    d. tracking.

16. As you are watching Sara and Ron talk about Charles, you notice that Charles is looking out the window. You are likely

    a. to ask him to pay attention to what his parents are saying.
    b. to have him move his chair close to or between his parents.
    c. ignore him and listen to his parents.
    d. ask him what he is feeling now.

17. When Sara and Ron talk about how they had a difficult time with Charles at home about not doing his history assignment, you may

    a. suggest that they be more encouraging.
    b. act out the situation right now with Charles, having his parents talk to him now about history.
    c. suggest that he start first with math (something he likes) and later do history.
    d. get Charles' attention and explain why it is important for him to listen to his parents.

18. After the session is over and you make a map of the family, the map would include

    a. a diagram of Sara and Ron's relationship to their parents.
    b. lines to indicate the type of boundaries that exist within the family.
    c. changes in the seating that took place within the session.
    d. directions to the family's house.

STRATEGIC THERAPY

Strategic therapy focuses on the clients' symptoms or problems that they describe to the therapist. Like structural therapists, strategic therapists attend to relationships within families and triangles that exist. However, strategic therapists concentrate on symptoms, often seeing them as metaphors for problems within the family.

GOALS OF STRATEGIC THERAPY

The basic goals are to remove the symptoms that families bring to therapy. The goals must be specific so that the therapist can find out which family member is experiencing which symptoms, in what ways, and in which situations. There must be enough information so that the therapist can decide how to reach the goals.

TECHNIQUES OF STRATEGIC THERAPY

Strategic therapy is one of the most difficult of the therapies covered in this text for therapists to learn and implement. The therapist devises and assigns tasks to the family. Such tasks would be ones that the family has not implemented. The two types of tasks that are used to bring about change are straightforward and paradoxical. The tasks are often metaphors for solving family problems. For example, asking a father and daughter to go shopping together would be a metaphor for improving the relationship between the father and daughter. Paradoxical tasks are particularly difficult to devise.

straightforward task A task that the family is intended to accept and perform as stated.

paradoxical task A task in which a therapist gives a client or family a directive that is likely to be resisted. Change takes place whether or not the task is completed.

QUESTIONS

Because strategic therapy is complex, you are likely to find questions OE2 and OE3 very difficult to answer. Take a guess and don't worry if you can't think of possible solutions. Some solutions are offered at the end of the chapter.

*OE1. State the goal of strategic therapy for the Green family.

_____

_____

*OE2. Describe a straightforward task that you would give to the family.

_____

_____

*OE3. Describe a paradoxical task that you would give to the family.

_____

_____

EXPERIENTIAL AND HUMANISTIC THERAPY

Both Carl Whitaker and Virginia Satir used approaches that encouraged open communications within the family. Whitaker used an intuitive approach, trusting his reactions to the family. Whitaker used confrontation, exaggeration, and absurdity as techniques. His approach was creative and energetic.

Noted for her communication skills, Virginia Satir was often empathic with the family. She identified five styles of relating within the family. To explore relationships within the family, she used techniques such as family sculpting and taking a family life chronology.

family sculpting A technique in which family members are physically molded or directed to take characteristic poses to represent a view of family relationships.

family life chronology A way of recording significant events in a family's development.

QUESTIONS

19. If Charles says "Nobody pays attention to me unless I'm in trouble," a humanistic therapist might respond in this way:

    a. Why don't you sit closer to Vivian.
    b. Sometimes you really hurt inside if you feel your parents are too busy to be with you.
    c. When you are at school and the teacher asks a question, raise your hand and try to answer it.
    d. Sara, did you feel ignored by your mother when you were Charles' age? What did you do to feel closer to her?

20. When Vivian starts to cry because of Charles's outbursts in therapy, a humanistic or experiential family systems therapist might

    a. tell Charles to be careful not to shout so as not to upset Vivian.
    b. ask Ron to caution Charles not to shout.
    c. ask whether what has just happened in therapy happens at home.
    d. empathize with Vivian, discussing her fear of Charles' shouting.

INTEGRATIVE APPROACHES

Several of the different family systems theories may seem quite distinct from each other. However, many family therapists make use of some of these approaches or even all of them. The training of family therapists and the perception that family therapists have of the best approach to treating the family is likely to influence the therapists' approach. Also, their own personality is likely to influence which theories therapists choose to use.

THEORIES OF INDIVIDUAL THERAPY AS APPLIED TO FAMILY THERAPY

Each of the theories in the text with the exception of Jungian therapy, applies its theoretical approach to helping families. The method for doing this is summarized in the following chart that lists the chapter, the theory, and the basic approach to family therapy.

Chapter 2	Psychoanalysis	The object relations approach is influential in focusing on nurturing and caring provided by family members to each other. Interpretation of past behavior and therapeutic resistance is common.
Chapter 4	Adlerian Therapy	Using an educational approach, Adlerians teach parents how to deal with children by pinpointing the problem and reaching agreement.
Chapter 5	Existential Therapy	Therapists are aware not only of relationships between family members but also each member's sense of being in the world. Keeping diaries is an example of a method to do this.

Chapter 6	Person-Centered Therapy	Family therapists may empathize with family members who are present at the session, as well as those who are not.
Chapter 7	Gestalt Therapy	Gestalt therapists help members to be aware of their own issues. They may also have family members enact problems.
Chapter 8	Behavior Therapy	Behavioral family therapists often teach parents how to use behavioral methods with their children.
Chapter 9	REBT	Family therapists identify irrational beliefs among family members. They then dispute *shoulds* and *musts* and other irrational beliefs. They also use cognitive and behavioral change techniques.
Chapter 10	Cognitive Therapy	Education is a part of family therapy as is challenging and changing distorted beliefs. Suggestions for changing beliefs are given to family members.
Chapter 11	Reality Therapy	Reality therapists observe choice systems of family members. They help family members meet their own needs while promoting harmony in the family. They focus on activities family members can do together.
Chapter 12	Feminist Therapy	Feminist family therapists may focus on how political and social factors influence the family. They attend to the effect of gender and cultural issues that affect the family.

BRIEF FAMILY SYSTEMS THERAPIES

Although most family therapeutic approaches tend to be brief, some were designed to produce change quite quickly or to require relatively few sessions. Even though the approaches are symptom focused (first-order change), they are designed to bring about lasting change (second-order). Brief family therapy may be for fewer than 5 or 10 sessions.

first-order change A temporary change in the family system to solve a specific problem. Such changes do not alter the basic system of the family.

second-order change A change that produces a lasting change in the family as well as fundamental changes in the family's structure and organization.

THE MENTAL RESEARCH INSTITUTE BRIEF FAMILY THERAPY (MRI) MODEL

One of the earliest approaches, the MRI model, focused on communication patterns. Its goal was to resolve problems in the family and relieve symptoms. Often MRI therapists try to make small changes and build on them. As Haley does in structural therapy, they make use of straightforward and paradoxical tasks. Some of their communication concepts include the following:

complimentary communication A relationship in which there is inequality in two or more members. One is usually submissive to the other.

symmetrical communication A type of communication characterized by equality among individuals. Such communication can result in one angry remark following another, leading to an argument.

punctuation The concept that each person in a transaction believes what he or she says is caused by what the other person says. Basically the individual holds the other responsible for his or her reactions.

Focus is more on communication patterns rather than on coalitions and alliances as used by Minuchin in structural therapy or on parental hierarchies as in Haley's strategic therapy.

LONG BRIEF THERAPY OF THE MILAN ASSOCIATES

Although there are several different approaches within the Milan group in Italy, their focus has been somewhat similar to the MRI model. They have used dramatic interventions. They also have had consulting therapists watch sessions of the family therapy and then make suggestions to the therapists. Two techniques that they are particularly known for are circular questioning and the invariant prescription.

circular questioning An interviewing technique designed to elicit differences in perceptions about events or relationships from different family members.

invariant prescription A single directive given to parents, designed to create clear boundaries between parents and children.

SPECIAL TOPICS

OE4. Why do you think psychoeducational approaches have become more popular recently in working with families with schizophrenic members than have traditional therapeutic approaches? (512)

_____

_____

OE5. Why is it helpful for family therapists to have a knowledge of legal issues? (513)

_____

_____

OE6. What impact can feminist therapy's view of gender role have on the practice of family therapy? (516)

_____

_____

OE7. If you were a family therapist, in what ways would knowledge of your clients' family background and culture be helpful to you? (517)

_____

_____

_____

OE8. How can ideas from family systems therapy be applied to individual therapy? (545)

_____

_____

_____

STRENGTHS AND LIMITATIONS

What do you believe are the strengths and limitations of family systems therapy?

Strengths	Limitations
_____	_____
_____	_____
_____	_____
_____	_____
_____	_____
_____	_____
_____	_____
_____	_____

FAMILY SYSTEMS THERAPY: A QUIZ

True/False Items. Decide if the following statements are "more true" or "more false" as they apply to family systems therapy.

T F Q1. Family systems therapy focuses on each individual equally.

T F Q2. The genogram would be a useful assessment device in Haley's strategic therapy.

T F Q3. Only family systems therapies try to help families with problems.

T F Q4. Other theories of therapy do not work with families.

T F Q5. Bowenian therapies are interested in family relationships that may include grandparents.

T F Q6. In the 1930s, it was almost unheard of for a family therapist to meet with the whole family.

T F Q7. Experiential therapy has a set of specific techniques that are applied to the experiences of different family members.

T F Q8. A structural therapist might ask a family member to move closer to another member in order to realign boundaries.

T F Q9. Psychoeducational approaches have been developed to help families with schizophrenic members develop methods for coping with and helping the schizophrenic member.

T F Q10. In family systems therapy, positive feedback refers to giving positive reinforcement to a family member.

Multiple choice items: Select the best answer from the alternatives given. Most of the questions ask you to choose the theory of family therapy that most closely fits the question.

_____ Q11. How do other theories of family therapy differ most clearly from family systems therapy?

        a. do not apply as many directive techniques
        b. do not adhere to the same strict code of ethics
        c. do not view the family as a single system
        d. are less likely to use paradoxical interventions

_____ Q12. A family that has a severely depressed parent is most likely to experience

        a. a double bind.
        b. marital schism.
        c. marital skew.
        d. pseudomutuality.

_____ Q13. Family systems therapists view the communication within the family as

        a. linear.
        b. contrived.
        c. dysfunctional.
        d. circular.

_____ Q14. In assessing family problems, which type of family therapy is most likely to use family mapping?

        a. Bowen's intergenerational therapy
        b. existential therapy
        c. structural therapy
        d. strategic therapy

_____ Q15. In assessing family problems, which type of family therapy is most likely to examine distorted thoughts of family members?

        a. Bowen's intergenerational therapy
        b. cognitive therapy
        c. structural therapy
        d. strategic therapy

_____ Q16. The use of straightforward tasks to bring about change in the family is most often used in

    a. Bowen's intergenerational therapy.
    b. cognitive therapy.
    c. structural therapy.
    d. strategic therapy.

_____ Q17. Discussion of family interaction style of grandparents is most likely to occur in

    a. Bowen's intergenerational therapy.
    b. rational emotive behavioral therapy.
    c. structural therapy.
    d. strategic therapy.

_____ Q18. Having a family act out a conflict is a technique that is most commonly associated with structural family therapy and

    a. Bowen's intergenerational therapy.
    b. existential therapy.
    c. Gestalt therapy.
    d. psychoanalytic therapy.

_____ Q19. Which of these theorists was most concerned about education as a way of helping families with problems?

    a. Adler
    b. Bowen
    c. Freud
    d. Jung

_____ Q20. Determining the degree to which family members are differentiated is most likely to be done in

    a. Adlerian therapy
    b. Bowen's intergenerational therapy.
    c. structural therapy.
    d. strategic therapy.

_____ Q21. Focusing on helping families develop authenticity and meaningfulness in their lives is most associated with

    a. Adlerian therapy.
    b. existential therapy.
    c. psychoanalytic therapy.
    d. strategic therapy.

_____ Q22. Empathy and warmth in relating to the family are most often associated with the work of

    a. Murray Bowen.
    b. Jay Haley.
    c. Virginia Satir.
    d. Carl Whitaker.
    e. the Milan group.

_____ Q23. The use of the invariant prescription is an approach associated with

        a. Murray Bowen.
        b. Jay Haley.
        c. Virginia Satir.
        d. Carl Whitaker.
        e. the Milan group.

_____ Q24. Which of these approaches to family therapy is the most difficult for therapists to use well?

        a. Adlerian therapy
        b. Bowenian therapy
        c. person-centered therapy
        d. strategic therapy

_____ Q25. Which of the following is NOT a current issue in family systems therapy?

        a. the impact of medication of family therapy
        b. psychoeducational methods with families with members who have severe psychological disturbance
        c. concern about vulnerability to malpractice suits
        d. the impact of intersubjectivity theory on the therapeutic relationship with the family

ANSWER KEY

1.	a	11.	a	Q1. F	Q11. c	Q21. b
2.	c	12.	d	Q2. F	Q12. c	Q22. c
3.	d	13.	b	Q3. F	Q13. d	Q23. e
4.	c	14.	d	Q4. T	Q14. c	Q24. d
5.	b	15.	c	Q5. T	Q15. a	Q25. d
6.	d	16.	b	Q6. T	Q16. b	
7.	d	17.	b	Q7. F	Q17. a	
8.	c	18.	b	Q8. T	Q18. c	
9.	b	19.	b	Q9. T	Q19. a	
10.	d	20.	d	Q10. F	Q20. b	

*OE1. The goal of strategic therapy would be to have Charles act friendly and verbally with his peers and sister. Another goal would be for him to complete his homework on time.

*OE2. Straightforward tasks might be to
    have him play football and have his father involved in coaching the team.
    have his father play sports with him.
    have Charles help Vivian with her math homework.
    have Charles teach Vivian an athletic activity.
    have Sara take Charles to school, go to a sports event, or do an activity with him.

(Most of these activities would be designed to channel Charles' aggressiveness into socially acceptable activities or to have Charles have a closer coalition with members of his family.)

*OE3. Paradoxical tasks might include
    telling Charles to continue to act out aggressively so he can make others do what he wants.
    telling Charles not to do his homework so he can be even more independent.
    telling the family to encourage Charles to not be friendly with children at school so he can be even more
       independent.

(Because the Green family is cooperative, paradoxical tasks may not be necessary. The paradoxical tasks above could have negative consequences that the therapist does not intend.)

CHAPTER 14

OTHER PSYCHOTHERAPIES

> Because this chapter contains relatively brief explanations of five different therapies, the format of this chapter is different from the other chapters. For each of the five theories, five questions are given to compare your view of therapeutic issues with those of the theory. Then the theory is summarized and important concepts are described. A quiz follows which includes five true and false questions and five multiple choice questions.

ASIAN THERAPIES

To compare your views of therapy with those who use Asian therapeutic approaches, put an "X" on the line that indicates how much you agree or disagree with the statement.

D_____A 1. Spiritual healing and therapy are closely related.

_____ 2. Clients can learn responsibility by learning how to act ethically.

_____ 3. To understand oneself, one has to understand other aspects of the universe.

_____ 4. Attending to one's own being and thoughts can be therapeutic.

_____ 5. Helping clients become less self-centered is an important goal of therapy.

BACKGROUND OF ASIAN THERAPIES

Dating back more than 3,000 years, Asian philosophy and psychology have been influenced by Hindu and Buddhist teachings. In Indian psychology, four concepts have been key to understanding philosophical beliefs that relate to Asian psychology.

dharma Rules that describe goodness and appropriate behavior.

karma Movement from past incarnations that affect the present.

maya A concept referring to the distorted perception of reality and experience. Only by directing attention to one's awareness, through concentration or meditation, can reality and experience be perceived more accurately.

atman A concept of universality in which the self is not seen as an individual but as part of the entire universe.

These concepts are learned, in part, through yoga and Hatha-yoga.

yoga Hindu teachings dealing with ethics, life-style, body postures, breath control, intellectual study and meditation.

Hatha-yoga Deals with the physiological discipline required in separating the self from thought processes.

Other concepts that are derived from Buddhist teachings are the four noble truths and the eightfold path. These values have had a major influence on Asian psychology and philosophy.

ASIAN THEORIES OF PERSONALITY

Thousands of years of the history of Asian philosophy and religion are condensed into less than eight pages on Asian therapy. There are major differences between several Asian philosophies and religions. The commonalities between these philosophies, rather than the differences, are described in the text. These include:

The self is closely related to the universe.

Deemphasis on the individual, emphasis on the whole of humanity.

Interdependence as seen by involvement with the family and the extended family is important.

There are different states of consciousness.

Psychological health can be seen as freedom from fears, compulsions, and anxieties.

Being able to observe one's fears, compulsions, and anxieties is helpful in being psychologically healthy.

ASIAN THEORIES OF PSYCHOTHERAPY

Three Asian therapies are described in the text. They can be called "quiet" therapies because of their focus on spending time in isolation to deal with thoughts and varied states of awareness. Meditation is the most ancient and is closely associated with Buddhism and Hinduism. Naikan and Morita therapies were both developed in Japan.

MEDITATION

Used widely in Asia to seek higher psychological or religious levels of self-development, it is used much less commonly in the West. In the West, it is often used for stress management and relaxation. By focusing on consciousness itself, individuals can become aware of distortions in perceptions (maya).

meditation Methods for controlling one's mental processes. In concentration meditation, the focus is on a stimulus such as the act of breathing. In awareness meditation, the purpose is to examine consciousness and the mind.

zazen A Zen Buddhist approach to meditation.

Meditation, when practiced 30 minutes a day, can have positive physiological and psychological effects. To try out meditation, sit in a straight-backed chair for 10 to 30 minutes following this instruction:

Count each inhalation and exhalation up to ten; then start over, or count only exhalations; if you want, extend the exhalations and the internal count as ooooone, then twooooo, threeeee, and so forth.

190

NAIKAN THERAPY

A Japanese therapy in which patients focus on their mistakes in past relationships, Naikan therapy helps patients improve relationships with others so that they may contribute to society. In Japan, it is a strict inpatient therapy. In the West, it has been modified so that isolation and activity restriction is not so strict. Three important questions guide patients in their self-observations of past relationships:

1. What did I receive from this person?
2. What did I return to the person?
3. What troubles and worries did I cause this person? (Reynolds, 1993, p.124)

MORITA THERAPY

Originated around 1915, Morita therapy is designed to help patients redirect tension away from themselves. It is an inpatient therapy lasting 4 to 5 weeks. There are four phases starting with isolation and moving towards doing mundane tasks.

Following this regimen, patients learn to be practical and specific so that actions can be taken to reduce symptoms. Originally designed to treat obsessive-compulsive, panic, and phobic disorders, it has been used for other psychological disturbances as well. When used in the United States, the severe isolation aspects are modified. Writing down one's thoughts and the therapist's comments are an aspect of Morita therapy.

QUESTIONS

True/false items. Decide if the following statements are more "true" or more "false".

T F Q1.   Asian therapies are derived from Western existential philosophy.

T F Q2.   Meditation is viewed in Asia as a form of psychotherapy.

T F Q3.   Meditation interferes with the ability to observe one's own fears.

T F Q4.   Assertiveness training is very different in focus than Naikan therapy.

T F Q5.   The purpose of isolation in Morita therapy is to help patients experience their symptoms and appreciate the need for changing one's lifestyle.

Multiple choice items. Select the best answer from the alternatives given.

_____ Q6.   Which of the following concepts refers to distortions of perceptions of experience?

        a. dharma
        b. karma
        c. maya
        d. atman

_____ Q7.   Which of the following concepts refers to seeing oneself not as an individual but as a part of the universe?

        a. dharma
        b. karma
        c. maya
        d. atman

_____ Q8. Which of these therapies sees overcoming self-centeredness as an important therapeutic goal?

        a. meditation
        b. Naikan therapy
        c. Morita therapy
        d. existential therapy

_____ Q9. Learning to be more practical and less idealistic is an important therapeutic goal for

        a. meditation.
        b. Naikan therapy.
        c. Morita therapy.
        d. existential therapy.

_____ Q10. In Naikan therapy, the therapist's role is similar to that of a

        a. coach.
        b. confessor.
        c. evaluator.
        d. facilitator.

BODY PSYCHOTHERAPIES

To compare your views of therapy with those who use body therapy approaches, put an "X" on the line that indicates how much you agree or disagree with the statement.

D_____A 1. Bodily and psychological processes are one and the same.

_____ 2. Attending to patients' breathing, posture, and physique is useful in assessing patients' problems.

_____ 3. Touching the patient is appropriate in therapy as long as it is done in accordance with ethical guidelines.

_____ 4. Personality of individuals can be assessed by attending to how patients move and stand.

_____ 5. Early traumatic experiences can affect how people breathe, stand, walk, or run.

BACKGROUND OF BODY THERAPY

Developed by Wilhelm Reich, body therapies seek to integrate the body and mind. Reich developed *vegetotherapy* in which he sought to release life forces so that they could flow through the body. He did this by observing and manipulating the body. For Reich, orgone was a central concept.

Alexander Lowen, a patient and student of Reich's, developed bioenergetic analysis. It differed from Reich's method in that it used a more varied approach to treatment, was more closely aligned with psychoanalysis, and attended to grounding. Lowen's work has been popularized to some degree through his writings. The most significant concepts from Reich's and Lowen's work are described here.

body armor or *muscular armor* A protective mechanism in the individual to deal with the punishment that comes from acting on instinctual demands such as defecating in public.

orgone A physical force that powers all physiological and psychological functions. Developed by Wilhelm Reich.

bioenergetic analysis Developed principally by Alexander Lowen, this is a method of understanding personality in terms of the body and its energy flow. Attention is given to physiology, breathing, and bodily movement.

grounding A concept developed by Alexander Lowen which emphasizes being in contact with the ground literally, through feet and legs, as well as figuratively being grounded in the real world.

PERSONALITY THEORY AND THE BODY

Attending to the ways that individuals conduct themselves physically is an essential aspect of understanding personality. Body therapists especially attend to the ways in which individuals breathe. Changing breathing patterns can bring about momentary changes in affect. Likewise, changing other bodily positions and movements can bring about other changes. Psychological disorders are affected by physiology. Physiology may be affected by past events.

Lowen described five types of character structures. They are explained in the text along with their psychological attributes. The physiological characteristics associated with them are pointed out here.

schizoid character The individuals' upper and lower body parts may not seem to go together. The head may be held to one side, and there may be a lack of energy in face, hands, and feet.

oral character The legs and feet are likely to be underdeveloped and thin. Tension in the shoulders and legs may symbolize that the person has been left alone or abandoned.

narcissistic character A sense of superiority may appear in the overdevelopment of the upper half of the body. Tension appears in the legs and back of the person when standing.

masochistic character Because such individuals tend to hold in feelings, tension can be seen in the arms and legs. Often the eyes have a look of suffering, and the individual has a whining voice.

rigid character The posture is erect, with rigidity in the back muscles and stiffness in the neck.

It is important not to take these descriptions out of context. They are provided to show how Lowen makes a link between the physical and the psychological. As he points out, he treats people not character types. Individuals combine different character types.

PSYCHOTHERAPEUTIC APPROACHES

Body therapists integrate assessment with therapy. As individuals change their body positions and breathing, body therapists reassess these changes, and therapists use this information to make therapeutic interventions. Body reading and body awareness methods are used for assessment. Soft and hard techniques are used for helping individuals with their psychological problems.

body reading Systematic observations used to understand energy blockages and tensions within the body.

body awareness Patients may move or change positions and develop more awareness of their body.

soft techniques A way of asking the patient to assume a gentle posture or softly touching a patient so that psychological awareness or change may occur.

hard techniques A method of asking the patient to assume an uncomfortable or painful position or touching a patient in a somewhat painful way which may bring about intense emotional responses.

ETHICS AND BODY PSYCHOTHERAPY

Because of the use of touch, ethics are of primary importance in body psychotherapies. Focus is on patient growth. Therapists should not use therapy to satisfy their own needs. Erotic intentions are prohibited. Ethics also apply to group workshops. Therapists must be aware when members are in therapy and that contact with all workshop participants may be limited to the single event.

QUESTIONS

True/false items. Decide if the following statements are more "true" or more "false".

T F Q11. Body psychotherapists use similar techniques to those of physical therapists.

T F Q12. The concept of muscular armor is a protective mechanism to deal with punishment for acting on instinctual demands.

T F Q13. In the assessment process, body psychotherapists may touch the patient's body to assess blockages in energy flow.

T F Q14. The use of the orgone box to help a variety of patients' problems led to Reich's eventual imprisonment.

T F Q15. Because of their use of touch, body therapists are particularly concerned with following ethical guidelines closely.

Multiple choice items. Select the best answer from the alternatives given.

_____ Q16. To have firm contact with the real world refers to the concept of

        a. orgone.
        b. grounding.
        c. soft therapeutic techniques.
        d. hard therapeutic techniques.

_____ Q17. Vegetotherapy is a technique associated with the work of

        a. Lowen.
        b. Reich.
        c. Sheldon.
        d. Smith.

_____ Q18. Which of the following is not a part of Lowen's group of character structures?

        a. schizoid
        b. grounding
        c. oral
        d. masochistic
        e. rigid

_____ Q19. Calling attention to when a patient stops breathing for a moment is an example of a body therapy

    a. soft technique.
    b. hard technique.
    c. grounding technique.
    d. use of a technique from a different theory.

_____ Q20. In body therapy, touching a female patient's breast would be an example of

    a. a soft technique.
    b. a hard technique.
    c. grounding.
    d. unethical behavior.

INTERPERSONAL PSYCHOTHERAPY

To compare your views of therapy with those who use interpersonal therapy, put an "X" on the line that indicates how much you agree or disagree with the statement.

D_____A 1. Therapy should be designed to treat specific disorders.

_____ 2. In developing a theory of therapy, attention should be paid to research that supports the use of certain methods rather than relying solely on clinical hunches.

_____ 3. Treatment of depression should focus on interpersonal relationships.

_____ 4. Encouragement and support are essential elements of therapeutic treatment.

_____ 5. Treatment manuals are a valuable asset in the application of psychotherapy.

BACKGROUND

Developed by Gerald Klerman and his colleagues, interpersonal therapy differs from other therapies in several respects. It was designed using a medical model, being exposed rather quickly to tests of its effectiveness. Not only was it designed to be subject to research, but its rationale and techniques were built on prior research. Its original application was to depression. Other applications have generally been to disorders that are somewhat similar to depression such as dysthymia. Because it was designed to be subject to research, treatment manuals that clearly spell out procedures for therapists to follow were implemented and refined. The manuals plan for therapy to be completed in approximately 12 to 16 sessions.

A psychiatrist, Klerman was influenced by medical research and, more specifically, research into the treatment of depression. Three theorists were particularly important in the early development of interpersonal therapy.

Adolf Meyer emphasized the importance of both physiological and psychological forces on treatment of psychiatric disorders.

Harry Stack Sullivan showed how peer relationships in childhood and adolescence affect later interpersonal relationships.

John Bowlby's work on attachment explained the importance of early bonding with the mother.

One of the most important influences on Klerman's development of interpersonal psychotherapy was his review of specific factors that contributed to depression.

INTERPERSONAL THERAPY PERSONALITY THEORY

Designed for assisting depressed patients, Klerman focused on those factors that contributed specifically to depression. He asked, What problem areas contribute to depression? After reviewing literature on depression, he identified four: grief, interpersonal disputes, role transitions, and interpersonal deficits.

grief Although a normal process, grief can contribute to depression. When the loss is severe and lengthy or there is more than one loss, depression can last a long time.

interpersonal disputes Ongoing struggles, disagreements, or arguments with others can contribute to depression. The disputes may occur in the family, at school, at work, or in other situations.

role transitions Life changes such as illness, divorce, marriage, or having children leave home can create stress and contribute to depression.

interpersonal deficits Social isolation or the lack of social skills may cause loneliness and related problems.

Note that all four of these categories deal in some way with interpersonal relationships.

GOALS

The goals of interpersonal therapy are developed from the four types of problems that relate to depression. Typically, interpersonal therapists will only work on one or two of these goals due to the short duration of interpersonal therapy.

grief To reestablish interest in relationships and become more involved with others and to help with the mourning process.

interpersonal disputes To understand how disputes and arguments relate to depression and to resolve these disputes to bring about change.

role transitions To move from one role to another. To mourn the loss of one role and develop mastery of a new role, resulting in increased self-esteem.

interpersonal deficits To reduce isolation from others, develop new relationships and improve old ones.

TECHNIQUES OF INTERPERSONAL THERAPY

Interpersonal therapy is done in three phases: the initial, the intermediate, and the termination phase. The first and third phases last for two or three sessions each. All phases focus, in different ways, on one or two of the four problem areas.

Initial phase Diagnosis of depression is made. Referral may be made if interpersonal therapy is not appropriate. Assessment is focused on placing the problem into the four problem areas. Diagnosis is shared with the patient. Encouragement and hope for the problem are given to the patient.

Intermediate phase In this phase, attention is addressed to the four problem areas. A good therapeutic relationship not only encourages participation in therapy but provides a model for outside relationships. Techniques for change are not very different than those used by other therapies, but the techniques are designed to address those problem areas as appropriate.

starting the session Klerman suggested that therapists ask: "How have things been since we last met?" Because the question focuses on recent events, it helps to focus the patient on specific problem areas.

encouragement of affect Expression of painful emotions is encouraged so that the therapist can show understanding and explore ways to remedy the situation.

clarification Interpersonal relationships are clarified so that patients can better understand an interpersonal situation.

role playing This is one of several techniques used to help the patient try out or explore new methods for improving interpersonal relationships.

Termination phase Explicitly discussing the approaching end of therapy, a focus is put on the patient becoming more independent. Emphasis on gains and discussion of relapse prevention also takes place.

Interpersonal therapy flows from one phase to another. The attention to the appropriate problem areas (grief, interpersonal disputes, role transitions, or interpersonal deficits) occurs in all three phases.

Although interpersonal therapy was designed for the treatment of depression, it has been applied to other problem areas. Before it is applied to a new area, a new treatment manual is developed. The new areas of treatment are often quite close to the original area: distressed but not clinically depressed individuals, people with a depressive mood disorder (dysthymia), pregnant women with depression, and adolescents with depression. In general, results have been more positive when interpersonal therapy was applied to these groups than when it was applied to substance addictions.

QUESTIONS

True/false items. Decide if the following statements are more "true" or more "false".

T F Q21. Klerman's interpersonal therapy focuses on different styles of communication among people.

T F Q22. Interpersonal therapy was developed to treat anxiety disorders.

T F Q23. The duration of interpersonal therapy is approximately three months.

T F Q24. Past interpersonal relationships are the major emphasis of interpersonal therapy.

T F Q25. Treatment manuals were written in such a way to encourage the use of support rather than to explore unconscious motivations.

Multiple choice items. Select the best answer from the alternatives given.

_____ Q26. A significant aspect of interpersonal therapy is its

    a. tie to existentialism.
    b. grounding in constructivism.
    c. focus on enactment.
    d. use of treatment manuals.

_____ Q27. Which of the following is not a problem area that interpersonal therapy addresses?

    a. anti-social behavior
    b. grief
    c. interpersonal disputes
    d. interpersonal deficits
    e. role transitions

_____ Q28. In interpersonal therapy, which of the following areas is considered the most difficult to address?

    a. anti-social behavior
    b. grief
    c. interpersonal disputes
    d. interpersonal deficits
    e. role transitions

Q29. Which of the following problems is interpersonal therapy LEAST likely to address?

    a. loss of a spouse
    b. panic disorder
    c. disputes at work
    d. lack of friends

Q30. Which of the following techniques is most likely to be used by an interpersonal therapist?

    a. behavioral analysis
    b. boundary analysis
    c. communication analysis
    d. psychoanalysis

PSYCHODRAMA

To compare your views of therapy with those who use psychodrama, put an "X" on the line that indicates how much you agree or disagree with the statement.

D_____A   1. Individuals learn about themselves by examining the different roles that they play in life.

_____   2. Spontaneity and creativity are characteristics of living a full and healthy life.

_____   3. Enacting one's problems can provide new and creative solutions to them.

_____   4. Expressing feelings that have been held in is a significant goal of therapy.

_____   5. Other people can provide valuable insights into your problems by playing roles of important people in your life.

BACKGROUND

The theatrical nature of psychodrama reflects the flair for the dramatic and the interest in drama of its founder, Jacob Moreno. As a student of philosophy, he enjoyed watching the play of children. While a medical student in Vienna, he was interested in social injustice and in helping socially disenfranchised groups. His development of psychodrama in the 1930s laid the groundwork for group therapies that were to follow. The technique of role playing, adopted by many theories, was developed by Moreno as he created new therapeutic techniques to be used in psychodrama.

Moreno worked in a variety of settings. He developed impromptu theater in Vienna. In 1925, he moved to the United States. In one sanatarium, he built a theater to be used for psychodrama. He brought psychodrama to schools, prisons, and hospitals. Moreno's focus on the different roles people play and the use of the group in therapy provided an impetus for other therapeutic interventions that were to follow.

THEORY OF PERSONALITY

In his view of personality, the roles that people played at various times in their lives with other people were of paramount importance. He developed sociometry as a way of studying roles and the relationships between people. He was interested in activity that was taking place in the present. The past is important as it influences the present. Noted for his spontaneity and creativity, Moreno valued these characteristics in others and saw them as a part of acting in a healthy way. His major concepts of personality relate to roles, the present, creativity, and energy.

sociometry A method of learning the nature of relationships between people in a group by getting feedback from members about their interpersonal preferences.

role distance By playing parts connected to or associated with an event, individuals become more objective (or more distant) from their roles.

encounter The dialogue that takes place between two individuals or two aspects of the same individual meeting another individual or another part of themselves.

tele The energy that is present in an interaction between two people in an interpersonal exchange. Moreno frequently used *tele* to refer to a sense of caring that developed in group members in the process of psychodrama.

PSYCHODRAMA THEORY OF PSYCHOTHERAPY

The basis of psychodrama is role playing. By playing different roles through the use of enactment, individuals can view their lives differently. They can experience *catharsis*, the expression of feelings that have been previously repressed. In psychodrama, individuals can play different roles. The therapist functions as a director.

director The person who manages the participants in a psychodrama. The director initiates and organizes a psychodrama and works with the protagonist, auxiliaries, and the audience.

protagonist The individual who presents a problem that will be the focus of a psychodrama.

auxiliaries Members of a group or audience who play significant roles in the life of the protagonist.

audience People present during the enactment who observe the psychodrama. They may be involved at some point as protagonists or auxiliaries.

In psychodrama there are three basic phases: the warmup, action, and discussion and sharing. During all of these phases, the therapist creates an atmosphere of sharing and trust.

warm-up Describes the purpose of psychodrama and encourages sharing among participants, often in small groups.

action Auxiliaries and the protagonist work through the protagonist's issues guided by the director.

sharing and discussion Auxiliaries and the audience share their observations with the protagonist. The director guides the process so that the feedback is helpful rather than critical.

A variety of psychodrama techniques are used to help individuals learn about their relationships with others through enactment. These can involve just the protagonist or the protagonist and one or more auxiliaries.

monodrama A dialogue with oneself in which an individual plays both parts in a scene by alternating between them.

role reversal A technique in which individuals play the part of someone else in their life to get a better perspective of their relationships with others.

double technique A role in which an auxiliary takes the part of the protagonist and expresses his or her perception of the protagonist's thoughts or feelings.

mirror technique A process in which the auxiliary tries to copy the postures, expressions, and words of the protagonist so that the protagonist can view the perceptions of his or her behavior as held by another person.

surplus reality Experiences that are not physical reality but rather may refer to fantasies, dreams, hallucinations, or relationships with imagined people.

future projection Playing a situation that could occur at some time in the future. For example, playing out an interaction with a future mother-in-law.

QUESTIONS

True/false items. Decide if the following statements are more "true" or more "false".

T   F   Q31. Understanding one's relationships with others is the primary focus of psychodrama's approach to understanding personality.

T   F   Q32. The role of the director is to encourage the audience and auxiliaries to express their unchecked emotional feelings regarding the protagonist's problems.

T   F   Q33. Bringing past experiences and relationships into the present through enactment is a primary purpose of psychodrama.

T   F   Q34. Sociometry is a systematic way of studying the relationships between people.

T   F   Q35. Assessment in psychodrama occurs throughout the entire process of the psychodrama, not just at the beginning.

Multiple choice items. Select the best answer from the alternatives given.

_____ Q36. Which of the following does NOT describe psychodrama?

   a. creative
   b. cognitive
   c. encounter
   d. spontaneous

_____ Q37. Psychodrama is based on a belief that individuals' personality is based in large part on

   a. each individual's relationships with his or her parents.
   b. responsibility for one's own actions.
   c. the different roles that individuals play in their lives.
   d. how individuals cope with choices that concern behaving authentically.

_____ Q38. In studying roles, Moreno used _____ as a method for determining how individuals related to each other.

   a. genograms
   b. sociograms
   c. diagrams
   d. anagrams

_____ Q39. When Mary plays the role of Margaret's grandmother and then gives up the role so that Margaret, the protagonist, can play her own grandmother, the director is using

   a. the double technique.
   b. surplus reality.
   c. future projection.
   d. role reversal.

_____ Q40. If Mary, an auxiliary, now plays the role of Margaret, the protagonist, the director is using

   a. the double technique.
   b. surplus reality.
   c. future projection.
   d. role reversal.

200

CREATIVE ARTS THERAPIES

To compare your views of therapy with those who use creative arts therapies, put an "X" on the line that indicates how much you agree or disagree with the statement.

D_____A 1. Non-verbal expressions by patients as acted out in art, music, dance, or drama can be a helpful adjunct to therapy.

_____ 2. Acting out one's problems can be a helpful therapeutic approach.

_____ 3. Listening to music or watching drama and discussing its relevance or value for individuals can contribute to personal growth.

_____ 4. Social skills can be learned by interaction with the therapist and group members while using a variety of creative arts therapies.

_____ 5. Having art work that can be looked at from time to time and discussed in therapy provides a dimension that verbal expression does not.

OVERVIEW OF CREATIVE ARTS THERAPIES

By expressing themselves through the use of creative arts therapies, individuals can understand their feelings and beliefs in new ways, become more productive, develop self-esteem, develop new forms of self-expression, and/or improve their social interaction with others. The most common creative arts therapies are art, drama, dance movement, and music. The text describes each briefly, giving one or two case examples of each. The use of an artistic medium or form of expression is an element that all four have in common.

Creative arts therapy training programs exist for each of these areas. More recently there has been a trend for creative arts therapists to learn more than one form of the creative arts therapies.

Creative arts therapists often work as a part of a team. Although the traditional area of employment is psychiatric hospitals, this trend is changing with creative arts therapists working in a variety of employment settings. Regardless of setting, creative arts therapists combine their knowledge of an area of artistic skill with knowledge of psychotherapy to help patients. The four types of creative arts therapies are defined here.

art therapy A method of helping patients deal with emotional conflicts and awareness of their feelings by using a variety of art media such as paints, crayons, paper, or sculpting materials.

dance movement therapy A method of helping individuals integrate psychological and physiological processes so that they can better understand their own feelings, thoughts, and memories by expressing themselves through movement or dance.

dramatherapy A means of making psychological change by involving individuals in experiences that are related to theater. Sometimes patients may enact their own spontaneous drama, play the parts of a play that has been written, or observe a play and discuss it. Psychodrama is considered to be one form of dramatherapy.

music therapy Patients may listen or participate in musical experiences through singing or using musical instruments to improve emotional expression, reduce stress, or to deal nonverbally with a variety of issues.

QUESTIONS

True/false items. Decide if the following statements are more "true" or more "false".

T F Q41. Art therapists should use their work as examples to stimulate client creativity.

T F Q42. An advantage of art therapy is that it can create physical works that can be discussed, whereas words are lost once they are spoken.

T F Q43. More than most therapists, creative arts therapists often work as part of a team.

T F Q44. Video recording equipment is too complex to be used in art therapy.

T F Q45. Music therapy involves making sounds or music, not listening to it.

Multiple choice items. Select the best answer from the alternatives given.

_____ Q46. Exaggeration is a technique that is most likely to be used in

    a. art therapy.
    b. dance movement therapy.
    c. dramatherapy.
    d. music therapy.
    e. all of the above.

_____ Q47. Psychodrama can be viewed as a subset of

    a. art therapy.
    b. dance movement therapy.
    c. dramatherapy.
    d. music therapy.
    e. all of the above.

_____ Q48. Dance movement therapy is least likely to include

    a. movement exercises.
    b. spontaneous movement by patients.
    c. dancing with other patients.
    d. structured dances.

_____ Q49. In creative arts therapies, suggestions for creative expression come from

    a. the client.
    b. the therapist.
    c. treatment manuals.
    d. both a and b.

_____ Q50. Issues of boundaries, transference, and ethics are most likely to be found in

    a. art therapy.
    b. dramatherapy.
    c. music therapy.
    d. all of the above

ANSWER KEY

Q1.	F	Q11.	F	Q21.	F	Q31.	T	Q41.	F
Q2.	F	Q12.	T	Q22.	F	Q32.	F	Q42.	T
Q3.	F	Q13.	T	Q23.	T	Q33.	T	Q43.	T
Q4.	T	Q14.	T	Q24.	T	Q34.	T	Q44.	F
Q5.	T	Q15.	T	Q25.	T	Q35.	T	Q45.	F
Q6.	c	Q16.	b	Q26.	d	Q36.	b	Q46.	b
Q7.	d	Q17.	b	Q27.	a	Q37.	c	Q47.	c
Q8.	b	Q18.	b	Q28.	d	Q38.	b	Q48.	d
Q9.	c	Q19.	a	Q29.	b	Q39.	d	Q49.	d
Q10.	b	Q20.	d	Q30.	c	Q40.	a	Q50.	b

CHAPTER 15

CONSTRUCTIVIST AND INTEGRATIVE APPROACHES

Constructivist and integrative therapies go beyond a single theoretical approach. In constructivist approaches, the therapist focuses on understanding problems, not from theory, but from the client's point of view. Integrative approaches combine two or more theories in various ways.

In this chapter of the Student Manual, the case of Wanda is used to help you better understand two constructivist theories, solution-focused and narrative therapy and three integrative approaches. These are summarized and questions are asked about each.

CONSTRUCTIVIST THEORIES SELF-INVENTORY

D _____ A   1. Theories can get in the way of understanding a client.

_____   2. Therapists can learn much about a client by understanding her story from her point of view.

_____   3. Theory does not help clients move toward solving their problems.

_____   4. Approaching a client's problems as if they are short stories or novels can be helpful.

_____   5. Solutions to problems should be the therapist's focus, not underlying reasons for the problem.

_____   6. I enjoy understanding themes and characters in novels.

_____   7. For some client problems, theories of psychotherapy are not necessary.

_____   8. Individuals have basic ways they see or construct their world.

_____   9. A client's view of the world is more important than the therapist's theory of psychotherapy.

_____   10. In therapy, subjective perceptions that clients have are more important than an objective diagnostic system like the DSM-III-TR.

INTEGRATIVE THERAPIES SELF-INVENTORY

Put an "X" on the line so that it indicates how much you agree or disagree with the statement: A=Agree, D=Disagree.

D_____A 1. Several theories can be combined together to be used in psychotherapy and counseling.

_____ 2. Theories provide a consistent way to conceptualize client problems.

_____ 3. Using more than one theory can be helpful in understanding the personality of a client.

_____ 4. Concepts from psychoanalysis and behavior therapy can be combined while still presenting a consistent theoretical approach.

_____ 5. Using only one theory can limit a therapist's flexability.

_____ 6. Concepts from many theories can be combined to make an entirely different theory that is internally consistent.

_____ 7. If I were counseling, I would want to use more than one theory.

_____ 8. Some theories are better than others for certain types of client problems.

_____ 9. Research is important in determining which theories to use with clients.

_____ 10. Counseling or therapy without a grounding in theory tends to make it difficult to develop clear goals and know which techniques should be used with clients.

SOLUTION-FOCUSED THERAPY

Therapists want to know how the family views possible solutions to the problem. They are not particularly interested in discussing the causes of the problem. The focus is on the expectations that family members have for change.

GOALS

Goals should be clear, specific, and small. Therapists want to know how things would be different in life if the goals were met. Progress on goals is often measured in therapy using a 0 to 10 scale. At the end of a session, the therapist may ask for feedback about meeting goals as well as give written or oral feedback to the family about their progress in meeting goals.

TECHNIQUES USED IN SOLUTION-FOCUSED THERAPY

Most techniques used in solution-focused therapy are questions. These are usually goal related, often dealing with progress in meeting goals. Some questions inquire about ways the family may have tried to solve the problem and when they were successful, even if briefly, in making their problems better. Questions may try to focus on what worked rather than what didn't work.

change questions Questions are asked about what positive changes in solving the problem took place prior to therapy.

miracle questions What would be different if a miracle happened? Questions like this help to further define the goal.

exception finding questions Therapists ask about exceptions to the problem. When is the problem not there and what is life like when the problem is not there?

coping questions These questions ask about successful experiences that individuals have had in dealing with the problem. They highlight the person's ability to cope with problems.

scaling questions Asking individuals to rate their progress on a goal from 0 to 10 is the basic approach in using scaling questions.

CASE EXAMPLE

Wanda is a 9 year old girl who is in the third grade. She has a 12 year old sister, Jill, who is in the sixth grade. Wanda's parents have been concerned because Wanda has started to scream at Jill and at Wanda's classmates if Wanda does not get her way.

Wanda's parents, Harry and Mary Balto, have become concerned because the relationship between Jill and Wanda has gotten worse. Because Mary works at a chemical plant as a technician and Harry is a self-employed electrician, they have depended on Jill to take care of Wanda after school. Wanda complains about Jill being mean to her and Jill complains about Wanda's rudeness and uncooperativeness.

Harry and Mary have sought help in dealing with Wanda because they have seen her becoming more defiant and less cooperative recently.

QUESTIONS

1. As a solution-focused therapist, which of the following questions are you most likely to ask in counseling the Balto family?

    a. How did Wanda's angry behavior start?
    b. When have you noticed that Wanda plays well and is cooperative?
    c. What has happened at home that has caused Wanda to act out angrily?
    d. When did Jill start to have difficulty with Wanda?

2. The answer to question 1 is "b", because all other questions deal with causes rather than solutions. What type of solution-focused question is "b"?

    a. change
    b. miracle
    c. exception finding
    d. coping
    e. scaling

3. As a solution-focused therapist, which of the following questions are you most likely to ask in counseling the Balto family?

    a. Jill, how do you feel when Wanda is angry at you?
    b. Mary, were you at all like Wanda when you were growing up?
    c. Mary, if something wonderful could happen with your family and there were no longer any problems, how would your family be different?
    d. Wanda, the solution to the problem can be easy if you want it to be. Do you need to control your temper when you are angry?

4. The answer to question 3 is "c", because all other questions deal with feelings, past behavior, or simplistic solutions. What type of solution-focused question is "c"?

   a. change
   b. miracle
   c. exception finding
   d. coping
   e. scaling

5. If you say to Jill, "How were you able to talk calmly to Wanda and get her to enjoy playing with her Barbies rather than have a tantrum?", you would be asking a (an) _____ question.

   a. change
   b. miracle
   c. exception finding
   d. coping
   e. scaling

NARRATIVE THERAPY

Changing or retelling stories so that more positive resolutions can occur is the basis of narrative therapy. The narratives can deal with issues in people's lives that are political, cultural, economic, or social. Negative or problem-oriented stories can affect the attitudes or lives of families.

CONCEPTS OF NARRATIVE THERAPY

Clients' perceptions of events and the world around them are of great interest to narrative therapists. They listen for problem-oriented or problem-saturated stories, thinking about how these can be reconstructed so that the solutions can be changed to be more productive. Attending to themes and meanings of stories is a major focus of narrative therapists. Many narrative therapists use terms that are used in literature classes to analyze stories or novels:

setting When and where the story takes place. This promotes a background for understanding the clients' description of the problem.

characterization The people in the story are the characters. The client is often the protagonist as well as the narrator. People who have conflicts with the client are often the antagonists.

plot The plot refers to actions that take place in the story. Plots may have several episodes and/or actions. The story may be told more than once. Different plots or views of the plot may develop.

themes The themes are the meanings that the story has for the client. What does the client find important or meaningful in the story? Clients may understand the story in one or more of these ways: cognitively, emotionally, or spiritually.

GOALS

A significant goal of narrative therapy is to help clients see their lives or stories from a more positive rather than a problem saturated point of view. Clients try to derive meaning from examining the characters and plots in their lives. Achieving a resolution to a problem can come from examining a story in new ways to bring about new alternatives to events in the story.

TECHNIQUES OF NARRATIVE THERAPY

Narrative therapy techniques are all related to the telling of stories. Narrative therapists have developed new ways to look at stories and retell them.

narrative empathy Fully understanding the story of the family or client.

reconstructing The process of telling a story in a different way to bring about positive change.

externalizing the problem Making the problem, not the child or family, the opponent. Thus, removing Guilt becomes the focus of therapy rather than the person's guilty feelings.

unique outcomes Sometimes called sparkling moments, unique outcomes are thoughts, feelings, or actions that occur when the problem starts to dissolve.

alternative narratives The process of exploring strengths, special abilities, and aspirations of the family to tell a positive story with good outcomes rather than a problem-saturated story.

QUESTIONS

6. Mary tells of a time recently when the four of them went to a large shopping mall. Wanda went with Jill into a toy store and patiently listened to Jill give her opinion of some toys. Narrative therapists would call this a(an)

    a. reflective moment.
    b. alternative narrative.
    c. reconstruction.
    d. unique outcome.

7. When Wanda describes how she just got so angry at a classmate and yelled at her, you, as a narrative therapist, might say:

    a. Weren't there any other alternatives?
    b. What were you feeling at the moment?
    c. What would you like to do when Anger appears?
    d. Wanda, what would you like to say to that girl now?

8. As a narrative therapist, you would try to find a(an) _____ for the Balto family that would lead to Wanda dominating Anger.

    a. reflective moment
    b. alternative narrative
    c. reconstruction
    d. unique outcome

9. As a narrative therapist, which theoretical background would provide the best approach to using narrative empathy with a family?

    a. psychoanalytic theory
    b. person-centered theory
    c. structural therapy
    d. strategic therapy
    e. no theory

(e. This may seem like a trick question, but a narrative therapist would not want theoretical or other preconceptions to interfere with her understanding the family's story.)

THERAPEUTIC INTEGRATION

There have been three major systematic approaches to integrating theories of therapy. Each approach has had several different models within it. In the text, one example or model is given to illustrate each approach to integrating theories of therapy. These three approaches are defined here.

transtheoretical A psychotherapeutic approach in which concepts common to many theories are used to develop a new theory of psychotherapy.

theoretical integration A psychotherapeutic approach in which concepts of personality and techniques of psychotherapy from one theory are combined with those of one or more other theories.

technical eclecticism A psychotherapeutic approach in which the personality concepts of one theory provide the rationale for using psychotherapeutic techniques from many theories.

PROCHASKA'S TRANSTHEORETICAL APPROACH

Perhaps the most well known transtheoretical approach, Prochaska's system, focuses on readiness for change, types of problems, and change processes. The change processes have been adapted from different theories of therapy and are applied only to certain types of problems or stages. For this approach, theories serve as a source of developing therapeutic techniques and are not used directly as they are in theoretical integration and in technical eclecticism. To provide an overview of Prochaska's transtheoretical approach, the five stages of readiness for change, the five types of problems, and the ten change processes are listed here.

READINESS FOR CHANGE	TYPES OF PROBLEMS	CHANGE PROCESSES
pre-contemplation	symptoms	consciousness-raising
contemplation	maladaptive thoughts	catharsis/dramatic relief
preparation	interpersonal conflicts	self-reevaluation
action	intrapersonal conflicts	environmental reevaluation
maintenance	family conflicts	self-liberation
		social liberation
		counter conditioning
		stimulus control
		contingency management
		helping relationships

The text presents just a sketch of Prochaska's well-developed transtheoretical model. That overview should be sufficient to show how a psychotherapy theorist could draw concepts from other theories to develop his or her system.

THEORETICAL INTEGRATION

At its most basic, theoretical integration takes two theories and combines them. Their personality theories are combined to provide an assessment of patients' problems and an understanding of their personality. The techniques are combined in prescribed ways to bring about change. Sometimes more than two theories are used in this way. Although a number of different theoretical integrative models have been developed, one which has probably generated the largest following is Wachtel's cyclical psychodynamics.

cyclical psychodynamics An example of the theoretical integration approach to psychotherapy that was developed by Paul Wachtel. Concepts from psychoanalytic theory are combined with those from behavior therapy (and also cognitive and family systems approaches). The cyclical aspect of his view refers to the belief that psychological problems create problems in behavior, and problems in behavior create psychological conflicts or problems.

TECHNICAL ECLECTICISM

Unlike the unsystematic (hodgepodge) eclectic approach, technical eclecticism is quite systematic. One personality theory forms the basis for assessing patients' problems and understanding their personality. For therapeutic techniques, the theorist draws from many theories, making the application of the technique consistent with the personality theory. The most widely used technical eclectic approach is that of multimodal therapy.

multimodal A therapeutic approach developed by Arnold Lazarus which uses personality theory concepts from social cognitive theory and takes techniques from many other theories which it applies in a manner that is consistent with social cognitive theory. The seven major modalities are represented in the acronym BASIC I.D.

BASIC I.D. An acronym that includes the seven fundamental concepts of multimodal therapy: Behavior, Affect, Sensation, Imagery, Cognition, Interpersonal relationships, and Drugs/biology.

In order to assess client problems and to make changes in the seven modalities, Lazarus has developed techniques that help in the observation of modalities and in tracking clients as they switch modalities.

firing order The sequence of modalities that occurs when an individual perceives an event. For example, Interpersonal-Sensation-Imagery.

tracking Observing and responding to the sequence or firing order of the seven modalities (BASIC I.D.) of different clients.

bridging Being aware of and responding to a client's current modality before introducing another modality to the client.

Two other techniques are helpful in multimodal therapy. Time tripping deals with the Imagery modality, and the deserted island technique can be helpful in learning more about all of the modalities.

time tripping A technique in which clients are asked to picture themselves going backward or forward in time to deal with events or issues.

deserted island technique A fantasy experience in which clients are asked what the therapist would learn if he or she were alone with the client on a deserted island. It is designed to help the therapist learn more about the client's seven modalities.

QUESTIONS ABOUT THREE TYPES OF THERAPEUTIC INTEGRATION

10. If you question Wanda's commitment to changing behavior, you would probably be conceptualizing using

    a. Prochaska's transtheoretical model.
    b. Wachtel's theoretical integration.
    c. Lazarus's technical eclecticism.

11. As a therapist, you observe that Wanda imagines her classmates not liking her and then yells or hits them. You notice a switch from Imagery to Behavior. You are probably using this approach:
    a. Prochaska's transtheoretical model.
    b. Wachtel's theoretical integration.
    c. Lazarus's technical eclecticism.

12. Lazarus would describe the technique that you use to observe Wanda a
    a. coping.
    b. firing order.
    c. miracle question.
    d. tracking.

13. Because of Wanda's age, you decide to make use of behavioral, cognitive, and family systems therapy as a way to understand her problems and as a way to help her with her problems. You are using which integrative approach?

    a. a transtheoretical model
    b. theoretical integration
    c. technical eclecticism
    d. unsystematic eclecticism.

14. Imagine that you were unfamiliar with theories of psychotherapy, which approach are you most likely to have taken with Wanda?

    a. a transtheoretical model
    b. theoretical integration
    c. technical eclecticism
    d. unsystematic eclecticism

15. You decide that you are going to help Wanda by using specific techniques that you have gathered from several theories. These techniques include catharsis/dramatic relief, stimulus control, and contingency management. You would be using

    a. Prochaska's transtheoretical model.
    b. Wachtel's theoretical integration.
    c. Lazarus's technical eclecticism.

SPECIAL TOPICS

OE1. Why do you think therapists continue to be attracted to the idea of integrating two or more theories into their work? (594)

_____

_____

_____

OE2. How does the construct of gender fit into the techniques of solution-focused and narrative therapies? (596)

_____

_____

_____

OE3. What multicultural issue can hinder the application of solution-focused therapy in non-English speaking languages? (597)

_____

_____

OE4. How could Wachtel's cyclical psychodynamic approach to theoretical integration include a sensitivity to multicultural issues? (597)

_____

_____

STRENGTHS AND LIMITATIONS

What do you believe are the strengths and limitations of constructivist therapy?

Strengths	Limitations
_____	_____
_____	_____
_____	_____
_____	_____
_____	_____

What do you believe are the strengths and limitations of integrative approaches?

Strengths	Limitations
_____	_____
_____	_____
_____	_____
_____	_____
_____	_____

CONSTRUCTIVIST AND INTEGRATIVE APPROACHES: A QUIZ

True/False Items. Decide if the following statements are "more true" or "more false" as they apply to constructivist and integrative therapies.

T   F   Q1.   George Kelly believed most people, not just scientists, construct hypotheses and test them against their view of reality.

T   F   Q2.   Solution-focused therapists can work with vague and unclear goals as well as those that are specific.

T   F   Q3.   Reflection of feelings rather than questions are a basic tool of solution-focused therapy.

T   F   Q4.   In narrative therapy, clients' problems can be analyzed the way one would analyze a novel.

T   F   Q5.   Narrative therapists and solution focused therapists look for times in their patients' lives when the problem did not occur or when the problem started to dissolve.

T F Q6. The transtheoretical approach to integrating theories draws effective techniques from other theories to make a new theory.

T F Q7. Unlike many theories, Prochaska and Norcross's transtheoretical model describes levels of readiness for theoretical change.

T F Q8. A theoretical integration model is one which combines theories of personality and theories of psychotherapy of two or more therapies.

T F Q9. Therapists who practice technical eclecticism draw techniques from other theories without systematically integrating them.

T F Q10. In multimodal therapy, Lazarus uses social cognitive theory as a means for understanding the behavior and personality of his clients.

Multiple choice items: Select the best answer from the alternatives given. Many of the questions ask you to choose the constructivist or integrative therapy that most closely fits the question.

Q11. In narrative therapy, therapists try to determine the meaning of the story the client tells. The therapist is listening for the

    a. miracle.
    b. theme.
    c. solution.
    d. unconscious.

Q12. Externalizing the problem is a technique used in

    a. solution-focused therapy.
    b. narrative therapy.
    c. transtheoretical therapy.
    d. technical eclecticism.

Q13. Which of the following therapies is most likely to ask about positive changes in solving a problem that took place prior to therapy?

    a. solution-focused therapy.
    b. narrative therapy.
    c. transtheoretical therapy.
    d. technical eclecticism.

Q14. Time-tripping is a technique used in

    a. narrative therapy.
    b. solution-focused therapy.
    c. Prochaska's transtheoretical approach.
    d. Wachtel's cyclical dynamics.
    e. Lazarus's multimodal approach.

Q15. Rating the clients' progress on a goal from one to ten is a technique found in

    a. narrative therapy.
    b. solution-focused therapy.
    c. Prochaska's transtheoretical approach.
    d. Wachtel's cyclical dynamics.
    e. Lazarus's multimodal approach.

Q16. What would be different if a miracle happened? is a question most likely to be used in

   a. narrative therapy.
   b. solution-focused therapy.
   c. Prochaska's transtheoretical approach.
   d. Wachtel's cyclical dynamics.
   e. Lazarus's multimodal approach

Q17. A theory that combines the personality theories and techniques of cognitive therapy and Asian therapies would be called

   a. a transtheoretical approach.
   b. theoretical integration.
   c. technical eclecticism.
   d. solution-focused therapy.

Q18. A theory based on the existential understanding of personality yet uses techniques derived from many theories would be called

   a. a transtheoretical approach.
   b. theoretical integration.
   c. technical eclecticism.
   d. unsystematic eclecticism.

Q19. If a therapist selects techniques from various theories and shows how they help with different problems and also provides a new system for assessing client concerns, her approach would be

   a. narrative therapy.
   b. a transtheoretical approach.
   c. theoretical integration.
   d. technical eclecticism.
   e. unsystematic eclecticism.

20. Observing and responding to clients' switching from one type of modality to another is associated with

   a. Prochaska's transtheoretical approach.
   b. Wachtel's cyclical dynamics.
   c. Lazarus's multimodal approach.
   d. solution-focused therapy
   e. unsystematic eclecticism.

21. Attention to clients' readiness to change is an aspect of

   a. Prochaska's transtheoretical approach.
   b. Wachtel's cyclical dynamics.
   c. Lazarus's multimodal approach.
   d. unsystematic eclecticism.

22. Combining the personality theory and change techniques of both behavior therapy and psychoanalysis is the basis of

   a. Prochaska's transtheoretical approach.
   b. Wachtel's cyclical dynamics.
   c. Lazarus's multimodal approach.
   d. unsystematic eclecticism.

23. The use of the BASIC I.D. to establish goals is associated with

    a. Prochaska's transtheoretical approach.
    b. Wachtel's cyclical dynamics.
    c. Lazarus's multimodal approach.
    d. narrative therapy.

24. A therapist who does not use a theoretical rationale but changes approaches as the client changes her statements in therapy is using

    a. Prochaska's transtheoretical approach.
    b. Wachtel's cyclical dynamics.
    c. Lazarus's multimodal approach.
    d. unsystematic eclecticism.

25. Being aware that a client is changing from Affect to Behavior in multimodal therapy would be called

    a. bridging.
    b. environmental reevaluation.
    c. stimulus control.
    d. time tripping.

ANSWER KEY

1. b	11. c	Q1. T	Q11. b	Q21. a
2. c	12. d	Q2. F	Q12. b	Q22. b
3. c	13. b	Q3. F	Q13. a	Q23. c
4. b	14. d	Q4. T	Q14. e	Q24. d
5. d	15. a	Q5. T	Q15. b	Q25. a
6. d		Q6. T	Q16. b	
7. c		Q7. T	Q17. b	
8. b		Q8. T	Q18. c	
9. e		Q9. F	Q19. b	
10. a		Q10. T	Q20. c	

CHAPTER 16

COMPARISON AND CRITIQUE

Because this final chapter seeks to summarize and integrate the theories discussed in previous chapters, the format in this study guide is different from that of other chapters. I provide a format for you to make notes about pertinent information that will help you prepare for a final exam.

To help you identify concepts from theories, I will give you a case example and follow it with a dialogue with the client. You will be asked to identify the theory that best fits the therapist's response. Finally, a quiz with 25 multiple choice questions will help you test your knowledge of theoretical concepts and therapeutic techniques.

BACKGROUND

Perhaps the best way to review the background for each theory is to go over the section in this study guide that summarizes the background for each theory. Doing this prior to completing the following section may be helpful.

PERSONALITY THEORY, GOALS, ASSESSMENT, AND THERAPEUTIC TECHNIQUES

These four sections represent the core of the textbook and of theories of psychotherapy and counseling in general. Personality theory, goals, assessment, and therapeutic techniques are summarized in Chapter 16 separately. Reviewing these sections should prove useful. Another way to further review the material is to test yourself on it by filling out the following charts which are designed to summarize the four areas for each chapter. Using this section to make notes and to list important concepts in the text may be helpful.

DIFFERENTIAL TREATMENT

You may find it helpful to review cases in the text to better understand the application of theory to actual psychotherapy. Table 16.5 on page 612 in the text provides a useful overview of the ways each theory can be applied to depression and anxiety. Cognitive therapy and psychoanalysis are two theories that have developed different techniques for different disorders. Behavior therapy and Adlerian therapy have done this also but to a lesser degree. Other theories apply similar approaches to different disorders, focusing more on attending to patient issues and problems than on diagnostic classification systems.

PSYCHOANALYSIS

PERSONALITY THEORY	GOALS AND ASSESSMENT	THERAPEUTIC TECHNIQUES
Drive Theory		
Ego Psychology		
Object Relations		
Self Psychology		
Relational Psychoanalysis		

JUNGIAN ANALYSIS

PERSONALITY THEORY	GOALS AND ASSESSMENT	THERAPEUTIC TECHNIQUES

ADLERIAN THERAPY

PERSONALITY THEORY	GOALS AND ASSESSMENT	THERAPEUTIC TECHNIQUES

EXISTENTIAL THERAPY

PERSONALITY THEORY	GOALS AND ASSESSMENT	THERAPEUTIC TECHNIQUES

PERSON-CENTERED THERAPY

PERSONALITY THEORY	GOALS AND ASSESSMENT	THERAPEUTIC TECHNIQUES

GESTALT THERAPY

PERSONALITY THEORY	GOALS AND ASSESSMENT	THERAPEUTIC TECHNIQUES

BEHAVIOR THERAPY

PERSONALITY THEORY	GOALS AND ASSESSMENT	THERAPEUTIC TECHNIQUES

RATIONAL EMOTIVE BEHAVIOR THERAPY

PERSONALITY THEORY	GOALS AND ASSESSMENT	THERAPEUTIC TECHNIQUES

COGNITIVE THERAPY

PERSONALITY THEORY	GOALS AND ASSESSMENT	THERAPEUTIC TECHNIQUES

REALITY THERAPY

PERSONALITY THEORY	GOALS AND ASSESSMENT	THERAPEUTIC TECHNIQUES

FEMINIST THERAPY

PERSONALITY THEORY	GOALS AND ASSESSMENT	THERAPEUTIC TECHNIQUES

FAMILY THERAPY

PERSONALITY THEORY	GOALS AND ASSESSMENT	THERAPEUTIC TECHNIQUES
Bowen's intergenerational		
Minuchin's structural		
Haley's strategic		
Experiential		

CONSTRUCTIVIST AND INTEGRATIVE APPROACHES

PERSONALITY THEORY	GOALS AND ASSESSMENT	THERAPEUTIC TECHNIQUES
Solution-focused		
Narrative therapy		
Prochaska's transtheoretical approach		
Wachtel's theoretical integraion (cyclical psychodyamics)		
Lazarus's technical eclecticism (multimodal therapy)		

BRIEF THERAPIES

More than any other theory, psychoanalysis has been applied to short term psychotherapeutic treatment. Brief psychodynamic therapy varies in length from 12 to 50 sessions. Most brief psychoanalytical approaches are 12 to 20 sessions. One of over a dozen short-term psychoanalytical therapies is described in the text.

Brief approaches have not usually been applied to Jungian or person-centered therapies. Gestalt, Adlerian, and reality therapy tend to be briefer than psychodynamic and Jungian therapies.

Cognitive, behavioral, and REBT therapies are generally brief. However, the number of problems, their severity, and their strength influence the length of therapy for these theories.

Family systems therapies tend to be brief. A few, the MRI model and the long brief therapy of the Milan school, are very brief, often less than 6 to 10 sessions. Solution-focused and narrative therapy are also brief, meetings may not be weekly and may be less frequent as therapy proceeds.

CURRENT TRENDS AND INNOVATIONS

The text has focused on two specific trends in terms of the way they affect many theories: treatment manuals and constructivism. A third trend has been towards the integration of theories.

Reviewing answers to questions about current trends and innovations in this study guide will help to remind you of specific trends within each theory.

USING THE THEORY WITH OTHER THEORIES

Most practitioners of a theory often look outside of it to add new techniques or concepts. A notable exception is person-centered theory that continues to focus on genuineness, empathy, and unconditional positive regard as the only conditions that are necessary and sufficient for change. Reality therapy has a focus on responsibility and planning that tends to limit its use of techniques from other theories. Feminist and existential therapies tend to borrow heavily from other theories as they have relatively few of their own techniques. The three integrative approaches in Chapter 15 demonstrate different ways of incorporating concepts and methods from various theoretical approaches.

RESEARCH

Research has not been addressed in this study guide, in part because research is summarized briefly in the text and is difficult to summarize or abstract further. However, I have done this in Table 16.6 on page 618. As this table shows, much research has been done with cognitive, behavior, and REBT therapies. Some research has been conducted with psychoanalysis, person-centered, and family systems therapies. Relatively little research has been done with other theories of therapy. Two specific concepts that are useful in understanding research issues are process and outcome research.

process research The study of various aspects of how psychotherapy works. Examples include comparing two or more psychotherapeutic techniques and monitoring a change in personality as a result of the introduction of a technique. It is used in contrast to outcome research.

outcome research A systematic investigation of the effectiveness of a theory of psychotherapy, a technique of psychotherapy, a comparison of techniques or theories of psychotherapy, in contrast to process research.

GENDER ISSUES

Feminist therapy has had the greatest influence on gender issues within the field of psychotherapy. However, within each theory this issue has been addressed to varying degrees. The earliest theory, psychoanalysis, was the one

224

that was most often criticized by theorists and practioners for its gender bias. Many feminist psychodynamic writers have added to the literature on psychoanalysis.

In the following space, it would be helpful for you to summarize your comments from the Special Topics section of this study guide that refers to gender to provide you with an overview of how gender issues affect therapy.

_____

_____

_____

_____

_____

MULTICULTURAL ISSUES

Clients who sought therapy prior to the 1950s tended to be white and have at least a moderate income. In recent years, there has been an emphasis on the need to provide therapy for individuals from a variety of cultures. Feminist therapy has probably done more than other theories to provide techniques and support for mental health services to people from a variety of backgrounds. Asian therapy, discussed in Chapter 14, has also had an influence on an awareness of cultural differences and the application of meditation and other methods. Jung and Erikson were particularly interested in studying other cultures and learning about how these cultures could help inform their own theoretical development.

Family systems therapists have been quite aware of the different traditions and customs that affect family interaction. Behavioral, cognitive, and REBT theories have been slower to study the relationship between culture and their theoretical approaches.

In the following space, it would be helpful for you to summarize your comments from the Special Topics section of this study guide that concerns multicultural issues to provide you with an overview of how culture affects therapy.

_____

_____

_____

_____

_____

_____

GROUP THERAPY

Some theories, such as person-centered, Gestalt, and feminist therapy clearly value the importance of group therapy. Others provide group approaches to a variety of problems. Jungian therapists tend to see group as an adjunct to individual therapy. Table 16.7 on pages 622 and 623 summarizes each theory's approach to group therapy.

CASE STUDY

The purpose of the following case study is for you to practice identifying personality theory concepts and techniques from different theories that have been described in the text. This case is not meant as a demonstration of how to do therapy, but merely as a way to learn about and test your ability to identify theoretical concepts and techniques. I will briefly describe a case, then I will provide a client statement followed by a therapeutic statement or question. I will ask you to choose the theory that fits with that therapeutic response.

Chris is a 42-year-old married woman with a 10-year-old son and a 12-year-old daughter. She works part-time in an insurance office, mainly when her children are in school. Before she was married, 12 years ago, she had worked at a small office. Her employers were pleased to have her back when she decided three years ago that she wanted to return to work part time.

Her husband, Desmond, is currently unemployed. He had worked for the phone company until nine months ago. After repeated warnings and a suspension, he was terminated for drunkenness on the job. His drinking has been a considerable problem for the past five years. When drunk, he gets violent, yelling at Chris and hitting her. At those times, he blames her for his problems. He is particularly critical of her cooking and complains about the lack of cleanliness in the house. He also blames her for the problems that their daughter, Amanda, is having at school which include not doing her work and talking in class.

Chris agrees that she is responsible for many of these problems. Since childhood, she has had low self-esteem. Her father, like Desmond, was an alcoholic. He was often critical of Chris, her brother, and their mother. Her father died in an automobile accident when Chris was 17. A shy child, Chris often hid in her room, sometimes in her closet, when she heard her father come home drunk. She could tell by the way he opened the back door to the house, how drunk he was. As a child, Chris was often sickly. She complained of a nervous stomach and heart palpitations. She has had these symptoms all of her life.

Chris has been very anxious since she was hospitalized for a concussion. Desmond hit her with his fist. She fell back and hit her head against the refrigerator, causing her to be hospitalized overnight for observation. Since she has come home, she has been very anxious. She complains of headaches, possibly related to the concussion. Her stomach is upset, and Chris has little appetite. At 5'4", she is very thin, weighing 101 pounds. She feels tense in her neck and shoulders and has heart palpitations frequently. She now seeks help from a therapist for her anxiety symptoms, her lack of self-esteem, and her fears of Desmond's violent behavior.

QUESTIONS

In the following questions, choose the theory that most closely fits the therapist's conceptualization or response.

1. C: I seem to live in constant fear of doing something wrong or saying something wrong. I feel miserable.

   T: Chris, tell me more about what you are afraid of. (T thinks: I want to learn specific details about Chris's fears.)

   a. behavior therapy
   b. Gestalt therapy
   c. existential therapy
   d. person-centered therapy

2. C: I am afraid of the stove boiling over, of my children getting sick, of giving the wrong phone messages at work, and of Desmond hitting me.

   T: Be aware how you clench your fist now. Could you put words to that clenched fist?

   a. behavior therapy
   b. Gestalt therapy
   c. existential therapy
   d. person-centered therapy

3. C: I feel so angry. I want to do something, but I don't think anything will work. I have got to do something about my fears of cooking, of making mistakes at work (cries).

   T: You are so full of rage now, but there seems no place for it. Then you quickly worry about making mistakes.

   a. behavior therapy
   b. Gestalt therapy
   c. existential therapy
   d. person-centered therapy

4. C: I am so worried about making mistakes. I check and recheck my work at the agency. My boss, Bob, has never been critical, but I am so worried about making mistakes. Sometimes I lose my concentration and day-dream. I often daydream of this ugly vampire with an axe killing me and the whole office.

   T: It is possible that this monster, a common symbol, represents the anger inside of you, aggressive impulses that you are not aware of.

   a. Gestalt therapy
   b. Jungian therapy
   c. object relations therapy
   d. reality therapy

5. C: Ever since I have been a child, I have dreamed of monsters at night and had day dreams about them. The dreams always frighten me. They were really bad when I was younger. I would hide under my covers and suck my thumb.

   T: Tell me more about how you behaved when you woke up then. (T thinks: I wonder if she regressed to an earlier period of development.)

   a. cognitive therapy
   b. ego psychology
   c. object relations therapy
   d. Jungian therapy
   e. existential therapy

6. C: I remember a time when I cried and Mom came; I felt fine until she left. Then I got scared again, afraid something bad would happen.

   T: Having your mother there provided comfort for you. (T thinks: Her mother was an important holding environment, but she wasn't there often enough, it seems.)

   a. cognitive therapy
   b. ego psychology
   c. object relations therapy
   d. Jungian therapy
   e. existential therapy

7. C: My mother had to work a lot. I can remember standing at the window waiting for her to come home. Sometimes she would be late and I would get scared, wondering if she had been killed in a car accident.

   T: Tell me more about your thoughts about the possibility that your mother could die and thoughts about the possibility of your own eventual death.

   a. cognitive therapy
   b. ego psychology
   c. object relations therapy
   d. Jungian therapy
   e. existential therapy

8. C: When I had thoughts about my mother dying, I would get very frightened and be so scared. I wouldn't know what to do if she died.

   T: Can you feel your neck tightening and your breathing change? Can you finish this sentence? "I'm aware that ..."

   a. behavior therapy
   b. Gestalt therapy
   c. existential therapy
   d. person-centered therapy

9. C: I am aware that I feel so frightened now. I am here with you, and I feel safe. But I think I was aware of how scared I was as a child sometimes. That scare comes back to me at times when I'm at home and Desmond starts drinking.

   T: The safety you feel here is in such contrast with the terror you experienced as a child and now with your husband. (The therapist responds in a way that helps Chris think about her own mortality and the threat her husband poses to her own life.)

   a. behavior therapy
   b. Gestalt therapy
   c. existential therapy
   d. person-centered therapy

10. C: I think: I must be strong for the children. I'm so weak, such a failure.

    T: It would be nice to be strong for the children, but you don't HAVE TO be strong for them.

    a. Adlerian therapy
    b. behavior therapy
    c. cognitive therapy
    d. reality therapy
    e. REBT

11. C: But I know that they expect me to be with them all the time and take care of them like my mother did sometimes.

    T: You seem to be able to read their minds, but it really isn't possible to know what they are thinking, is it?

    a. Adlerian therapy
    b. behavior therapy
    c. cognitive therapy
    d. reality therapy
    e. REBT

12. C: No, I want to be strong for them. I want to be confident with them and not anxious like I am.

    T: I think that it would be helpful for you to act as if you are strong, to pretend that you know how to discipline them, how to encourage them.

    a. Adlerian therapy
    b. behavior therapy
    c. cognitive therapy
    d. reality therapy
    e. REBT

13. C: When my son, Paul, acts up, I get so tense. I'm not sure what to do.

    T: That might be a good time to try the relaxation procedures that I have taught you.

    a. Adlerian therapy
    b. behavior therapy
    c. cognitive therapy
    d. reality therapy
    e. REBT

14. C: I will try them, but I always mess up everything I do.

    T: Perhaps, this thought "I always mess up everything I do" is an overgeneralization. Do you mess up everything that you do at work?

    a. Adlerian therapy
    b. behavior therapy
    c. cognitive therapy
    d. reality therapy
    e. REBT

15. C: I don't mess up everything I do. I do what I need to do at work.

    T: But those are someone else's needs. Let's look at your own needs, such as your needs for belongingness and for fun.

    a. Adlerian therapy
    b. behavior therapy
    c. cognitive therapy
    d. reality therapy
    e. REBT

16. C: I would feel a lot better if I had time to enjoy myself, like going out dancing with my husband. But when we go out, he gets smashed.

    T: Well, it might be helpful for us to consider how best to work with his problems. (T thinks: Desmond seems to have a great deal of difficulty separating his intellectual processes from his emotional ones.)

    a. Bowen's intergenerational approach
    b. Minuchin's structural approach
    c. Haley's strategic approach
    d. solution-focused therapy
    e. narrative therapy

229

17. C: He always gets drunk when we go out, so it would be hard to work with his problems.

    T: Can you think of an exception to this when you go out and he is not drunk?

    a. Bowen's intergenerational approach
    b. Minuchin's structural approach
    c. Haley's strategic approach
    d. solution-focused therapy
    e. narrative therapy

18. C: Yes, I went to Paul's school with Desmond for a teacher's conference. He was fine. He was sober. He asked the teacher good questions. He really cares about Paul. I worry because he isn't close to Amanda.

    T: Perhaps the four of you can come in and we can approach this as a family. (T thinks: If the family comes in together, perhaps I can join with them and help them change their current boundaries.)

    a. Bowen's intergenerational approach
    b. Minuchin's structural approach
    c. Haley's strategic approach
    d. solution-focused therapy
    e. narrative therapy

19. Taking the entire sequence of 18 therapeutic responses, the therapist's approach could best be described as

    a. transtheoretical.
    b. theoretical integration.
    c. technical eclecticism.
    d. hodgepodge or unsystematic eclecticism.

20. If this were an actual therapeutic dialogue instead of an exercise, how would you rate the therapist's pattern of responses?

    a. excellent
    b. good
    c. average
    d. terrible

The answer to questions 19 and 20 is "d". The therapist changes his theoretical approach with each statement. There is no rationale for the therapist's switch from one theory to another. Chapter 15 describes appropriate integrative approaches that use more than one theory. These approaches do not present a random, hodgepodge approach to combining therapies as this dialogue does. If the current dialogue were to continue, both therapist and Chris are likely to end up quite confused about the goals and methods used in therapy. Contrast the clarity of theory presented in the other chapters with the lack of direction and purpose in this exercise.

STRENGTHS AND LIMITATIONS

You may find it helpful to summarize your view of the strengths and limitations of each theory. You may do this by looking at the strength and limitation sections from each chapter in this study guide and by consulting the Critique of theories on pages 624 to 631 of the text.

A QUIZ ON ALL THEORIES OF THERAPY

The following 25 multiple choice questions cover all theories except those described in Chapter 14. Most questions ask you to identify which theory a certain concept or technique is associated with.

_____ Q1. Social interest was a characteristic that _____ believed healthy individuals should possess.

    a. Alfred Adler
    b. Erik Erikson
    c. Sigmund Freud
    d. Carl Jung

_____ Q2. The shadow is a(an)

    a. alter ego in ego psychology.
    b. former self in self psychology.
    c. archetype in Jungian psychology.
    d. an elusive contact boundary in Gestalt therapy.

_____ Q3. Analyzing the client's life style is an assessment approach in

    a. Adlerian therapy.
    b. object relations psychology.
    c. Jungian analysis.
    d. existential therapy.

_____ Q4. Projective techniques, such as the Rorschach Test, are LEAST likely to be used in

    a. psychoanalysis.
    b. behavior therapy.
    c. Jungian analysis.
    d. existential therapy.

_____ Q5. The therapy that is specifically designed to treat individuals with narcissistic characteristics is

    a. drive theory.
    b. self psychology.
    c. Jungian analysis.
    d. existential therapy.

_____ Q6. The therapy that is most likely to ask a client to put words to his tight stomach is

    a. existential therapy.
    b. behavior therapy.
    c. Gestalt therapy.
    d. feminist therapy.
    e. person-centered therapy.

_____ Q7. Client: I can't stand the way my mother is always butting into my relationship with my husband.

Therapist: You are so angry at your mother for not respecting you and interfering with your relationship with your husband.

The therapist's response is most consistent with

a. existential therapy.
b. behavior therapy.
c. Gestalt therapy.
d. feminist therapy.
e. person-centered therapy.

_____ Q8. Introjection, swallowing whole the opinions of others, is a concept that is most consistent with

a. existential therapy.
b. drive theory.
c. Gestalt therapy.
d. feminist therapy.
e. object relations.

_____ Q9. Stimulus control, a change method in Prochaska's transtheoretical approach, has been taken from

a. cognitive therapy.
b. behavior therapy.
c. rational emotive behavior therapy.
d. feminist therapy.
e. reality therapy.

_____ Q10. A goal of _____ is to help clients learn a philosophy that will help them reduce the chances that they will be disturbed by overwhelming irrational thoughts.

a. cognitive therapy
b. behavior therapy
c. rational emotive behavior therapy
d. feminist therapy
e. reality therapy

_____ Q11. Power analysis is a technique used most often in

a. cognitive therapy.
b. behavior therapy.
c. rational emotive behavior therapy.
d. feminist therapy.
e. reality therapy.

_____ Q12. Making plans and following through on them is a characteristic of

a. cognitive therapy.
b. behavior therapy.
c. rational emotive behavior therapy.
d. feminist therapy.
e. reality therapy.

_____ Q13. The therapy that is LEAST concerned about using techniques is

    a. existential therapy.
    b. Jungian therapy.
    c. Gestalt therapy.
    d. feminist therapy.
    e. reality therapy.

_____ Q14. Questioning is a technique that is LEAST likely to be used in

    a. existential therapy.
    b. behavior therapy.
    c. Gestalt therapy.
    d. feminist therapy.
    e. person-centered therapy.

_____ Q15. Guided discovery is an active technique most often associated with

    a. cognitive therapy.
    b. behavior therapy.
    c. Gestalt therapy.
    d. feminist therapy.
    e. reality therapy.

_____ Q16. A sociological approach to understanding the client's problem is most likely to be found in

    a. cognitive therapy.
    b. behavior therapy.
    c. Gestalt therapy.
    d. feminist therapy.
    e. reality therapy.

_____ Q17. Which of these therapies is LEAST likely to use role playing as a therapeutic technique?

    a. cognitive therapy
    b. behavior therapy
    c. Gestalt therapy
    d. feminist therapy
    e. person-centered therapy

_____ Q18. To become a more authentic individual is the goal of

    a. existential therapy.
    b. behavior therapy.
    c. Gestalt therapy.
    d. feminist therapy.
    e. person-centered therapy.

_____ Q19. Which of the following is most likely to have a different therapeutic approach depending on the client's psychological diagnosis?

    a. cognitive therapy
    b. behavior therapy
    c. Gestalt therapy
    d. feminist therapy
    e. reality therapy

_____ Q20. Client: I have to get my boss to like me and appreciate my work.

Therapist: It would be nice to have your boss like you, but you don't HAVE to get him to like you and your work.

The therapist who made this statement is most likely practicing

a. cognitive therapy.
b. behavior therapy.
c. rational emotive behavior therapy.
d. feminist therapy.
e. reality therapy.

_____ Q21. Taking responsibility for oneself and meeting one's own needs without interfering with the needs of others is most likely to be a goal of

a. cognitive therapy.
b. behavior therapy.
c. rational emotive behavior therapy.
d. feminist therapy.
e. reality therapy.

_____ Q22. Although disputing is a technique that cognitive therapists might use, it is particularly associated with

a. behavior therapy.
b. rational emotive behavior therapy.
c. feminist therapy.
d. reality therapy.

_____ Q23. Many therapies can be used alone. Which of the following cannot be used alone?

a. cognitive therapy
b. behavior therapy
c. Gestalt therapy
d. feminist therapy
e. reality therapy

_____ Q24. The psychoanalytic concept of splitting is most similar to which one of these concepts from cognitive therapy?

a. all or none thinking
b. labeling
c. magnification
d. Socratic dialogue

_____ Q25. Which of the following theories is LEAST similar to psychoanalysis?

a. Jungian analysis
b. Adlerian therapy
c. Bowen's intergenerational approach
d. reality therapy

ANSWER KEY

1. a	11. c	Q1. a	Q11. d	Q21. e	
2. b	12. a	Q2. c	Q12. e	Q22. b	
3. d	13. b	Q3. a	Q13. a	Q23. d	
4. b	14. c	Q4. b	Q14. e	Q24. a	
5. b	15. d	Q5. b	Q15. a	Q25. d	
6. c	16. a	Q6. c	Q16. d		
7. e	17. d	Q7. e	Q17. e		
8. b	18. b	Q8. c	Q18. a		
9. c	19. d	Q9. b	Q19. a		
10. e	20. d	Q10. c	Q20. c		